Europeanization and Foreign Policy

This book examines the relationship between the European Union (EU) and its member states by analysing how the process of integration in the field of foreign policy is shaping member states' identities.

Focusing on the mutually constitutive aspects of the relationship between the EU and its member states, Jokela argues that we need discourse analytic and comparative tools for analysing foreign policy in the EU context and draws on the contributions of poststructural international relations. Providing empirically rich and comparative case studies that explore the impact of the Europeanization of foreign and security policy on Finnish and British foreign policy discourses as well as these states' identities, Jokela generates detailed knowledge about the interplay of national and supranational foreign policy discourses.

Making an important contribution to Europeanization studies, foreign policy analysis and discourse analysis, this book will be of strong interest to students and scholars of European politics, comparative politics, foreign policy and international relations.

Juha Jokela is the director of the European Union research programme at the Finnish Institute of International Relations.

Routledge Advances in European Politics

Europeanization and Foreign Policy

State identity in Finland and Britain

Juha Jokela

Routledge
Taylor & Francis Group

LONDON AND NEW YORK

First published 2011
by Routledge
2 Park Square, Milton Park, Abingdon, Oxfordshire OX14 4RN

Simultaneously published in the USA and Canada
by Routledge
711 Third Avenue, New York, NY 10017, USA

First issued in paperback 2016

*Routledge is an imprint of the Taylor and Francis Group,
an informa business*

Typeset in Times New Roman by
Florence Production Ltd, Stoodleigh, Devon

British Library Cataloguing in Publication Data
A catalogue record for this book is available from the British Library

Library of Congress Cataloging in Publication Data
Jokela, Juha.
    Europeanization and foreign policy: state identity in Finland and
    Britain/Juha Jokela.
        p. cm. – (Routledge advances in European politics)
    Includes bibliographical references and index.
    (alk. paper)   1. European Union countries – Foreign relations.
    2. European Union.   3. Finland – Foreign relations – 1981–
    4. Great Britain – Foreign relations – 1997–   5. Intergovernmental
    cooperation – European Union countries.   6. European cooperation.
    I. Title.
    JZ1570.J65 2011
    341.242'2–dc22   2010025351

ISBN 13: 978-1-138-96914-8 (pbk)
ISBN 13: 978-0-415-57787-8 (hbk)

To my Mum, Dad, Ville,
Heikki and Antti

Contents

Illustrations

Figures

Tables

Acknowledgements

Writing this book would not have been possible without generous support received from a University of Bristol Postgraduate Scholarship, the Economic and Social Science Research Council, a British Council Chevening Scholarship, the Finnish Cultural Foundation and a Kone Foundation Postgraduate Scholarship.

I am also most grateful for the guidance and advice provided by Richard Little and Jutta Weldes. You formed a brilliant supervisory team for my doctoral research. I have warm memories of our joint meetings, lively discussions and friendly debates. Much gratitude also goes to the staff and students of the Department of Politics at Bristol University, especially to Dibyesh Anand, Terrell Carver, Michelle Cini, Eric Herring, Vernon Hewitt, Johanna Kantola and Judith Squires. Your comments were most valuable for my doctoral studies. I am also most grateful to Brian White and Judith Squires for their sharp observations and brilliant suggestions as the examiners of my PhD dissertation.

The initial idea of this book developed at Birmingham University's Department of Political Science and International Studies. I would like to especially thank Stuart Croft, David Marsh and Collin Hay for inspiration and support. I also thank the Finnish Institute of International Affairs as well as my colleagues in the Network for European Studies at the University of Helsinki where this book was finalized. In particular, I wish to thank Teija Tiilikainen, Teemu Palosaari and Bart Gaens for their dedication to incorporate me into the Finnish university world. To all my friends in Turku, Birmingham, Bristol and Helsinki I am very grateful. You have been a source of support and always a delight.

Two people have been most important for this study. My deepest thanks go to Johanna. You have been a true friend and companion since the very first idea of this book. You have helped me to keep this endeavour on track and my life in perspective. Thank you for sharing your professional and personal life with me, thank you for everything. My loving thanks go to my partner Marko, whom I met while I was conducting field research for this book in Helsinki. Your love, kindness and curiosity towards life have been a unique source of inspiration and support. I also want to thank your family for helping me to rediscover Finland.

Finally, this book is dedicated to my family. To my mother Ritva, my father Timo and my brothers Ville, Heikki and Antti. Your love and support have been the most significant source of self-reliance, and crucial for this book and my life in general.

Abbreviations

APEC	Asia Pacific Economic Cooperation
CFSP	Common Foreign and Security Policy
CIS	Commonwealth of Independent States
CoE	Council of Europe
CSCE	Conference on Security and Cooperation in Europe
CSDP	Common Security and Defence Policy
EC	European Community/Communities
ECAP	European Capabilities Action Plan
ECSC	European Coal and Steel Community
EEA	European Economic Area
EEAS	European External Action Services
EEC	European Economic Community
ESS	European Security Strategy
EFTA	European Free Trade Area
EIS	European integration studies
EPC	European Political Cooperation
ESDP	European Security and Defence Policy
ETA	European Trade Area
EU	European Union
Euratom	European Atomic Energy Community
FCMA	Treaty of Friendship, Cooperation and Mutual Assistance
FPA	Foreign Policy Analysis
G7/G8	Group of Seven/Group of Eight
GPD	great-power discourse
IMF	International Monetary Fund
IR	International Relations
ISAF	International Security Assistance Force
KFOR	Kosovo Force
MERCOSUR	Common Market of the Southern Cone (Argentina, Brazil, Paraguay, Uruguay)
MP	Member of Parliament
NACC	North Atlantic Cooperation Council
NAFTA	North American Free Trade Area
NATO	North Atlantic Treaty Organization

OSCE	Organization for Security and Cooperation in Europe
PfP	Partnership for Peace
SDE	Statement on the Defence Estimate
SDR	Strategic Defence Review
TEU	Treaty on European Union
UK	United Kingdom of Great Britain and Northern Ireland
UN	United Nations
US	United States
WEU	Western European Union
WTO	World Trade Organization

1 Introduction

This book sheds light on the relationship between the European Union (EU) and its member states in analyzing how the Europeanization of foreign and security policy is shaping the identities of two different member states, Finland and Britain.[1] The analytical rationale emerged from empirical observations related to the variation in the debate on foreign and security policy in Finland and Britain in the 1990s. In Britain there were some far-reaching generalizations suggesting that attempts to establish a Common Foreign and Security Policy (CFSP) and a Common Security and Defence Policy (CSDP) for the EU were delusional.[2] It was argued that the EU treaty declarations on these twin policies lacked political support, institutional capabilities and military resources. Consequently, the CFSP and the CSDP played a marginal role in the British political and scholarly debate. In Finland, meanwhile, the government argued that membership of the EU reinforces Finnish security. Consequently, the CFSP and the CSDP became the buzzwords of the new EU member state's foreign and security policy and a central element in the political and scholarly debate. Against this background, two particularly puzzling and interrelated questions arise. What accounts for the differences? What do these differences tell us about the European foreign and security policy?

The central assumption of this book is that we have witnessed the emergence of a distinct European foreign and security policy system, at the core of which is the European Union. It is a system that is based not on traditional state boundaries but on a progressively robust form of multi-level governance. European-level decision-making brings the vast majority of European states into constant interaction, and European institutions play an increasingly important role in the process. EU developments are of particular importance given the EU's increasing powers over its member states. Although these are more evident in monetary policy and single market, they have also been gradually strengthened in the field of foreign and security policy. Moreover, it has become increasingly difficult to distinguish between the more supranational EU external relations – such as trade and development policies – and the more intergovernmental CFSP and CSDP. For instance, implementation of the crisis-management decisions made by the intergovernmental Council of the European Union under the auspices of the CFSP and CSDP often draw on the resources governed by the more supranational

European Commission. On the other hand, the Commission-based EU trade and development policies must be taken into account in the formulation of the CFSP.

Moreover, the Lisbon Treaty, which came into force in 2010, aims to overcome the coordination problems resulting from the complex institutional and procedural web of the EU's external relations. The new institutional set-up brings the majority of its external policies under the leadership of the High Representative of the Union for Foreign Affairs and Security Policy, with the assistance of the European External Action Services (EEAS). The High Representative is the Vice-President of the Commission. She chairs the Foreign Affairs Council comprising the member states and conducts the CFSP. Given the aim to bridge the Commission- and Council-based external activities of the EU, the distinction between the intergovernmental and supranational features of its external relations is increasingly difficult to sustain in practice. Arguably, it is the expansion of the supranational elements of EU's foreign and security policy that marks the difference between the EU and the other European or international security organizations. It is further suggested that this constitutes a challenge to the traditional analysis of foreign and security policy.

Although there is nothing inherently wrong in analyzing European foreign and security policy within an intergovernmental or supranational framework, the idea in this book is to investigate whether it is feasible to study the different levels concurrently within a single theoretical framework by utilizing the concept of Europeanization in a novel way. Europeanization studies have represented an analytical move from explaining the process of European integration to examining its effects on European (states') politics. In other words, instead of seeking to explain the integration process and European-level institution building from a bottom-up perspective, scholars have become progressively more interested in analysing the effects of EU institutions and policies on its member (and neighbouring) states within a top-down frame. The concept has recently been applied in analyses of European foreign and security policy, and some scholars have studied national adaptation to the CFSP and the CSDP (within a top-down frame). However, and given the continuing salience of the state in this field, the Europeanization of foreign and security policy has also been studied from a bottom-up perspective in terms of the national projection of state interests on the EU level. Similarly, some researchers have emphasized the reciprocal features of the process, thereby explicitly drawing on international relations (IR) theories. In so doing, they have often turned towards social constructivism and poststructuralism, and many have focused on change and continuities in national discourses and identities.

Against this background, this book contributes to two contemporary theoretical and methodological debates. First, it combines Europeanization with the study of identity within a discourse-analytical framework, thus explicating what social constructivism and poststructuralism can bring to EIS. It is argued that this facilitates more detailed and context-specific analysis of Europeanization, and hence complements the overall rationale of Europeanization studies – to account for national variation in light of increasing EU governance. Second, the study embraces the recent tendency within discourse theory to adopt a comparative framework, the aim being to contribute to the emerging literature on comparative discourse analysis (Howarth 2005, J. Kantola 2006).

European foreign and security policy

EU developments in foreign and security policy are notable in light of the theoretical developments in the study of IR. The emphasis on globalization (Clark 1999, Held 1999), regionalization (Fawcett and Hurrell 1997), Europeanization (Tonra 2001, Featherstone 2003, Radaelli 2004) and transnational (Keohane and Nye 1971) as well as multi-level governance (Hooghe and Marks 2001, Bache 2008) is challenging the autonomy of the state and emphasizes other institutions and interdependency. However, the state has largely retained its dominance and autonomous character, especially in the study of foreign policy. In light of this theoretical drift, the posited supranational tendencies of the EU's foreign and security policies are of particular empirical interest in that they connect these policy fields more directly to theories of general transformation suggesting the diminishing role of the state in international relations. Analytically they also allow the incorporation of theoretical innovations from European integration studies (EIS) into the study of international relations and vice versa.

Thus far the debate on European foreign and security policy has largely focused on three interrelated dimensions (White 2001: 40–41, Carlsnaes 2004: 1). The first of these relates to the traditional and distinguishable activities of European states in the context of foreign and security policy. Despite the increasing cooperation and rapid institutional developments on the European level, these activities have increased rather than decreased. The second dimension concerns the development of the EU's foreign and security policy, referring to the increased coordination of the member states' political and military relations with the outside world, and the third reflects developments in other fields of the EU's external relations such as financial, trade and development. In these areas the EU is becoming increasingly recognized as a key player in world politics. As a result of rapid developments related to the second and third dimensions, a fourth distinct dimension has become increasingly visible in that a number of scholars are focusing on the EU as an international actor in world affairs. As such it has thus been used as an empirical example in many analytical approaches, highlighting the increasing regional and global governance in foreign and security policy.

Given the broad scope of scholarly interest, the terms used to clarify and define the subject matter are numerous. In recent years two terms have become dominant in book and journal articles: whereas some refer to European or Europe's foreign policy, others call it EU or the EU's foreign policy (S. Smith 1994, Hill 1996a, Nuttall 2000, Zielonka 2002, K.E. Smith 2003, M.E. Smith 2004, Tonra and Christiansen 2004). Furthermore, some influential accounts employ longer expressions such as 'the foreign policies of the European Union member states' (Manners and Whitman 2000). Although the different labels are mostly carefully considered choices reflecting the author's take on the different dimensions of the debate, at times they are used interchangeably. In order to establish conceptual clarity for the analysis, a brief discussion about the subject matter and focus of this book is called for.

Although this book focuses largely on developments in the EU and two of its member states, it adopts the broad definition of European foreign policy, rather than the narrower EU foreign policy. The analytical rationale behind this choice comes from the recognition that given the EU's pivotal role, foreign policy activities in Europe are not coterminous with the institutional and discursive boundaries of the European Union. Norway, for instance, is not an EU member state, but its foreign policy has been shaped by the CFSP and the CSDP to a significant degree (Sjursen 2003: 7–8). On the other hand, some of the EU member states' foreign policies seem to be remarkably detached from the CFSP and the CSDP, but not, for instance, from North Atlantic Treaty Organization (NATO) policies. The broader definition also accommodates the increasing interplay among European security organizations, most crucially the EU, NATO and the Organization for Security and Cooperation in Europe (OSCE). The term 'European foreign policy', which incorporates individual states' foreign policies and the increasing role of European-level institutions and policies, therefore serves this book well in that it incorporates all the key actors and institutions, as well as the complex processes among them.

The conceptualization of foreign policy constitutes another challenge for this study. The broad scope of this policy area is recognized, and the book draws on theoretical approaches questioning narrow conceptualizations. Although global and regional regulation has penetrated many areas of national politics, domestic actors increasingly bypass the state and operate directly in other states, as well as regionally and globally. Indeed, the processes of globalization and regionalization have blurred the previously sharp distinction between domestic and foreign policy, thereby challenging state-centric accounts of domestic and international politics. This has paved the way for broader research agendas – a move often labelled a shift from government to governance. This is symptomatic in the European context in at least two ways. Regional institutions such as the EU are shaping the domestic politics of EU member states to an increasing degree, and many areas of internal policy are high on their external agendas. This has certainly broadened the scope of foreign policy in Europe. On the other hand, the EU has been recognized as a particularly influential actor in world affairs, mainly in other fields than traditional foreign policy. This has also widened the focus of foreign policy analysis. Accordingly, a growing number of policy-makers and scholars are referring to external relations rather than foreign policy, especially in the context of the EU's policies towards other states, regions and international organizations. This being said, the focus and the empirical material of this book rely largely on documentation reflecting rather conservative foreign policy matters, such as security and defence. There were practical and analytical reasons for this choice. On the practical level these areas have been predominant in the debate on European foreign policy in light of the development of the CFSP and the CSDP. Analytically these areas are pivotal in that they are widely held to be immune to the process of European integration, and to be one of the strongholds of state power. Given the focus on traditional foreign policy matters, largely but not exclusively related to state security and defence, the term 'European foreign and security policy' is applied throughout.

Although the aim of the book is to shed light on European foreign and security policy, and in so doing to make a valuable contribution to foreign policy analysis in general, it is not in itself a book of foreign policy analysis: it is about Europeanization and foreign policy. Whereas European foreign and security policy refers to the overall context in which EU and state-level policy-making take place, the term 'Europeanization of foreign policy' relates to the process of ongoing transformation in this context. In other words, Europeanization is symptomatic of the emergence of a distinct European foreign and security policy system and of the increasing importance of European-level governance in this context, namely but not exclusively the CFSP and the CSDP.

Comparing state identities

The recent theoretical developments within IR triggered the choice of national and state identity as a key concept of this study. Whereas the concept of national identity – predominantly associated with the nation-state – is broadly applied within different theoretical orientations in IR, analysts have also written about state identity. This terminological and conceptual choice is often left without explanation, however. Although some accounts seem to favour the term on account of an explicit focus on the state (Wendt 1999, Mitzen 2006) others use it to elucidate the relationship between state and nation (Biswas 2002). The concept of state identity is preferred here given the focus of the study first and foremost on state practices, specifically their foreign and security policies. On the more implicit level, this conceptual choice highlights the need to problematize the amalgamation of state and nation in IR. On the one hand, states may comprise more than one nation, and nations' borders do not necessarily coincide with the borders of the state in question. On the other hand, although state practices constitute a major site for the reproduction of national identities, the identities cannot be reduced to such practices: other important and often institutionalized sites include for example ethnicity, language and religion, often directly and indirectly linked to the state.

Similarly, the reproduction of state identity should not be reduced to state practices or certain policy fields such as foreign and security policy. Non-state institutions and other policy fields also play a role. Nevertheless foreign and security policy is largely considered critical to the existence of the state, and is understood almost exclusively in terms of the state. Indeed, the EU appears to be the only non-state actor that explicitly claims to have a foreign and security policy. As such, the state and its foreign and security policy constitute a privileged site for the construction of the state identity.

Against this background, states' foreign and security policies are understood in this book as boundary-producing political practices. As such they do not merely reflect state identities, but are rather part of their reproduction (Weldes 1996, Campbell 1998, Weber 1998). In order to examine this reproduction, specifically what difference, if any, the EU foreign and security policy has made to Finland and Britain, the study turns towards discourse analysis, which has proved increasingly valuable in IR and EIS but is rarely applied in Europeanization studies. The premise in this book is that discourse analysis provides the analytical tools with which to elucidate the relationship between the EU and its member states.

The core ideas of this work are pursued through a comparative study of Finland and Britain. These two states provide rich and analytically interesting material with which to investigate what difference, if any, the Europeanization of foreign and security policy made to the Finnish and British foreign policy discourses in the 1990s and early 2000s, as well as to these states' identities. Whereas Finland represents a small and previously neutral state, and is a relatively new EU member, Britain stands for a major state and an internationally engaged security actor with long-term membership of the European Union. Interestingly, both share a problematic historical relationship with European integration: Finland in terms of its neutrality and special relationship with the Soviet Union and Russia, and Britain due to its great-power status and special relationship with the United States. Given the differences, both states have re-articulated their relationship with the EU: Finland after its accession in 1995 and Britain in the 1998 British–French joint declaration on European security and defence signed in St Malo.

Although the Europeanization of foreign and security policy does suggest a degree of convergence in member states' identities, divergence should not be ruled out either. Comparison of the similarities and differences between Finland and Britain in light of Europeanization thus highlights the need for a context-specific theory of foreign policy. The assumptions on which the book is based and the theoretical framework thus point away from the idea of a grand theory and general laws, which tend to highlight particular actors such as states with given identities and interests. Accordingly, the key characteristics of a particular state, such as Finland's smallness and Britain's greatness, are not taken for granted but are seen as socially constructed through specific state discourses and practices. Similarly, comparison of the discourses of foreign and security policy and state identity does not necessarily correspond with the conventional methods of comparative politics: it rather reflects the methodology of discourse analysis, which suggests a problem- rather than a method-driven approach, as well as a broad historical and contextual understanding of the case studies. Thus this volume also aims to add to our knowledge of Finnish and British foreign and security policy in the 1990s and 2000s.

Structure of the book

The book is organized along the following lines. Chapter 1 begins with a description of European foreign and security policy with the EU at its core. It outlines some of the key institutional developments of the CFSP and the CSDP, and highlights the importance of the EU. The literature focusing on recent developments reflects two distinct approaches, labelled the intergovernmental and the supranational approaches. Whereas the former draws largely on the IR literature, the latter is more closely associated with EIS. In light of globalization and regionalization and the development of the EU's foreign and security policy, the exchange of ideas between these approaches is becoming more lively, and it is suggested that contrasting them would be analytically valuable. Weighed against supranational approaches, the prevailing state-centrism of the majority of European foreign policy analysis, including the accounts that draw on neo-liberal institutionalism and need to account for interdependence and non-state actors, becomes apparent. On the other hand, the more limited supranational analysis is weak in accounting for the role of the states. It is argued that the recent theoretical interest in the concept of Europeanization within the study of European foreign and security policy has reproduced these problems to some extent. Consequently, the Europeanization of foreign and security policy has been approached largely as a top-down or bottom-up process. However, some of the accounts drawing on social constructivism and poststructuralism suggest that a third way highlighting the reciprocal features of Europeanization is possible, and that conceptualizations of it as both a top-down and a bottom-up process deserves closer analytical attention.

The main objective in Chapter 2 is to identify an approach that is able to account for the complexity of the reciprocal relationship between the EU and the foreign and security policies of its member states. Drawing on the literature concerning the Europeanization of foreign and security policy, the chapter contributes to the expanding body of work focusing on the Europeanization of state identities, and thereby lays out the theoretical and methodological framework of the study. It begins with a discussion about some of the theoretical issues involved in the methodological question of structure and agency that lies at the heart of the current debate on global and regional governance. It then outlines a theoretical and methodological framework based on a discourse-analytical approach, clarifies the methods of analysis used and presents the comparative research design. It is stressed that the purpose is not to construct a conventional comparative model or framework, but rather to explore novel ways of conceptualizing and analyzing the Europeanization of foreign and security policy.

Chapter 3 discusses the role of the EU foreign and security policy in the Finnish discourse on foreign and security policy and state identity. It analyses the key foreign, security and defence policy documents generated in the 1990s and early 2000s, as well as the associated parliamentary debates. The findings suggest that a significant turn took place in the mid-1990s. Drawing on historical Finnish state discourses, and on contemporary discourses of post-Cold War Europe and the developing foreign and security policy of the European Union, it articulates a new and radically different discourse on foreign and security policy that highlights alignment with the West rather than neutrality. Although initially resisted, this new discourse had become dominant by the early 2000s. It is argued that the EU foreign and security policy was an essential element of the new discourse and thus of the Finnish state identity.

Chapter 4 assesses the impact, if any, of EU foreign and security policies on the seemingly rigid foreign policy discourse in Britain. It therefore analyses foreign and security policy documentation in Britain from the 1990s prior to the launch of the Strategic Defence Review (SDR) in 1997. It is suggested that EU policies had a marginal role in the discourse during this time period, that its influence increased after 1997; and that a novel position was articulated in the joint British–French St Malo Declaration in 1998. The impact of the increasing weight given to EU foreign policies in Britain is assessed through the analysis of related documents and parliamentary debates. It is revealed that the increasing Europeanization of foreign and security policy assumed significance in the 1998 re-articulation of the British foreign policy discourse. However, this re-articulation represented a twist rather than a turn: in other words, the key elements remained largely unchanged. Analyses of the subsequent white papers and the parliamentary debates shed light on how this re-articulation developed in light of intensifying Europeanization. It seems that the traditional British great-power identity was largely reproduced in the official discourse.

Following this analysis of Finnish and British discourses concerning the Europeanization of foreign and security policy, Chapter 5 turns to the relationship between the European Union and the member state foreign policies. Specifically, the aim is to discuss the similarities and differences between Finland and Britain in light of the findings of the case studies. It seems that EU foreign policy played a central role in the re-articulation of both foreign policy discourses. As such, it shaped the reproduction of these states' identities. However, the process had very different effects. Whereas the Europeanization of its foreign and security policy was fundamental in the transformation of Finland's neutrality identity to an alignment identity, in Britain it enabled the reproduction of the traditional great-power identity. Three key arguments are put forward: first, the findings indicate that Europeanization in foreign policy can even transform state identities; second, the variation between these two cases highlights the importance of the national context in reproducing them; and third, the results highlight the contribution of the comparative discourse analysis. It is suggested that discourse-analytical approaches are valuable in accounting for the interplay between EU and national levels in the field of foreign policy, whereas comparative analysis is needed to explicate what, if anything is context-specific in the process of Europeanization. By way of illustration the chapter first revisits the broader background of the book in light of two questions: Why the comparison? Why these cases? Second, it compares and contrasts the findings of the case studies, and third it discusses their relevance to the analysis of European foreign policy/ies.

In conclusion, the empirical findings of the book suggest that the official foreign policy discourse in Finland changed during the 1990s from one of neutrality to one of alignment, whereas the British discourse showed continuity. Taken together, this generates a third finding: that EU policies have a differential impact on the foreign policy discourses and identities of member states. The analytical findings of the volume comprise two elements: first, comparative discourse methodology offers new insights into the process of Europeanization, and second, Europeanization should be theorized as both a top-down and a bottom-up process in which state identities are both transformed by and shape EU discourses (differentially depending on prior identities).

2 The Europeanization of foreign policy

Introduction

How should one approach and account for European foreign policy? This is a question that has attracted an increasing amount of attention among scholars and policy-makers alike in recent years. At its core is the expanding and deepening European integration, and in particular the development of the CFSP and the CSDP. These twin policies show how European integration has spilled over into the most sensitive field of state sovereignty. European foreign and security policy is no longer based on individual states and inter-state cooperation, but rests on a progressively robust form of multi-level governance. The growth of this complex and multilayered foreign policy system is also challenging as far as conventional foreign policy analysis is concerned – in particular with regard to its state-centric nature.

This chapter examines recent attempts to respond to this challenge that have utilized the concept of Europeanization in the analysis of European foreign and security policy. It draws on the work of international relations and European integration studies scholars, who have adopted various theoretical perspectives in their analyses, generally falling into the two broad categories of the inter-governmental and the supranational. It is posited that the way in which the concept of Europeanization has been applied reflects the respective theoretical orientations. Conceptualized as the national projection of state interests (bottom-up process), on the EU level it has its roots in state-centric realism and inter-governmentalism, whereas in terms of national adaptation (top-down process) it reflects some of the key ideas in theories of European integration. It is suggested that the recent engagement of foreign policy scholars with Europeanization clarifies the process as both bottom-up and top-down.

The chapter comprises three sections. The first one lays out some of the empirical developments at the heart of the debate on European foreign policy. The second section focuses on the CFSP and the CSDP, examining both the intergovernmental and the supranational approaches to European foreign and security policy and including the recent literature on Europeanization. Finally, attention is given to the emerging literature on the Europeanization of foreign and security policy, and specifically on the reciprocal aspects. In conclusion, it is suggested that deeper social constructivist and poststructuralist engagement would benefit analysis of the reciprocal aspects of the Europeanization of foreign policy.

The CFSP and the CSDP

> Today virtually no major foreign policy issue goes unexamined by the EU, and cooperation is under serious consideration in related areas such as security and defence.
>
> (Smith 2004: 17)

EU policies in the areas of foreign relations, security and defence have developed significantly since the 1990s. Earlier attempts to coordinate member states' external policies, known as European Political Cooperation (EPC), were renamed and reformulated in Maastricht in 1992. The second pillar of the Treaty on European Union established the Common Foreign and Security Policy for the European Union 'including the eventual framing of a common defence policy, which might in time lead to a common defence' (Official Journal 1992). Following the developments towards the end of the 1990s the defence aspect of the policy came to be known first as the European Security and Defence Policy (ESDP), and was renamed under the Lisbon Treaty the Common Security and Defence Policy (CSDP). Whereas the aim of the CFSP is to create a common voice for the European Union in world politics, the purpose of the CSDP is to increase the Union's military capabilities to deal with identified security issues and threats.

Although the development of the CFSP and the CSDP is widely acknowledged, a powerful set of arguments has rightly highlighted the contradictions and problems within these twin policies. At the outset it was claimed that the acronyms reflected bold political rhetoric rather than a real political and material ability to formulate and implement policies. It was therefore argued that treaty texts created great expectations, but in practice the development of the CFSP and the CSDP was, at best, spasmodic. The European Union was widely held to lack institutional structures enabling strong and decisive decision-making (Hill 1993), and the military capability to back up its policies. Consequently, the power in foreign and security policy-making in Europe was assumed still to lie within the states.

The crisis related to the disintegration of Yugoslavia was at the heart of these arguments and of the development of the CFSP and the CSDP. Violent conflicts among and within the former republics of Yugoslavia intensified in the immediate aftermath of the Maastricht Treaty. These developments were broadly seen to require unitary EU action, and as such they constituted a test for the newly established CFSP – a test that it failed spectacularly. Most crucially, the EU member states could not agree upon a common position, not to mention on concrete policies for dealing with the crisis. Jacques Delors, then president of the European Commission, commented thus: 'I took part in all the Council of Ministers meetings during the Yugoslav crisis and can attest to the deep divisions, based upon history with the Balkans' (cited in Andreatta 1997). Even if it is true that the EU was neither politically nor militarily prepared for a crisis of such proportions (McCormick 1996: 281), the images of the bloody conflicts in the Balkans and the EU's inability to act are still seen as a failure of EU and European foreign and security policy. According to the popular view, indecisiveness, incapacity and inaction were brought to an end by sound United States (US) diplomacy backed up by decisive military action in Bosnia in 1995 and in Kosovo in 1997, both followed by NATO-led peacekeeping operations. The lessons of these events were studied carefully in EU offices as well as in many European capitals. Significantly, the crisis prompted political consensus, which materialized in the form of the institutional and operational development of European security organizations. The developments within the EU have been particularly profound, and some of these indicate transfer of power from member states to the EU institutions.

For example, qualified majority voting was introduced for the first time in the CFSP context under the Amsterdam treaty (Official Journal 1997). Although applicable only to common positions or joint actions arising from unanimously agreed common strategies, a move towards majority voting in the field of foreign and security policy is a notable development. In addition, the Amsterdam treaty also established the post of the EU's High Representative for the Common Foreign and Security Policy, whose duties include assisting the Council in foreign policy matters through contributing to the formulation, preparation and implementation of European policy decisions. The High Representative also acts on behalf of the Council (and therefore the member states) in conducting political dialogue with third parties. Although the post was designed to enable the EU to speak with one voice on CFSP matters, the role of the member states has not diminished. Indeed, many of the larger ones have tended to emphasize their pivotal role and resources in the formulation of both the CFSP and the CSDP, and the country holding the rotating EU presidency has kept on acting as the number-one EU representative. Therefore, and instead of establishing one telephone number for Europe in foreign policy matters – as infamously desired by Henry Kissinger – the CFSP has lengthened the list by adding new relevant actors to it. The number of the High Representative has steadily moved up on it, however.

Under the Nice Treaty the member states extended the policy-making mechanism known as enhanced cooperation to certain aspects of the CFSP. This may operate between several member states in areas in which the objectives of the European Union cannot be achieved by the member states as a whole. In the CFSP context, member states that are in a position to do so may cooperate in the implementation of a joint action or a common position (Official Journal 2001). This is symptomatic of the problems related to the implementation of the policies and the positions agreed. In terms of implementation capabilities, however, there has been a shift in the military field.

The member states decided in Helsinki in 1999 that by 2003 the EU would develop military and civil forces capable of acting under EU command in peacekeeping and conflict-management situations (Helsinki European Council 1999). On the one hand, this so-called Helsinki Headline Goal reflected the Franco–British Joint Declaration adopted at St Malo in December 1998, in which these two counties – which are pivotal in terms of European security – argued that the EU ought to have the capacity for autonomous action backed up by credible military forces. The declaration laid the political foundation between France and Great Britain, which in turn facilitated the launch of the CSDP. On the other hand, the decision was made only weeks after the end of NATO's 78-day bombing campaign in Kosovo, which had re-exposed huge equipment gaps between US armed forces and European armies (Grevi and Keohane 2009: 71). The Helsinki Headline Goal was further clarified in November 2000 in Brussels when the EU governments agreed to create a Rapid Reaction Force of 100,000 troops, 400 combat aircraft, 100 ships and 100 buildings from which a force of 60,000 troops could be put together and supplied, depending on the requirements of a given mission (Council of the European Union 2000). Although the goal was never fully met, the Council of the European Union confirmed in May 2003 that the EU now had 'operational capability ... limited and constrained by recognised shortfalls', and the EU's commitment to overcoming these obstacles was restated (Council of the European Union 2003). The EU member states had already agreed on a new implementation programme in 2002 – the European Capabilities Action Plan (EACP) – the aim of which was to focus European efforts on acquiring particular crucial assets. This development has continued. New Headline Goals have been agreed and the composition of the forces better reflects the demands of the operations on which they might be deployed. Moreover, the forces have been developed in continuous dialogue with NATO. The aim has been to complement rather than compete with NATO, although some US observers have asked whether EU commitments would, in practice, mean lower NATO spending (Grevi and Keohane 2009: 72).

Given the recognized difficulties in developing the CFSP and the CSDP, some significant improvement in EU action must be acknowledged and a brief overview of some of its CFSP and CSDP activities sheds light to its role in the European foreign and security policy. On the eve of the Stockholm European Council meeting in March 2001 an EU delegation, including External Affairs Commissioner Chris Patten, was due in Skopje to offer EU-wide support to the Macedonian government, and to appeal for a peaceful settlement to its conflict with the Albanian rebels. Javier Solana, the High Representative of the CFSP, had visited Macedonia and Kosovo two days previously, delivering a similar message. The EU policy was supported by NATO action to secure the border between Macedonia and Kosovo through its international Kosovo Force (KFOR) in the region. Three hundred British, Swedish and Finnish soldiers were moved to the border. Their brief was to intercept any logistic support for the rebellious National Liberation Army in Macedonia. After intense diplomatic negotiations led by the European Union and supported by the United States, the rival sides signed a peace accord on 13 August 2001 (Council of the European Union 2001). Moreover, an international NATO force of 3,500 troops led by the British 16th air assault brigade was sent to Macedonia to collect and destroy rebel arms. In March 2003 the EU took over the Macedonian peacekeeping project from NATO. The short-term disarmament project had turned into a longer-term peacekeeping mission.

Significantly, neither the CFSP nor the CSDP have confined their concerns to the European Union's near abroad in the early 2000s. Shortly after taking over the Macedonian mission the EU launched its second military operation in the Democratic Republic of Congo in Africa. It had been involved in efforts to bring about a peaceful settlement of the conflict since 1996, for instance through its Special Representative for the Great Lakes Region. This military operation gave 'further tangible evidence of the development of the European security and defence policy (ESDP) and of the European Union's contribution to the international community's efforts to promote stability and security' (Council of the European Union 2003b: 16). The EU has launched a total of 23 CSDP missions since 2003, nine in Europe, eight in Africa, three in the Middle East, one in Central Asia, and one in South-East Asia. Six of these were principally military operations and 13 were civilian missions, but four combined both military and civilian elements.

Seeking to extend its global reach, the European Union has mediated in the slow-moving peace process between North and South Korea. It has also taken an active role in international efforts to end the violence that followed the collapse of the Middle East peace process. Although there are differences of opinion among the member states on its position towards the conflict, it has been able to play a role. For instance, in 2002 other key players – the US, Russia and the United Nations (UN) – joined the EU in calling on Israel to withdraw from Palestinian cities. The EU has also assumed a key role in the continuing stand-off between Iran and the international community over Iranian efforts to develop a uranium enrichment capability, possibly enabling the production of fissile material for nuclear weapons. It can be granted some success in bringing together the initially differing US and European approaches in favour of diplomacy, backed by sanctions. Moreover, its High Representative has assumed a leading role in the negotiations with Iran. Furthermore, the EU has been a major actor in the rebuilding of Afghanistan, providing assistance worth over three billion Euro since 2002 (the US has provided $6.9 billion and Japan $1.2 billion). Although the CSDP as such has not been employed in the crisis, 25 of the 27 EU member states are contributing to the NATO-led International Security Assistance Force (ISAF), which works under a UN mandate to assist the Afghan authorities in maintaining security.

Despite the developments and the rather bold rhetoric, the residual doubts about the direction and further development of the EU foreign and security policy have not disappeared. Prominent observers have argued that there is no evidence of a convincing collective response to successive stages of multiple crises such as 11 September, the US-led war on terror or the war against Iraq (M. Smith 2003: 557). In particular, the deep divisions between the EU member states exposed in relation to the war on Iraq in 2003 have been considered indicative of the failure or even the demise of the CFSP. As Michael Smith pointed out, according to commentators, 'the cause for EU foreign and security policy was set back for years to come, if not permanently, and that the holy grail of unified European diplomacy – let alone defence activity – had become effectively unattainable' (ibid.). In the opinion of some the deep European and transatlantic divisions were connected to the larger context and presaged disunity and hence the 'death of the West', whereas for others it simply highlighted the profound limitations of the EU's international influence, and the CFSP was identified as 'the key area of self-deception' (ibid.). The post-Iraq development of the European foreign and security policy points in the other direction, however. In other words, EU-level foreign and security policy mediation has increased rather than decreased, and significant institutional reforms have been agreed on and are currently being implemented.

The Lisbon Treaty and the new CFSP and CSDP

The Lisbon Treaty currently in force will fundamentally change the institutional set-up and decision-making of the CFSP and the CSDP. It gives the EU a single legal personality, the aim being to strengthen its negotiating power and thus to make it more effective on the world stage and a more visible partner for third countries and international organizations. It has also established new actors and institutions and reformed existing ones. First and foremost, there is now a permanent President of the European Council – a body comprising member states' heads of state and government that guides the direction of the integration, and which under the treaty has become a fully-fledged EU institution. Second, the roles and functions of the current High Representative of the CFSP and the Commissioner for External Affairs are combined in the new position of High Representative of the Union for Foreign Affairs and Security Policy. Third, the European External Action Service has been set up to support the new High Representative. Fourth, there are several more specific innovations concerning the CSDP aimed at enhancing its decision-making capabilities and the implementation of the policy, including operational capabilities. The details of these reforms are fully documented elsewhere, and the number of analyses dealing with their impact is growing steadily. I will therefore limit discussion here to some of the key issues in the current debate on the CFSP and the CSDP in light of the European Security Strategy (ESS) agreed on 2003 and reviewed in 2008.

The ESS is perhaps the clearest indicator of the kind of foreign and security policy actor the EU is or intends to become, and how it positions itself vis-à-vis other actors (Ojanen 2006: 19). Moreover, many of the key reforms were agreed during the negotiation of the Constitutional Treaty in 2003 and 2004, parallel to the drafting of the EU's first security strategy. As such, it sheds light on the aims of the changes stipulated in the treaty reform. The ESS states that due to its population and economic power 'the European Union is inevitably a global player', and that 'Europe should be ready to share in the responsibility for global security and building a better world' (Council of the European Union 2003c). According to the document, the EU has a wide set of instruments with which to address security challenges such as international terrorism, instability and conflicts brought by environmental degradation, poverty and failed states, for instance. It has developed military capabilities, designed mainly for crisis management, and runs a large number of development programmes. It is further developing its political and institutional capabilities to formulate common policies and positions, and will therefore be able to utilize its economic and political power more effectively in its near abroad and globally. Although initially the CFSP and the CSDP largely reflected European security considerations, the further development of these policies is clearly connected to global competition, influence and security. One could even argue that they provide the impetus for further development in these policy fields, which are often considered the most difficult to integrate. The outgoing High Representative, Javier Solana, reminded his audience in one of his last public performances in 2009 that Europe had two options in world politics: to unite or to become irrelevant (EUISS 2009). Moreover, the nature of the threats and challenges requires a wide set of civilian and economic instruments, such as policing and judicial assistance and training as well as development aims. This indicates that the CFSP and the CSDP must be coordinated with several other areas of EU policy. Furthermore, better coordination will play a major role in the ongoing institutional reforms based on the Lisbon Treaty.

Interestingly, observers have pointed out that the external relations reforms, including the CFSP and the CSDP, were among the least contentious in the nego-tiation of the Constitutional Treaty signed in 2006 (Avery and Missiroli 2007: 6). This was also the case in the French and Dutch referendums that resulted in 'no' votes and the end of the ratification process of the Constitutional Treaty. Moreover, the established consensus largely prevailed in the negotiations over the Lisbon Treaty – which was set to replace it. The requested clarifications and subsequent changes made were mostly marginal, or restated the obvious (Missiroli 2007: 18). Whereas the title of the new chief of EU foreign policy was changed from Union Minister to High Representative of the Union for Foreign Affairs and Security Policy, some member states pushed forward a statement indicating that the treaty provisions related to the CFSP and the CSDP would not affect the prerogatives of the member states' national foreign and security policies, for instance.

Nevertheless, significant reservations about the possibility and future of the CFSP and the CSDP are justifiably expressed in both the policy-making and scholarly worlds. Some of these materialized in the attempt to update the EU's security strategy in 2008 (Council of the European Union 2008). It is widely agreed that both the European and the global security environments have changed significantly since early 2003. The EU has grown and the number of member states has almost doubled. Related to this, the EU was about to adopt the Lisbon Treaty signed in 2007, which would have significantly changed the formula-tion of its foreign and security policy. At the same time, events in Georgia and Ukraine, in the Middle East and across Africa, were demanding a coherent and updated strategic vision for the CFSP and the CSDP. Also, the shift in power relations due to the rise of emerging markets and multipolarity made the re-evaluation of the EU's key strategic goals – such as a world order based on effective multilateralism – highly topical.

Given the high expectations, the 2008 document fell short and introduced only minor changes. On the one hand, the process was undoubtedly influenced by the setback in the ratification of the Lisbon Treaty when Ireland turned it down in a referendum, and the long-awaited reforms were put on hold once again. On the other hand, a strong strategy paper corresponding to the EU's security challenges would have been most useful in order to reassure the member states and others about the urgent need for CFSP and CSDP reform. The failure to agree on a new strategy could therefore be seen as symptomatic of the increasing divergence between the member states' interests and EU strategic thinking.

As we move into the second decade of the twenty-first century the nation-state seems to be gaining more ground in many policy fields. This is a significant development given the trend in the 1990s and 2000s towards global and regional governance and the diminishing role of the state in the fields of politics, international relations and European integration. This also appears to be true in studies on (economic) globalization, in which market forces are largely seen to overshadow state power. In the face of increasing global competition, and long before the global financial crisis of 2008, concerns about the prominence of national economic thinking, even protectionism, were expressed in the EU. Whether this will be a major and long-term trend is debatable given that the relevance of even the largest EU member states has been called into question in light of the emerging new world order. As far as this book is concerned, the current developments are likely to highlight its relevance. It is necessary to recognize the increased EU-level governance in the field of foreign and security policy, and to thoroughly understand the relationship between the EU and its member states.

Theorizing European foreign and security policy

It is suggested in this book that two scholarly traditions have dominated analyses of European foreign and security policy. I label these the intergovernmental and supranational approaches, and argue that they differ considerably in their treatment of the conceptual and empirical puzzles of European foreign and security policy. Whereas intergovernmental approaches have largely maintained their focus on the state and inter-state relations, supranational approaches have highlighted European (mainly EU) institutions and interaction. Moreover, whereas the former reflects the study of international relations and its subfield of foreign policy analysis, the latter is interlinked with theories of European integration. Recently scholars have been increasingly applying the concept of Europeanization in their analyses. For some this has represented a new and distinct approach to the subject matter. The key argument in this chapter is that the main approaches in studies on the Europeanization of foreign and security policy also reflect traditional scholarly positions. The so-called *national projection* approach clearly falls within the intergovernmental tradition, and the *national adaptation* accounts draw on the supranational line of thinking.

Intergovernmental approaches: the prevailing state-centrism

Theorizing European foreign and security policy in light of the CFSP and the CSDP is predominately based on accounts that define these twin policies as examples of intergovernmental cooperation among EU member states. These approaches draw on the realism and neo-liberal institutionalism (including intergovernmentalism) that underpin the study of IR as well as foreign policy analysis. Although they differ in certain basic assumptions and foci, they are similar in ontology: they assume an anarchic international system within which the state is the prominent actor.[1]

Until recently they have tended to highlight the contradictions and problems of the CFSP and the CSDP. For instance, in the early years of the CFSP most of the arguments suggesting that the policy did not exist to the extent stipulated in the treaty texts and policy statements drew on intergovernmental approaches. State-centrism featured strongly in the debate related to the so-called 'capabilities–expectations gap' (Hill 1993) in the CFSP, for instance. As Hill notes, the treaty texts created great expectations, but in practice the development of the EU foreign and security policy was, at best, partial. Hill was mainly concerned about the EU's ability to formulate policies, but others highlighted the lack of military capability to implement the policies. As a result, the EU was generally seen to lack the institutional structures enabling strong and decisive decision-making as well as the military capability to intervene in crises and back up its policies. Consequently, the power in foreign and security policy-making in Europe was argued to lie within the states.

Realists suggest that states are key actors in world affairs, and rational agents operating according to principles of self-help within the structure of an anarchic international system (Morgenthau 1973, Waltz 1979). Although collaboration among states is possible, in practice it is restricted by the ubiquitous possibility of cheating. However, cooperation might emerge due to the presence of a dominant state (i.e. hegemon) or a common threat (Gilpin 1987, Walt 1987). For many realists the emergence of military alliances such as the Western European Union (WEU) and NATO, as well as the initial drive towards European integration in the 1950s, reflected the bipolar world order, the Soviet threat and US security interests. Further cooperation could be explained in terms of alliance dependency, meaning that the fear of abandonment or exclusion leads weaker members to support any cooperation advocated by stronger powers (M. Smith 2004: 20, footnote 4).

Initially the realists largely overlooked the emergence of the CFSP and the CSDP. One reason for this relates to the developments in the immediate post-Cold War world. Whereas the end of the Cold War was widely seen to demonstrate the limitations of realism, the emerging state fragmentation, globalization and environmental degradation constituted further challenges it was considered ill-equipped to address (Williams 2005: 1–2).[2] Indeed, the lack of analytical tools and the general decline of realism in the early 1990s partly explain the relatively modest amount of realist engagement in the increasing level of foreign and security cooperation in Europe. These conditions also shaped the outcomes of the early realist CFSP/CSDP analyses. In short, they rendered suspect the suggested supranational elements – which they were apparently not ready to explain – of the CFSP and the CSDP, and emphasized the fact that the common policies were reconcilable with the national interests of the member states (Pijpers 1991,

Jakobsen 1997, Regelsberger, Schoutheete *et al.* 1997, Tank 1998). Moreover, the alleged difficulties in establishing these policies were used as evidence of the timeless wisdom of core realist assumptions (Ojanen 2002), in other words the limitations of integration in the field of foreign and security policy.

Given the relatively modest amount of explicitly realist engagement during the early years of the CFSP and the CSDP, their grip over the public and over policy-makers should not been downplayed. Moreover, the realist contribution to the policy analysis is clearly on the rise. It has played a vital role in the political and academic debate on the transatlantic divide between the United States and Europe, for instance: some prominent observers such as Samuel Huntington have suggested that Europeans are teaming up against the US hegemon, and are creating a countervailing power (Kagan 2002). Moreover, the work of Adrian Hyde-Price (2006 and 2008) makes a substantial and explicitly neorealist contribution to European foreign and security policy and the development of the CFSP and the CSDP. His analysis is a direct response to and criticism of the liberal notion of the EU as a distinct normative (Manners 2006) or civilian (Duchêne 1973) power. He argues that structural realism can shed considerable light on the emergence, development and nature of both policies. Contradicting liberal and explicitly normative accounts of the EU as an international actor, he emphasizes their systemic determinant, such as the bipolarity shaping European integration and European Political Cooperation. Moreover, the development of the CSDP is considered a function of systemic changes in the structural distribution of power, which has created the US-led unipolar world and multipolar Europe. In this context, the development and functioning of the CFSP and the CSDP represent EU member states' aspirations to shape their external environment with a combination of hard and soft power. Hyde-Price's realist perspective further scrutinizes their ethical basis, which is highlighted in the EU's foreign and security policy rhetoric. First, he convincingly suggests that structural realism could explain the emergence of the EU as a self-proclaimed ethical power, embraced in much of the liberal and normative literature. Second, he argues that in a world of rival states with competing ethical visions EU policies risk leaving it as a weak and ineffective actor or as one that indulges in 'quixotic moral crusades' (Hyde-Price 2008: 29).

It is true that realism offers several intriguing insights into the topical debate on the fate of European integration, the development of the EU as an international actor, and the CFSP and the CSDP; and further realist engagement will surely be an asset in analyses of European foreign policy. Yet it apparently fails to account for the variation in member states' policies responding either to the systemic changes or the increasing supranational elements of the European foreign and security policy. Moreover, it tells us very little, if anything, about the complex institutional context in which the EU member states and other European states find themselves. Here neo-liberal institutionalism – highlighting the possibility of policy formulation through increasingly institutionalized international cooperation (Keohane and Nye 1977) – has offered a helping hand to the realists.[3]

Neo-liberal institutionalists argue that an array of sub-national, transnational and supranational actors have challenged the dominance of the state across a wide range of issues (S. Smith 1994: 4). The focus on the mixed-actor system has led to theoretical innovations that highlight, for instance, the role of international regimes defined as a set of implicit and explicit principles, norms, rules and decision-making procedures, around which actors' expectations converge in a given area of international relations (Krasner 1983: 2). Although the multi-perspective nature of the European project has been used as an exemplar of regionalization (Fawcett and Hurrell 1997) or the emergence of 'post-modern' governance (Ruggie 1993) or 'post-sovereign' foreign policies (M. Smith 2003), the CFSP and the CSDP have not occupied a central place in the general neo-liberal institutionalist literature on global and regional regulation. However, a particular form of neo-liberal institutionalism – known as liberal intergovernmentalism and associated with Andrew Moravcsik – has been influential in terms of theorization.

Intergovernmentalism has challenged functionalist-inspired accounts highlighting the role of an elite alliance between EC officials and pan-European business interest groups in negotiating the Single European Act (1986), in other words the centrality of the EU level of political and economic governance. Such accounts suggest that the negotiations were more consistent with the alternative explanation underlying inter-state bargaining between Britain, France and Germany (Moravcsik 1991), and that scholars should turn away from structural realist theories and towards domestic politics in the analysis of state interests. In this, however, the liberal intergovernmental approach 'stresses traditional conceptions of national interest and power, rather than supranational variants of neofunctionalist integration theory' (Moravcsik 1991: 219). It is suggested here that the Moravcsik's project is illustrative of the prevailing state-centrism of the many neo-liberal institutionalist accounts. These theories generally share ontology. They adopt assumpions of anarchy, state-centrism and an obsession with sovereignty and concerns over security and cheating. On the other hand they accept that institutions can serve as bargaining arenas in helping states to conclude agreements with each other, thus promoting cooperation (M.E. Smith 2004: 23). Like realism, intergovernmentalism also underlines the role of the major member states in integration, and downplays that of the minor states. Significantly, intergovernmentalism has been seen as particularly suitable theoretical approach to deal with areas of low-level integration. Hence it has contributed to the theorizing of the CFSP and the CSDP. Its focus on domestic interest formation is shared in many (European) foreign policy analyses.

The dominant view of these accounts is that a state's foreign policy comprises many competing (national) bureaucracies, and analyses should account for the competition and cooperation among them. Thus the foreign policy is understood as a compromise between various organizations' views of the national interest in the context of international politics (Allison 1971, Manners and Whitman 2000: 5–6), including increased interest in regional-level politics such as the CFSP and the CSDP. Although the EU level is recognized in these accounts, the focus is largely on the member states' responses to the external environment rather than the interaction between the EU and its member states. To some extent this reflects the dominance of the US research community – mainly preoccupied with US policy – in foreign policy analysis, which has certainly highlighted state-centric views on international institutional developments. This, in turn, raises concerns about the appropriateness of these accounts for analysing recent developments in European foreign and security policy. However, a more distinctly European foreign policy analysis emerged in the late 1990s and early 2000s (Carlsnaes, Sjursen and White 2004, Tonra and Christiansen 2004). Some of these accounts also applied theoretical EIS innovations, such as the concept of Europeanization. Although the emergence and application of this concept are discussed in more depth in the following sections of this chapter, it is worth noting here that some of these accounts reflect intergovernmental approaches, namely those conceptualizing the Europeanization of foreign and security policy in terms of the national projection of interests on the European level.

Thus, as in many of the intergovernmental approaches analysed above, these Europeanization accounts largely examine in which cases, in what ways and with what results the states have attempted to influence European-level institutions and, in particular, the CFSP and the CSDP. Even if the importance of the EU level is increasingly acknowledged, its impact on national policies and institutions, let alone identities, is not sufficiently addressed. Given the IR community's longer-term interest in increasing interdependence, as well as the more recent focus on regionalization (Fawcett and Hurrell 1997, Hay, Watson and Wincott 1999, H. Wallace 2000) and globalization (Held 1999, Marsh and Hay 1999), the tendency in the scholarly literature to view the CFSP and the CSDP through state-centric lenses is indeed puzzling. However, in light of the growing empirical evidence of the importance of these policies, intergovernmental approaches are increasingly being put under scrutiny. Consequently, the types of analytical engagement with the CFSP and the CSDP have diversified.

Supranational approaches: from functionalism to top-down Europeanization

As the EU institutions and policies in the field of foreign and security policy have developed, more and more studies focus on the CFSP and CSDP. Consequently, some scholars have explicitly underlined the supranational elements of the CFSP and the CSDP related to institutional development and policy-making processes at the EU level. In addition, there has been an increasing tendency to approach member-state politics in terms of top-down Europeanization, the aim being to map change in member states through participation in European integration.

Given the dominance of the intergovernmental approaches, it is worth noting that some alternative modes of thinking have prevailed in the analysis of European foreign and security policy throughout the post-war era. As Rosamond argues, the host of 'theoretical accounts that emerged in the 1950s and 1960s offered rival narratives of how closer cooperation in relatively narrow, technical, economic spheres of life could generate wider political integration among countries' (Rosamond 2000: 1). For instance, early functionalist integration theory was part of a broad movement that sought to theorize the conditions of the emerging human conflict in the turbulent political climate of the 1940s. On the familiar question of the avoidance of war, it attempted to encourage non-realist IR scholarship. Subsequently, some of the more integrationist theoretical innovations could have contributed to the analysis of European foreign and security policy. For instance, the works of David Mitrany on functionalism and Karl Deutch on transactionalism are closely related to the debates within IR.

Functionalism, as articulated in the work of Mitrany, emerged in opposition to the dominant rationale of Morgenthau's realist state-centric world-view (Rosamond 2000: 31), and Mitrany could be read as 'an intellectual ancestor' of interdependence theory, world-society approaches and regime theory (Taylor 1994: 125). Given that these approaches represented an attempt to move beyond the strict logic of state-centrism, this ontological assumption prevailed in many theoretical innovations related to European post-war developments. Deutsch's well-established theory of security communities serves as an exemplar. He argued that the level of communication (transactions) between states correlated with the sense of community among them. The more interaction there was between the states the greater their mutual relevance.[4] He also emphasized the continuing importance of the state, suggesting that security based on inter-state cooperation would be more likely to emerge in practice, and that it would be more durable (Deutsch 1968: 195–196).

The integration theory representing the most vigorous attempts to overcome state-centrism is neo-functionalism. The key proponent of neo-functionalist thought, Ernst Haas, defined integration as the formation of a new political community in which national political actors were persuaded to shift their loyalties, expectations and political activities towards a new centre, and the institutions of the new centre possessed authority over the states (Haas 1968). However, in their search for a non-state-centric theory of integration, neo-functionalists made an analytical move from 'high politics' to 'low politics'. They considered the key issues to be the satisfaction of welfare and material needs rather than matters of war and peace, suggesting that the 'ideological boundaries' that used to block inter-state cooperation in these areas were breaking down, and that a 'supranational scheme of government' was emerging on the regional level (Rosamond 2000: 56–57). In light of the developments in the economic field of European integration in the 1980s and early 1990s, neo-functionalism developed into a dominant integration theory (Sandholtz and Zysman 1989: 195). However, it started to feature in the analysis of European foreign policy only a decade later.

Towards the end of the 1990s the key concept in neo-functionalism, the spill-over of integration from one area to another, seemed increasingly relevant in analyses of European foreign and security policy. In other words, the development of the CFSP and the CSDP indicated that economic integration was spilling over into the field of foreign and security policy (Ojanen 2002: 6–7). Accordingly, neo-functionalism-inspired thinking underpinning the supranational theories of the so-called 'New Europe' (Rosamond 2000: 128) also spilled over to the analysis of European foreign and security policy. Two analytical approaches characterize this expanding body of literature: (i) studies focusing on the European Union's foreign and security policy; and (ii) analysis of the Europeanization of foreign and security policy.

Scholars taking the former approach have sought to demonstrate that the European Union has a foreign and security policy in accordance with both the broad and narrow definitions of the term (H. Smith 2002, K.E. Smith 2003, M. Smith 2003). The EU is assigned some state-like features in some of these accounts, whereas others emphasize that even if it constitutes an increasingly important element of European foreign and security policy, it cannot be fully accounted for by comparing it to a state (Gingsberg 2003: 12). Hence the increasing interaction within the EU framework is considered to represent a challenge to the conventional conceptualization of foreign policy (Tonra 2001, White 2001, M.E. Smith 2004, Tonra and Christiansen 2004, White 2004), and a distinct European foreign policy analysis has emerged. Within this movement scholars have tackled the question raised by Steve Smith in 1994: Can established foreign policy theories help us to understand and explain developments in Europe since the late 1980s? (S. Smith 1994).[5] As European foreign policy analysis has taken shape, a degree of convergence between IR and European integration studies is also to be observed. For instance, Manners and Whitman sought to formulate a comprehensive framework for comparative foreign policy analysis that would capture the diversity and complexity in the making of foreign policy among EU member states (Manners and Whitman 2000), and several other scholars have highlighted the process of Europeanization in foreign policy (Tonra 2001, White 2004, Wong 2005). Significantly, these approaches have made a substantial contribution to the analysis of European foreign and security policy.

Europeanization and the comparative turn

In the view of many, European integration has reached the stage at which its impact on European states must be taken into consideration. This line of thought is parallel to the scholarly interest in the EU as a political system (Hix 1999) rather than an international organization. In this context Europeanization is becoming an increasingly prominent analytical concept as well as a research agenda in explaining European politics (Vink and Graziano 2007). It is often connected to the so-called comparative turn in EIS and political science, in other words the tendency to account for convergence and divergence in institutional and policy changes among the European states within comparative frameworks (Hix 1994, Giuliani 2003).

Europeanization is an interdisciplinary term employed in sociology, economics, social anthropology, history and the political sciences. It has accumulated a wide set of meanings depending on the discipline and the specific questions on the different research agendas (Featherstone 2003: 3, Liebert 2003: 14). It has also been connected with the concept of multi-level governance. Although Europeanization generally concerns the vertical relations between the EU and the national entities, the notion of multi-level governance broadens the scope of the analysis in incorporating the horizontal level (Bache 2008: 1). Consequently the term is now widely deployed in the literature, which according to some reflects the emergence of a new and distinct field of inquiry (Börzel and Risse 2000, Featherstone 2003, Vink and Graziano 2007). Given the variation in approaches, a lively conceptual and theoretical debate has emerged. Some argue, for instance, that Europeanization as such is not an analytical solution or a theory, but is rather a phenomenon that needs to be explained (Bulmer 2007: 47, Radaelli 2004).

Within this debate it is helpful to distinguish between Europeanization as 'a background concept and a systematised concept' (Radaelli 2004: 4). As a background concept it refers to all the possible meanings we can think of whereas as a systematized concept its scope is more restricted. Within the community of scholars tackling questions related to European integration it reflects an increasing focus on the effects of the integration process, in particular in domestic arrangements (Knill 2001: 10). As such, Europeanization shifts the focus in relation to theories of European integration, theories of governance and classic themes of comparative politics (Radaelli 2004: 5). As Börzel and Risse (2000) note, for decades 'European studies have mostly been concerned with explaining European integration and Europeanization processes themselves'.[6] Accordingly, the debate between the intergovernmental and supranational approaches – liberal intergovernmentalism and neo-functionalism, for instance – has centred on the question of how to account for the emerging European polity. The study of Europeanization, however, adopts a different perspective in accepting that there is a process of European integration under way, and that the EU has developed its own institutions and policies over the last fifty years or so (Radaelli 2004: 5). Consequently, the studies are not preoccupied with questions related to the nature of the integration, such as why and how member states produce it, and whether the EU is intergovernmental or supranational. On the contrary, the theoretical aim is to bring domestic politics back into our understanding of integration by focusing on its impact on the domestic political and social processes of the member states (Börzel and Risse 2000, Radaelli 2004). The concept of Europeanization thus captures the way in which the European dimension has become an embedded feature framing policy, politics and polity within European states.[7] The issue is no longer whether Europe matters but how it matters, 'to what degree, in what direction, at what pace, and at what point of time' (Börzel and Risse 2000).

A key analytical observation and innovation in studies on Europeanization is that the domestic impact is differential (Jupille and Caporaso 1999, Green Cowles, Caporaso and Risse-Kappen 2001). For instance, it has been concluded that national administrative traditions have been able to both accommodate and modify or even neutralize European pressure for change (Hix and Goetz 2000: 216), and that the process has not replaced or rejected national administrative structures, cultures, rules and norms. In light of these findings, Europeanization has been defined as a process of convergence towards shared policy frameworks (Liebert 2003: 14–15), or of structural change, variously affecting actors and institutions, ideas and interests (Featherstone 2003: 3). It is nevertheless emphasized that it does not require assimilation, or indicate an erosion of the domestic level (Börzel and Risse 2000, Caporaso and Jupille 2001). On the contrary, the internal workings of member states are considered crucial for the process. Significantly, divergence is also a possibility.

There is, however, a relevant concern related to the ontological and epistemological assumptions in these approaches. Christiansen, Jørgensen and Wiener (2001: 1) argue, for instance, that the turn towards comparative frameworks could make the shape and type of polity less interesting than the variation in policy and politics. Hurrell and Menon (1996: 388–389) also dispute the desirability of the separation of analyses focusing on (European) 'politics' and 'integration' (Hix 1994). They suggest that studying these aspects separately, often in a rather mechanical fashion within rigid comparative frameworks, sidelines the crucial question of how the 'politics' feeds into the 'integration' and vice versa. Consequently, the top-down notion of Europeanization seems to accommodate only one direction of the reciprocal relationship between the EU and its member states. Although any approach is likely to be partial, it is suggested in this book that our understanding of the relationship between EU and member-state levels of governance will benefit from the fuller conceptualization that is often implicitly present in studies of the Europeanization of foreign and security policy.

The Europeanization of foreign and security policy: a top-down and bottom-up process?

The issue of Europeanization has also been raised in the context of foreign and security policy, connected to a process of incremental change that can be traced back to the post-war years. Scholars have recently found it useful in describing and analysing the increased interaction in European foreign and security policy-making, particularly with regard to issues related to EU foreign and security policy. It is also loosely connected with the literature on the EU as an international actor, and to studies on regional and global governance. It is suggested in this book that the concept has analytical value for the analysis of European foreign and security policy, and in particular that it captures the reciprocal features of the relationship between the EU and the member-state level of governance.

Scholars have been applying the concept of Europeanization in relation to European foreign, security and defence policies ever since the late 1940s when the post-war European defence cooperation was agreed (White 2001: 4–10).[8] Some started from the 1950s when attempts to establish an exclusively European Defence Community failed and the notion of the 'civilian power Europe' began to emerge (M. Smith 2003: 559).[9] On the other hand, a number of authors highlight European Political Cooperation as the beginning of a process in which the then EC member states sought to consult one another on foreign policy issues and to coordinate their respective national positions (M.E. Smith 2004: 17, Bretherton and Vogler 2006: 4). Common to all of these accounts is the notion of the modest accretion of cooperation and institutional evolution and the central role of the state in the process. It should also be noted that the Europeanization of foreign and security policy has not been restricted to the EU, and has included other institutions such as NATO and the Organization for Security and Cooperation in Europe. This being said, the recent literature on the Europeanization of foreign, security and defence policies has largely focused on the EU. As Featherstone argues, among IR scholars the use of Europeanization as a term has reflected the growth in EU foreign policy coordination (Featherstone 2003: 10). Indeed, one of the first authors to refer to the Europeanization of foreign policy in the mid-1980s examined the reorientation of the national foreign policy as a consequence of EC entry.[10] However, such application of the concept is rare, partly because EU competence in this field was considered modest and faltering.

Bottom-up Europeanization: a national projection approach

Some foreign policy analysts approach Europeanization as a bottom-up process, highlighting the national projection of interests and policies on the EU level. This could be a consequence of the relative weakness of EU competence in this area, compared with many aspects of market regulation (Featherstone 2003: 12). According to Wong, the national projection school maintains that states are the primary actors and agents of Europeanization (2005: 137). They are highly pro-active rather than passive in projecting their preferences, policy ideas and models onto the European level. As a consequence, participation on the EU level has increased the levels of communication and consultation among European states. This conception of Europeanization clearly shares many similarities with inter-governmental approaches, and hence its novelty is somewhat unclear. Although it is the antithesis of the top-down Europeanization approach, the state-centric argument is omnipresent in the literature and is not limited to the analysis of foreign and security policy. After all, the so-called Europeanization turn is largely based on increasing dissatisfaction with the dominant intergovernmental (bottom-up) and supranational (top-down) approaches to European integration and politics.

Top-down Europeanization: a national adaptation approach

Various authors attribute the reorientation of national foreign policies and related institutions to the European Union (Raunio and Tiilikainen 2003, Tonra 2001). For many, the amazingly rapid development of the CFSP and the CSDP both reflects and further enhances the Europeanization of foreign and security policy, and makes it sensible to focus on national adaptation (Howorth 2001, White 2001, Hansen 2002, Rieker 2005, Dover 2007). However, the continuing salience of the member states, especially in the formulation of the CFSP and the CSDP, could explain why the focus has, in a sense, been 'wider' in this area than in other fields of research on Europeanization. Rather than adopting a quantitative perspective on the 'mechanisms' through comparative frameworks, many scholars have taken a more qualitative approach, viewing the Europeanization of foreign and security policy as an elite socialization or cognitive process. Tonra (2000: 240), for instance, suggests that in terms of foreign policy it means changes in the way in which national foreign policies are constructed, in how professional roles are defined and pursued, and in the consequent internalization of norms and expectations arising from a complex system of collective European policy-making. M.E. Smith (2000: 617–628) notes that EU processes are having a stronger impact on national foreign policy in terms of elite socialization, bureaucratic reorganization, constitutional change, and an increase in public support for EU foreign policy. On the other hand, domestic procedures and cultures are conducive to the forging of common positions at the EU level. Tonra (2001: 279) arrives at a similar conclusion, suggesting that the relationship between national- and European-level foreign policies has been and continues to be reciprocal.[11]

This conceptualization of Europeanization is related to the methodological debate in IR, most importantly to the problems of structure and agency and levels of analysis. In their bridging attempts scholars working on the Europeanization of foreign and security policy have predominantly turned to social constructivism. Their main interest has been in the interaction between EU and member-state levels of governance, and its impact on the norms and rules, national cultures and identities in the foreign, security and defence policies of the member states (Manners and Whitman 2001, Tonra 2001, Aggestam 2004, Rieker 2005) or the EU (Fierke and Wiener 2001, Sjursen and K.E. Smith 2004). Europeanization, as a means of bridging levels of analysis as well as structure and agency, also has its critics. As White points out, some reviewers claim that it is a vague and widely applied concept that describes the process of integration rather than explaining how or why it occurs (White 2004: 21). As shown in the above section, however, scholars are increasingly preoccupied with defining the concept and its applicability in explaining both European politics and the process of integration. This growing body of literature also has value for scholars interested in the Europeanization of foreign and security policy, and encourages them to define their stance more precisely in light of their specific research interests.

Thus, and in light of the recent theoretical ferment focusing on the ontological and epistemological assumptions of IR, the gap in the literature on Europeanization might lie elsewhere. It is concluded in this chapter that whereas studies on the Europeanization of foreign and security policy provide an entry point for wider research agendas and qualitative methods of social constructivism in the more general literature, they largely lack a poststructuralist contribution, which has gained substantial ground in IR and political science though the emergence of discourse analysis, for instance. This is strange in that many of these accounts have explicitly addressed the theoretical and methodological problems related to complex and reciprocal relationships and levels of analysis. Poststructuralism has thereby questioned some of the theoretical and methodological assumptions in key social-constructivist accounts. Similarly, discourse analysis has provided novel ways in which to examine foreign and security policy, and these seem to be highly relevant in conceptualizing Europeanization as both a top-down and a bottom-up process.

Conclusion

This chapter outlined a particular approach to the Europeanization of foreign and security policy that highlights reciprocal elements of the process. It is suggested that the developments in European foreign and security policy challenge the dominant forms of analysis, which principally reflect either intergovernmental (bottom-up) or supranational (top-down) approaches. Given the two-sided character of the process, these approaches have a limited capacity to elucidate the relationship between the member states and the European Union, and the concept of Europeanization thus offers a way forward. Nevertheless, some of the studies on Europeanization conducted in the field of foreign and security policy reflect conventional approaches. The process has also been described as the national projection of interests on the EU level, or as national adaptation to the CFSP and the CSDP. Nevertheless, it has paved the way for arriving at a more comprehensive conceptualization of Europeanization as both a top-down and a bottom-up process. Many of these accounts draw on social-constructivist theory and methods, and the contributions of poststructuralism and discourse analysis are largely ignored. The aim in the following chapter is to narrow this gap.

3 Foreign policy and state identity

Towards comparative discourse analysis

Introduction

The developments in European foreign and security policy have been among the most salient issues in the scholarly literature of the late 1990s and early 2000s. It is generally assumed that EU countries are increasingly coordinating common policies within the context of the CFSP and the CSDP. This change is conventionally addressed within a intergovernmental framework highlighting the national projection of interests on the European level, and few accounts focus on the impact of these policies on the EU member states and their interests. The previous chapter demonstrated how the CFSP and the CSDP are increasingly shaping the environment in which European states find themselves. It is therefore plausible to integrate supranational elements into the analysis of European foreign and security policy. It was also suggested that such attempts could benefit from the application of discourse analysis, which is increasingly applied in IR, EIS and political science.

The purpose of this chapter is to determine how an approach conceptualizing Europeanization as a top-down and bottom-up process can be construed. It explores the links between Europeanization, social constructivism and discourse analysis, with a view to fostering interest in the Europeanization of national and state identities. Proceeding in three stages it sets out the theoretical and methodological framework of the empirical analysis of this book. The first part focuses on levels of analysis on the one hand, and structure and agency on the other in terms of social constructivism and poststructuralist-inspired accounts of foreign and security policy. The intention is not to solve these methodological 'problems', but rather to get round them by deploying a particular conceptualization of state identity. The second part describes the methods of discourse analysis used in IR and EIS, and further elucidates the theoretical context of the subsequent empirical analysis. The chapter ends with a discussion of the methods used and the comparative framework of the analysis. The conclusions are twofold. It is suggested on the one hand that studies on Europeanization – addressing the reciprocal relationship between national and European levels – could benefit from the application of discourse analysis, and that the comparative analysis underpinning much of the Europeanization research is valuable for discourse analysis in general.

Theoretical framework: bridging levels of analysis, and structure and agency

Even if state-centred accounts have dominated the analysis of European political integration, and supranational approaches have been applied mainly in the area of economic integration, alternative ways of theorizing structure and agency have emerged in studies on European foreign policy. This largely reflects the emergence of social constructivism in IR, which has spilled over to the field of European integration (Diez 1999, Christiansen, Jørgensen and Wiener 2001, Moravcsik 2001, Hansen 2002). These engagements reflect a similarly vibrant discussion between social constructivism and poststructuralism (Katzenstein 1996, Adler 1997, Campbell 1998, Hopf 1998, Weldes *et al.* 1999, Wendt 1999, Doty 2000, S. Smith 2000). Thus the process of European integration has recently been addressed in accounts highlighting the reciprocal and mutually constitutive features of the relationship between the regional context (structure) and state conduct (agency) (Christiansen, Jørgensen and Wiener 2001, Sjursen 2001, Tonra 2001, Rieker 2005). In other words, the existence of regional-level structural factors – such as the CFSP and CSDP institutions, procedures, norms and rules, and discourses – and state agency is considered relational: the state-agency is part of the reproduction on the regional level and vice versa.

It is clear from the debate between social constructivists and poststructuralists, however, that the mutual constitution of structure and agency on different levels of analysis is addressed rather differently depending on one's theoretical position. Whereas many social constructivists have attempted to solve the problem, poststructuralists suggested that it is not necessarily a problem that calls for a solution in the first place (Doty 2000, Hay 2002).[1] It is rather a theoretical assumption reflecting different ontological positions on the social world. In their endeavours to capture the mutually constitutive social and political relationships between structure and agency, both parties to the debate have made use of the concept of identity. However, the difference between 'solving' and 'moving beyond' this question has some significant analytical implications.

In searching for a theory that unites structure and agency through the concept of identity social constructivism is indeed a tempting option in that its main protagonists have often explicitly addressed the problem. This is certainly the case with Alexander Wendt, whose constructivism operates mainly at the level of the international system and individual states. Although the international system clearly constitutes the context within which the states find themselves, they are assigned a degree of agency. Their identity and interests are therefore constructed within, rather than derived from, the international system and other structural constraints. As Wendt argues, anarchy is what states make of it (Wendt 1992). In the context of the Europeanization of foreign and security policy, Wendt's constructivism would suggest that European integration and the structural factors it entails, such as the CFSP and the CSDP, are what states make of them. Hence they can contribute to the identity construction and interests of the EU member states. Given Wendt's focus on the external environment, the capacity of his account to capture the meanings generated from within the state – how each state, nation or unit creates its own identity – is however rather limited (S. Smith 2000: 161–162).[2] Thus it largely fails to bring the national context back into the analysis of European foreign and security policy, which is one of the key aims of Europeanization studies.

Some constructivists have attempted to address this shortcoming by focusing on the construction of the national identity through certain country cases (Katzenstein 1996). In these accounts a state's identity largely constitutes cultural and historical factors and narratives. These factors explain Germany's and Japan's relatively low political profile in the international arena, for instance (Berger 1996), and the continuities in Chinese foreign policy (Johnston 1996). However, there are also significant limitations. Crucially, the accounts largely fail to explain in a systematic way how the same cultural and historical background of a particular state can sustain highly contradictory foreign policies (Wæver 2002: 22). Whereas historical and cultural narratives in Britain allow both anti- and pro-European policies, the Finnish national culture has been able to accommodate aspirations for full neutrality and deep political alignment with the EU.

In moving from a somewhat fixed conceptualization of identity, constructed in relation either to the international system or the national culture, towards something more contingent the discussion easily turns to poststructuralism and discourse-analytical approaches. Significantly, the primary interest among poststructuralists has been in examining how structures of meaning – often called discourses – are constitutive of both social agents and structures (Weldes 1996). Accordingly, the focus of the analysis shifts from the grand narratives of the anarchical international system or national culture and history towards political practices within which the identity of the state in question is continuously being reproduced. Poststructuralists have been interested in elucidating the processes in which states and other agents gain a particular identity, which in turn allows a certain degree of agency and hence shapes the agents' reasoning about possible and feasible action (Doty 1993). It is significant that within these accounts the structural and agential aspects as well as the level of analysis are considered integral features of any explanation of European foreign and security policy. Moreover, whereas the interplay between these factors is seen as integral to the production and reproduction of state identities, discourse analysis has provided researchers with the necessary analytical tools.

Discourse analysis in international relations

In the late 1990s Jennifer Milliken noted how studies involving discourse as a key theoretical concept had become one of the most active and interesting areas of IR (1999: 225). This reflected developments in both theory and practice. On the one hand, theoretical and methodological developments in many fields of sociology and politics finally penetrated the discipline in the late 1980s. On the other hand, the difficulties of mainstream approaches in accounting for some key developments such as the end of the Cold War, the disintegration of the Soviet

Union and the integration of Western Europe underlined the need for alternative theories and methods. However, discourse analysis is often seen as a poststructuralist method rather than a theory or school of thought (Wæver 2004: 197). Indeed part of the difficulty of establishing discourse studies in IR and EIS is that methodologically the approach is not singular. It draws from different disciplines and canons, invoking different understandings of discourse (Laffey and Weldes: 2004: 28). For some, discourse analysis concerns the content or structure of written and spoken language, whereas others approach discourses as structures of meaning and analyse the interplay between discourse(s) and practice. Against this background, however, Milliken argues that given the divergent claims inherent in these approaches, discourse scholars in IR agree on the basic principles of how discourses work generally and in this particular subject field (1999: 225). This, in turn has led to common research interests. First, the overall aim in discourse studies has been to elucidate how discursive and social processes are intrinsically connected, and to analyse, in specific contexts, the implications of this connection for the way we think and act in the contemporary world. Second, scholarly interest in analysing discourses and the production of knowledge has been closely related to the critical analysis of power relations and inequalities, and in IR the field is often portrayed as a form of critical theory (ibid.).

Within IR the close relationship between discourse studies and so-called dissident, radical or critical IR has resulted in polarized positions, a focus on meta-theory and on the nature of the discipline (Wæver 1998). Notwithstanding the contribution of these accounts, this might have obscured the usefulness of the more operational analyses to broader audiences. Many discourse scholars have formulated innovative methods and focused on empirical questions.[3] On the other hand, many of these analyses focus on the United States and its foreign policy, and elucidate the construction of the other, such as enemies, allies, or crisis situations through which the US state identity emerge. Discussion on the broader applicability of discourse studies in analysing governance on local, state, regional and global levels is under-theorized in IR, however. This is unfortunate given the potential of such studies to offer an analytical frame within which to examine the links between actors located on various levels in international relations. They could, for instance, shed light on the changes and continuity in discourses concerning national foreign and security policy, which are increasingly shaped by global and regional contexts and institutions such as regimes and organizations. As argued in the previous chapter, there is an urgent need for analytical tools and research frameworks that are able to deal with these features of foreign and security policy. Interestingly, discourse studies addressing these issues have almost without exception come from European integration studies and/or political science.[4]

Discourse analysis in European integration studies

European integration studies now includes discourse-analytical approaches. Although discourse analysis has hardly achieved a prominent status – it has not been considered a serious rival of the main theories, nor has it provided a distinct interpretation of integration or of the EU itself (Wæver 2004: 197) – it has been successfully and increasingly applied in the analysis of EU politics. Unlike studies on international relations, discourse studies have not been linked with debates on the constitution of the discipline or the potential of knowledge and science. This is not necessarily surprising given that European integration studies are rarely considered an independent discipline in the first place, and rather tend to be located in between international relations and political science with some potential to bridge the divide between them. EIS has close links with European political science, in which discourse analysis – in particular the discourse theory developed by Laclau and Mouffe (1985) – is established as a valuable research tradition. As Wæver notes, although most political scientists have never heard of it and feel no need to relate to it, it has gained enough of a foothold in certain departments to establish its own sub-culture within the field (2004: 197).

There are two distinct approaches to discourse analysis in the field of European integration studies (ibid.). First, a relatively limited number of scholars attempt to develop it as a (general) theory of European integration, either to explain it and the emerging polity or to assess its impact on member states.[5] Second, a larger number of discourse studies have taken up some of the key questions in the field of European integration, conducted within several sub-fields and policy areas such as economic necessity (Hay and Rosamond, 2002), but also very much in the field of foreign, security and defence policy (Larssen 1997, Glarbo 2001). This more substantial body of literature resonates with the majority of approaches to discourse analysis in international relations, in which it is seen as a methodology rather than a theory.[6]

In relation to European integration, discourse-analytical approaches have been used to map out the features and forms of the European project, EU governance and national politics. All of these studies on different aspects of integration are closely linked to the concept of Europeanization, but the links are rarely explicitly addressed. The body of work analysing the European integration project frequently uses texts originating from the EU system and/or more general public debate on Europe, such as history books or the interventions of intellectuals. Here the focus is on how the integration project as such is conceptualized and what kind of identity it promotes. The key is to understand how discursive processes interact with general changes in Europe in areas such as legitimacy, history, the media, citizenship and politics (Wæver 2004: 207–209, Delanty and Rumford 2005). As Wæver notes, this approach to the study of discourse in European integration studies differs from the studies in IR, which have predominantly focused on the US and 'have tended to develop into rather monolithic stories of how the identity needs of the US state have demanded continued production of self/other images and foreign threats' (2004: 208, see also Doty 1993, Weldes 1996, Campbell 1998). In contrast, European institution building and EU development employ diverse and often contradictory discourses and project multiple identities. In terms of studies on Europeanization, this approach provides interesting insights into the development of regional and global discourses, which cut across conventional state boundaries. However, their suggested conceptual contribution to discourse theorizing is to be found in the studies on EU governance and national foreign policies. More specifically, it is suggested in this study that the concept of Europeanization enables us to bridge the two more explicitly.

Discourse scholars have contributed to the increasing body of literature on governance, and they have joint research interests with scholars highlighting the concept of multi-level governance. They are interested in 'polity ideas', defined as normative ideas about a legitimate political order (Jachtenfuchs, Diez and Jung 1998), for instance. A key question concerns whether these ideas are still relevant in a modern state – either in the intergovernmental sense of emphasizing EU member states, or in the supranational sense of highlighting the EU as a federal state – or whether they have moved beyond the state in terms of functionalism-inspired output legitimacy or network-stimulated legitimacy based on participation and identity (Diez 1999, 2001, Wæver 2004: 203). Thomas Diez (2001) addresses the legitimacy question explicitly via discourse analysis. He has applied and developed Laclau and Mouffe's (1985) concept of discursive nodal points, which are important junctures of discourses and hence significant for identity production. According to Diez, European governance is one of the current nodal points. Significantly, his analysis points towards increasing horizontal governance and interdependency, for instance among European political parties and other sub-state actors. On the other hand, his critics suggest that this approach downplays the national and state-level context. As Wæver notes, the focus on multi-level governance might initially seem like an interesting move to transcend the traditional limitations of intergovernmental approaches. However, the inter-connectedness of different discourses within the national context(s) and state institutions is easily overlooked. For instance, the transformation of the neutrality discourse to an alignment discourse in Finland in the early 1990s was based mainly on interaction between (vertically positioned) state and EU discourses, rather than horizontal discursive relations with neutrality discourses in other countries. Taking the opposite approach, however, easily creates the opposite problem, and points back to the value of EU governance.

The most substantial body of literature applying discourse theorizing in European integration studies is explicitly related to international relations. It was developed mainly to explain European foreign policies, and the prominent authors categorize it as a theory of foreign policy (Wæver 2002) rather than of European integration.[7] However, its value to integration theory has also been highlighted in that all of its main contributions have related to European policies, mostly those of EU member states. Significantly, the theory gives an explicit recommendation for analysing the interplay between 'on the one hand, national discursive struggles among competing articulations of national traditions and, on the other, the process (or not) of European integration' (Wæver 2004: 205). The main idea is to see how the general lines of foreign policy, and thereby European policy, are based on different concepts of Europe, and how these in turn are made possible by articulating differently concepts of state and nation, such as the French state-nation and the German concept of a romantic nation and a power state (ibid.). The explanatory power of the theory is partly related to the model of layered structures inspired by Kenneth Waltz's concept of international structure (1979). As Wæver explains:

> At the deepest level is the basic national concept of state-nation, at the second a purely relational conception of where the state-nation is in relation to Europe (internal, external, doubled, etc.), and at the third level are different concepts of Europe. The layered conception defines a way of studying stability and change because from any specific point, one can see possible changes as being more or less radial, and therefore more or less likely, depending on whether they happen at the third, the second, or the first layer.
>
> (Wæver 2004: 205)

This approach has many advantages and, for many, it is a practical application of discourse theorizing. It enables analysis of national European policies and sheds light on the direction(s) of European integration. As Wæver argues, European integration is only stable to the extent that the key countries can make sense out of their future within a discourse that includes the current European project (2004: 206). Significantly, in relation to Europeanization studies, these discourses do not need to be identical between countries; they only have to be compatible. Accordingly, divergence can be accommodated within this theory. Indeed, a relatively large proportion of the related empirical work has concentrated on the problems of advancing integration in countries such as Denmark and Norway, and the outcomes of the research could be seen as a warning of the fragility of European integration and an indication of the need to take the national context(s) seriously (ibid.).

The scholars themselves note that the approach is weak when 'discourses leave their national confines and meet directly in a European arena' (ibid). Arguably, this is currently the reality in several policy fields, including foreign and security policy. Although, the theory does allow the incorporation of the EU level as an overlapping layer, this is mostly considered secondary. The dominant view is that European processes are decided and guided by the key member states. The theory is therefore often loosely connected to intergovernmental analysis, and as such resonates with the conceptualization of Europeanization as national projection. Accordingly, it is suggested that the key puzzle confronting any student of European integration remains unsolved. Scholars still have to decide 'whether to approach Europe via national policies or by looking directly at the European project as such, 'its discourses and institutions' (Wæver 2004: 211).

It is nevertheless posited in this book that all discourse and some Europeanization studies approach this question very differently than conventional integration theories based on either state-centrism or supranationalism. As noted in the first chapter, the literature on Europeanization argues that both EU and national levels are important, and recently the relationship between them has been emphasized as the key to understanding and explaining governance in Europe. Similarly, discourse-analytical approaches have problematized the existence of given and fixed identities and subjects, such as states, and highlight the discursive construction of the state (or the EU) through complex relationships cutting across external/internal boundaries. It follows that we should avoid thinking of different levels of governance as ontologically separable; rather, they are mutually constitutive. The puzzle Wæver poses should therefore be read as an exercise in theoretical and methodological self-reflection as highlighted in discourse studies. For instance, his quasi-structuralist theory of discourse as layered structures makes plausible assumptions in prioritizing some layers in the analysis of the discursive possibilities of EU member states' European and foreign policies. Namely, it argues that foreign policy discourses are essential for the reproduction of states' identities, and that state actors and a national discursive context constitute the key to understand the interaction of governance in present-day Europe. Although these assumptions partly reproduce the traditional state-centric world-view they do not indicate fixed-state identities or levels and forms of governance.

In terms of its contribution to the literature on Europeanization, discourse theory can deepen our understanding of states' external and internal contexts (e.g. levels of governance). Externally it carries the potential to elucidate how discourses are established and reproduced in regional and global governance institutions, for instance, and internally it facilitates a better understanding of the domestic context and of why variation occurs. On the other hand, Europeanization studies pave the way for discourse analysis to connect the increasing interaction among the different levels with the internal and external contexts assumed in much of the literature on global, regional and domestic governance.

Methodological framework: towards comparative discourse analysis

Given the analytical purposes of this study, the methodological pluralism of discourse-analytical approaches has clear advantages – as a set of diverse analytical tools it is a strength in terms of examining complex and mutually constitutive relationships located on different levels. It should be stressed that such approaches are best seen as a version of problem-driven rather than method- or theory-driven research (Howarth 2005: 318). Method-driven approaches highlight the techniques of data gathering and analysis rather than the empirical phenomena under investigation, whereas the aim in theory-driven research is to support a particular theoretical proposition rather than to address a problem independently of the theory. However, problem-driven research should not be confused with problem-solving theory, which is valued in mainstream IR and EIS. As Howarth notes, the former is categorized in opposition to the latter in that problem-solving theory generally takes key units of analysis such as states and the levels of analysis as given. Nevertheless, the availability of methods also calls for clarification and reflection.

The social and political world is not understood as a simple reflection of ideas or material conditions in this study. In other words, the meaning the CFSP and the CSDP does not transparently correspond to something external; it is rather acquired through specific, mutable social processes, and is often generated by words, symbols and images, for instance (Squires 1999: 87). In accordance with anti-essentialist ontology and anti-foundationalist epistemology, it is assumed in the empirical analysis that the CFSP and the CSDP assume meaning through human agreement and social interaction, and hence not independently of our knowledge and conceptions of them. In other words, the meaning given to the suggested Europeanization of foreign and security policy is relational to the established system(s) of meaning manifested within the discursive field of European foreign and security policy. This is not to imply scepticism about the existence of the reality, however. Indeed, the claim that every object is constituted as an object of discourse has nothing to do with whether there is a world external to thought (Laclau and Mouffe 1997: 108). The establishment of the EU's rapid-reaction forces certainly took place independently of our thinking of it, but whether their specificity as forces is constructed in terms of 'peacekeeping' and 'crisis-management' on the one hand, or 'territorial defence' and a 'Euroarmy' on the other, depends upon the meaning(s) established in the discursive field. What is denied, then, is not that such armed forces exist externally to thought, but rather that they could constitute themselves as a particular kind of force outside any discursive conditions. This implies that institutional and material social conditions and practices interrelate with discursive practices. Further, it is their meaning and not their existence that matters in the context of this book.

There are various routes through which to examine links between the discursive field and political and institutional structures and policies. The aim in many studies is to make the relationship between discourses, institutions and political practices transparent (Wodak 1999, J. Kantola 2006). In terms of Europeanization, discourse analysis could therefore contribute to explanations of institutional change in the EU and its member states. The focus in this study is on the Europeanization of state identities however, and hence the analysis largely concerns change and continuity in the discursive field of foreign and security policy. Nevertheless, the Europeanization of state identities enables and constrains institutional and policy changes. Moreover, the relationship between discourse(s) and institutionalized political practices is significant in that it underpins the focus on official docu-mentation and policy-makers, for instance. It is suggested that institutionalized state practices carry more weight in discourses of foreign and security policy in that state institutions and officials indeed have a central role in generating meaningful articulations of the state and its environment (Weldes 1996). However, their privil-eged position is discursively constructed: their authority to speak and act becomes meaningful within the discursive context of foreign and security policy.

Four key arguments lie at the heart of the discourse analysis in this study. First, the methodology applied in the book builds on Foucault's definition of discourse(s) as those 'practices that systematically form the objects of which they speak' (Foucault 1972: 49). As such, discourse(s) are understood as 'concrete systems of social relations and practices' (Howarth and Stavrakakis 2000: 4); they reflect and reproduce structure(s) of meaning (Weldes 1996, Torfing 1999, Wæver 2002) that are constitutive of particular identities. While organizing knowledge systematically, they also set up the boundaries for the debate. They define what can be intelligibly said and what cannot (Wæver 2002: 29). In other words, they set up the rules governing sensible foreign and security policy statements at a certain juncture of time and place. Second, discourse and identity formation are relational and contextual (Torfing 2005: 14). In other words, identities do not occur independently of other meaningful actors and the environment constructed in the discourse(s) at a certain time and place. Moreover, the formative order of a discourse is not a stable self-reproducing structure, but a potentially precarious system that is constantly subjected to political attempts to undermine and/or restructure the discursive context (ibid.). Accordingly, analysis of discourses covering the Europeanization of foreign and security policy concerns the change and the continuity of these relationships.

Third, and related to this, identity is reproduced in and through struggles in the discursive field. According to discourse theory, there is no pre-given, self-determining essence that is capable of determining and ultimately fixing all other identities within a stable and totalizing structure (Torfing 2005: 13). In the context of this study this means that there is no essence of statehood reflecting ideas of sovereignty or security in relation to an anarchic international system, for instance. Because of the contingent nature of the system the identities need to be continuously reproduced. In this process, some discourses gain dominance and some become marginalized. Dominance is achieved when the discourse manages to provide a credible principle upon which read the past, present, and the future events (Torfing 2005: 15). In so doing it establishes common meanings that are, at times, held as objective truths (Squires 1999: 97). Similarly, the articulation of a foreign and security policy discourse and the reproduction of state identity are intrinsically linked to the construction of social antagonisms, which involves the exclusion of a series of identities and meanings (other subjects) that are articulated in terms of equivalence and difference. Antagonisms are manifested in and through the production of political frontiers, which often invoke stereotyped representations of friends and enemies, for instance (Torfing 2005: 15–16, see also Laclau and Mouffe 1985, Howarth and Stavrakakis 2000). Moreover, the exclusion and inclusion of actors in the dominant discourse is considered a significant political act, and is therefore a key focus in the empirical analysis of this study.

Finally, there is the question of the dislocation of dominant discourses. Most discourses are flexible and capable of integrating new elements into their existing structure of meaning. A dominant discourse becomes dislocated when it fails to explain, represent, or in other ways domesticate new events (Torfing 2005: 16), in other words when the rules structuring the meaning are seriously disturbed. When dislocation occurs a new terrain for political struggle opens up. Over time the debate is likely to lead to the emergence of a loose consensus, which may constitute a new dominant discourse. Given the purpose of this study to examine the reproduction of state identity through the analysis of change and continuity in foreign and security discourses in the face of increasing Europeanization, the question of whether national discourses have been dislocated in this process is a highly relevant one.

Comparison in discourse analysis

Although discourse analysts often use comparison, there is a lack of direct methodological reflection about it in the various approaches (Howarth 2005: 332). Moreover, the emergence of 'comparative discourse analysis' (J. Kantola 2006: 161), which highlights comparative case-study framework(s), is a novel, although significant, analytical and theoretical turn. The methodological dialogue between discourse studies and comparative analysis suggests that comparative discourse analysis deserves more scholarly attention. It is suggested here that combining elements of discourse and Europeanization studies will provide a way forward. Existing accounts (Howarth 2005, J. Kantola 2006) make the following two significant points. First, comparative discourse theory must be question-and-problem-driven rather than method-driven. In other words, the comparison is related to the questions raised and the problems addressed in the study rather than to rigid quantitative data-collection frameworks. In the case of Europeanization, for instance, the point is not to take a large number of cases (for instance EU member states), but to highlight the qualitative aspects in each one, such as analytical relevance to the specific questions addressed in the study. Second, the comparison must comprise extensive description and analysis of the historical context and the concrete specificity of the chosen cases (Howarth 2005: 332). This directs the comparative framework towards a rather limited number of cases. Moreover, it implies that the researcher's background knowledge of the chosen cases and his or her language skills play a constructive role in setting up a comparative framework. This is not to suggest that these aspects are more important than analytical reasoning based on the specific questions addressed, but in some cases if translations are not available or background knowledge of the relevant cases is hard to find, they might play a more significant role in the analysis.

Comparison also helps in putting some of the criticism of discourse studies into perspective. It has been argued, for instance, that discourse analysis does not take us very far because the findings are often so obvious (Doty 1993: 308). In response scholars claim that that we often do not have to look very far to find structures enabling and constraining the production of identities and interests (ibid.). Moreover, discourse studies allow (rather than foreclose) analysis of less transparent cases. Crucially, it enables us to explain, despite such obviousness, how the commonsensical identities enabling and constraining foreign and security policy were arrived at in a given context. Comparison adds to this: what might be obvious in one case or country is not necessarily so in others. The obviousness of any particular finding or argument is relative not only over time but also over space. In order to account for this relative character of the social world we should inquire more deeply into the common sense that shapes our reasoning. Thus comparative discourse analysis makes a broader methodological contribution. It facilitates explication of what is context-specific in a given (discursive) context, if anything is. This has particular relevance to discourse studies in IR given the inference among some of its critics that it focuses largely on one actor, namely the US.

Methods, research design and case selection

The rest of the chapter concerns the practical implications of the above theoretical and methodological discussion for the methods and research design employed in the empirical analysis that follows. It describes the analytical tools to be used in the discourse analysis, and clarifies the overall research design, the comparative framework and the case selection.

Given the key aim in this study to analyse the impact, if any, of the increasing Europeanization of foreign and security policy on state identities in Finland and Britain, the empirical material is examined largely through discourse analysis, which rests on interpretation. The analysis of the relationship between the EU and the Finnish and British foreign and security policies is based on an interpretation of foreign and security policy discourses within certain historical and political contexts. Thus the study is not merely a content analysis, the aim of which is to systematically map out and organize the substance of the discourses, nor is the sole focus on the frequency of terms or the function of the linguistic features. These elements do have a role to play, but the prime interest is in the discursive action taken by key state institutions in order to accommodate and shape EU-level foreign and security policy. Thus the focus is largely on the (political aspects) of the reproduction of state identities and the foreign and security environment, as well as the warranted action these representations uphold.

The concepts of *articulation* and *interpellation* are used in order to elucidate the open-endedness of discourses (Weldes 1996, Weldes 1999, Weldes *et al.* 1999) (Figure 3.1). Articulation here refers to the contingent and contextually specific representations of the world that produce meanings that come to seem natural and accurate descriptions of reality, such as the call for the CFSP and the CSDP in Finland and Britain, or the problematic nature of these twin policies. The study also investigates whether the re-articulations of the discourse(s) become dominant and 'interpellate' the state officials and wider publics, and become accepted as natural and accurate. The practical analysis therefore proceeds in two main stages.

First, the purpose of the analysis of articulation is to generate a picture of the dominant discourses that constitute Finnish and British state identities in the field of foreign and security policy. It is based on the reintroduction of a discourse through empirical analysis of its realization in political and social practices (Laffey and Weldes 2004: 28). The analysis moves backwards in order to discern a discourse from its empirical manifestations such as the representations generated in official documents (Figure 3.2). It focuses on the representations generated in the re-articulations of the dominant discourses and examines whether they are repeated, transformed or dismantled. This is done through *predication, presupposition* and *subject positioning* (Doty 1993). Although these tools are analytically separable, in practice they are interrelated. Predication is used for two purposes, to identify the subjects and objects – such as states and other actors – constructed in the discourse(s), and to examine their representations. The latter phase is based on an analysis of the use of predicates, adverbs and adjectives in conjunction with particular subjects and objects (Doty 1993, Weldes 1996).

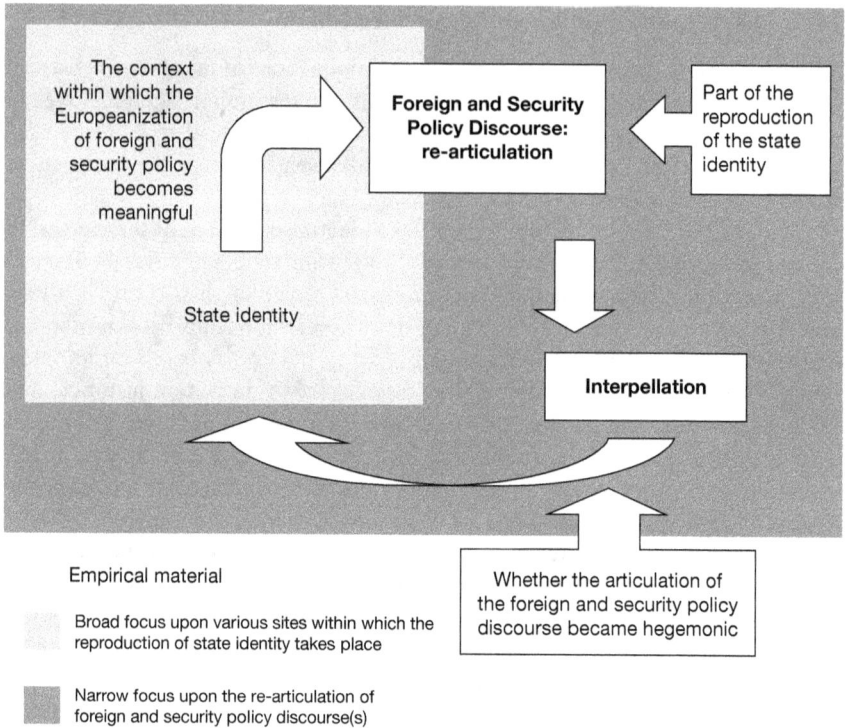

Figure 3.1 The reproduction of state identity in the field of foreign and security policy.

Presupposition is used to further analyse the representations generated by the discourse, the focus being on the background knowledge it generates. In other words, in explaining past, current and future developments in Finnish and British foreign and security policy certain knowledge is explicitly and implicitly assumed, and thereby constructed in the discourse. The construction of knowledge through presupposition operates through binary oppositions, which structure the meaning given to the states and other actors and simultaneously position them vis-à-vis each other. These relationships are predominantly constructed in terms of similarity, complementary and difference (Doty 1993: 306–308, Torfing 2005: 14). Finally, states and other actors are assigned a degree of agency through the construction of certain kinds of subject positions that are available to them. Significantly, predication and presupposition structure the availability of a particular subject position for a certain actor (Doty 1993). Moreover, the subject position available to the actors in the discourse is relational to the other subjects positioned in it. The breakdown of the discourse, manifested in the representations generated in the discourses of foreign and security policy, thus facilitates the analysis of change and continuity in the discourse of Finnish and British foreign and security policy.

Representation: method of predication
(discursive construction as a noun)

Articulation:
methods of presupposition and
subject positioning
(discursive construction as a verb)

Discourse: structure of meaning that sets out
the rules of representation

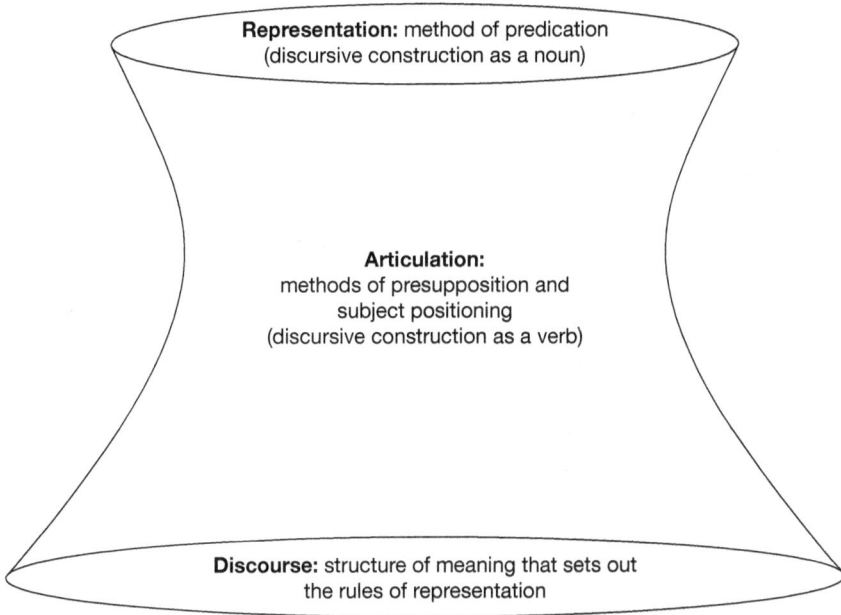

Figure 3.2 Representation, articulation and discourse.

The second stage is to examine whether the re-articulations of these discourses become accepted as accurate and natural, and in this the analysis draws on interpellation. A further question is whether the decision-makers were brought into the discourse (Laffey and Weldes 2004: 28). The first step in the process of interpellation is to create specific identities through the articulation and re-articulation of discourses. Second, in a successful interpellation individuals such as state officials and decision-makers come to identify themselves with the representations and subject positions generated by the discourse(s). As a result, the debate and disagreement over the re-articulation of discourse fades away. The analysis based on interpellation in this study systematically examines rival representations and subject positions, focusing on the inconsistencies in key documents such as white papers on foreign and security policy, and political discussion, such as parliamentary debates, of these documents.

Comparison and case selection

There are several ways of constructing a framework for comparison. It could be based on the 'most similar system design', for example, if the aim is to compare political systems that share several similar features in an effort to neutralize some differences while highlighting others (Van Evera 1997, Landman 2000: 27). Drawing on 'method of difference' logic, the purpose is to identify the key features that are different among similar states, and which account for the observed political outcome(s). This research design is considered to be well suited to area studies in particular (Landman 2000). Indeed, the intellectual and theoretical justification for area studies is that there is something inherently similar about the countries that comprise a particular geographical region, such as Europe, Asia, Africa or Latin America (Landman 2000: 28). The assumed similarities, in turn, make the comparison sensible.

In terms of the Europeanization of foreign and security policies in Britain and Finland, a comparative framework could be constructed around the fact that the foreign policy systems of both states share similar features: democratic control over the actors and bureaucracies, resulting in comparable if not identical decision-making systems. Moreover, Britain and Finland are becoming increasingly close in their foreign and security policy agendas, which address the so-called 'new security' threats in post-Cold War Europe such as ethnic conflicts, transnational crime, mass migration and environmental issues. The interest of both counties in the process of European integration has increased. Given their peripheral geographical locations at the rim of Europe, they both aim to take a central role in the EU defence policy. Although the joint Anglo–French declaration in St Malo (1998) launched a strong initiative aimed at building the CSDP, which was officially launched during the Finnish EU presidency in 1999, Finland has become one of the most active member states in crisis management in relation to its size. On the other hand, possible variation in policy outcomes could be attributable to the variables that differentiate them. For instance, they are unequal in terms of resources and capabilities. Britain has a more independent role in the international politics: it is a founding member of NATO, whereas Finland's defence policy is based on independent defence and military nonalignment. Britain has long-term membership in the EU (since 1973), whereas Finland is one of the more recent members (since 1995). Moreover, even though both member states are, in a sense, peripheral, Finland's geopolitical location in the North, between the cultural spheres of the East and the West, is different from that of Britain. Given these differences, a comparative framework could also be based on the 'method of agreement' (Landman 2000). In this case the comparison would be based on the 'most different system design', highlighting the fact that the two states do not share similar features in the field of foreign and security policy apart from the particular outcome to be explained, its Europeanization.

The research design of this study does not rest on generating testable hypotheses, however, or on isolating variables as in conventional social-scientific epistemology and methodology (cf. King, Keohane and Verba 1994). The study addresses a different set of questions than the more conventional approaches to Europeaniza-tion. The purpose is not to ask 'why questions' in order to discover the reasons for certain political outcomes, such as convergence or divergence in the Finnish and British foreign and security policies in the face of Europeanization. It is rather to examine how the assumed Europeanization is discursively constructed in two different states, and to explicate what the comparison of the findings generated in answering this 'how possible' question (Doty 1993, Weldes 1996) tells us about the relationship between the European Union and its member states. Accordingly, the above-mentioned similarities and differences between Britain and Finland are not to be taken as given facts. They are to be seen as points of contestation rather than fixed characters of these states' identities. At the heart of this study, then, is how these similarities and differences emerged. The comparison is not between the British and Finnish states as such, but between the discursive and political debates surrounding the CFSP and the CSDP in the two countries.

In sum, the chosen comparative approach is based on strong analytical justification. The number of cases is limited in order to produce a comprehensive study of the research topic that is rich and complex (Titscher 2000: 43). The study has two comparative elements. First, in order to examine the impact of Europeanization on the foreign and security policies of Britain and Finland it analyses the re-articulation of the related discourses in these states *over time*. Second, in order to elucidate the relationship between the European Union and its member states' foreign and security policies, the findings of the discourse analyses are compared *over space*.

Data collection and analysis

The empirical material used in this study requires clarification in order to highlight the self-reflective character of the discourse-analytical approaches used and to make the research practice transparent (A. Kantola 2002). The following discussion illustrates what the material reveals about the Finnish and British state identities in the face of the Europeanization of their foreign and security policies. As such it sheds light on the interplay between empirical material and discourse-analytical methods.

On the theoretical level it appears that state institutions and officials occupy a central place in the construction of the state's identity within the field of foreign and security policy, but they are by no means the only relevant actors generating representations of the state and its environment. High and popular cultural institutions, the media and cyberspace, educational establishments and many social institutions such as marriage and the family all have a role to play in this process. On the other hand, on the discursive level, state institutions and officials are widely acknowledged as the ones with the authority and legitimacy to speak and act.

Consideration of the relevant empirical sources for the study was limited to the material available in the public domain. The reasons for this were two-fold. First, the archives holding key documents concerning the Finnish and British foreign policies from the late 1980s onwards were largely closed for years to come. Second, although history writing will probably shed new light on British and Finnish foreign and security policy in the 1990s and 2000s, this is not a major concern here because the aim is not to discover hidden policy agendas or the concealed preferences of the decision-makers. The purpose is rather to analyse the impact of the Europeanization of foreign and security policy on official and publicly articulated discourses in Finland and Britain.

Official documentation such as policy reports and white papers as well as other statements constitutes the core empirical material of the study. This clearly establishes the Finnish and British states as certain kinds of political communities with particular interests. The other states and actors articulated in these texts 'hang together' in a certain way, and the relationships among them appear logical and uncontroversial. The documents construct a particular kind of reality in foreign and security policy within which the Finnish and British policies appear sensible. Moreover, several of them address topical issues concerning the CFSP and the CSDP. As such they proved to be highly suitable as the core material for the analysis. They made it possible to investigate the dominant discourses that were constitutive of the Finnish and British state identities. Moreover, given the interest in finding out how these particular identities were arrived at, the findings are taken as potential points of contestation rather than conclusive evidence of certain identities (Weldes 1996, Hansen 2002). The core material would have benefitted from sources presenting competing yet still official representations in the field of foreign and security policy, which could be gathered through interviews of the state officials. These were however problematic for two reasons. First, it was difficult to generate comparable material based on interviews from both sides due to the sensitive nature of the subject matter. Generally speaking, Finnish state officials and institutions were more open than their British counterparts. Second and more seriously, interviews conducted in early 2000 would have been problematic on account of the temporal aspect: they would have comprised a collection of state officials' memoirs of issues and events in the 1990s rather than a set of primary material providing access to the issues covered in political debates at different points of time.

Media coverage of Finnish and British foreign and security policy was another potential yet problematic source of empirical material giving opposing views on the CFSP and the CSDP. State officials were quoted and referred to in news reports, newspaper columns and editorials, for example, and conflicting views emerged. However, in many cases it was rather difficult to distinguish the articulations of the state officials from those of journalists. Even direct quotations, which could be taken as the state official's 'own words', were inserted into edited texts and hence mediated through the journalist.

Eventually, parliamentary debates on key foreign and security policy documents were chosen as the primary material. These are accurately recorded in both Finland and Britain, and the documentation provided rich material within which the key articulations related to the CFSP and the CSDP were contested or agreed upon. However, the material proved to be too broad for detailed discourse analysis. The focus is therefore on the key debates, in other words those in which change and continuity in foreign and security policy in the face of Europeanization constituted a clear element. In Finland these included the 1995 debate on the Government's foreign and security policy report and the subsequent debates in 1997 and 2001 on the Government's report on security and defence policy, and in Britain they included the debates related to the Strategic Defence Review (SDR) in 1998, the Defence White Paper in 1999 and the Policy Paper on European Defence in 2001.

Importantly, the parliamentary debates in Finland and Britain also produced material that could be compared and contrasted. Regardless of certain major differences, such as in the electoral systems that reflect distinct political traditions resulting in different political systems, the similarities in the field of foreign and security policy-making were striking. In both cases the key institutional actors such as the president and the prime minister, as well as the ministries for foreign affairs and defence, were largely in charge of the construction of the policy documents, which were then given to parliament to be debated. Parliament's role was also highly limited in the decision-making in both countries. In practice it was extremely difficult to reject or change the policies outlined in the papers given the majority governments and the constitutional factors limiting parliamentary power in these fields. Nevertheless, the parliamentary debates had a particular political significance in terms of the political legitimacy of the policy and the governments.

Several secondary sources are referred to throughout the empirical chapters, complementing the primary material. They constitute factual historical material, however, and are used as interpretations of the actual events (Wodak 1999, Hay 2002, A. Kantola, 2002). As such it could constitute part of the primary discourse-analysis material. On the other hand, it is used as supportive material in order to elucidate the Finnish and British historical contexts in which the EU foreign and security policy was made meaningful in the 1990s and early 2000s.

Conclusion

This chapter justifies the use of poststructuralist theories incorporating the concept of discourse in shedding light on the Europeanization of foreign and security policy. It is suggested that the methodological move in which the question of structure and agency is dissolved rather than solved has particular value in the analysis of complex relationships among different policy-making levels, and this makes it plausible to examine the Europeanization of state identities in this field. Methods associated with discourse analysis are adopted, and a comparative element is introduced.

4 The Europeanization of Finnish foreign and security policy discourse

From neutrality to alignment identity

Introduction

For almost half a century Finland had a unique position in European foreign and security policy. In the context of the Cold War confrontation between the East and the West, Finland claimed a neutral status in the late 1950s, yet it was the only neutral country with a security pact with the Soviet Union.[1] This gave the policy of neutrality a particular meaning. On the one hand it was meant to limit further Soviet involvement in Finnish foreign and security policy, and on the other it acknowledged Finland's special importance to Soviet security interests. Significantly, it limited Finland's participation in Western European integration. Indeed, full involvement in Western economic and political organizations was said to undermine Finland's neutrality and as such it was construed as detrimental to good neighbourly relations with the Soviet Union. Although many Finnish state officials and scholars suggest that neutrality was a pragmatic policy in the challenging Cold War context, it is argued in this chapter that over time it constituted a key feature of the Finnish state identity.

A major transformation in policy and discourse took place when Finland applied to join the European Union in 1992, and joined in 1995. The security arrangements with the Soviet Union and its successor, the Russian Federation, were dissolved in 1991, and Finland joined the EU as a previously neutral and militarily non-aligned state. However, the policy of military non-alignment did not constitute a problem in terms of full participation in the CFSP and the prospective CSDP. Conversely, Finland argued that its membership of the European Union reinforced the foundations of Finnish security (Council of State 1995: 5), and it became one of the key supporters of both policies.

This case study concerns the Europeanization of the Finnish state identity within the field of foreign and security policy. It concentrates on Finnish foreign and security policy discourse(s) re-articulated in official documents from the 1990s and early 2000s, and debated in parliament. The chapter proceeds in three stages. The first part briefly elucidates neutrality discourse, situating it in a historical and political context and then examining its articulation. The second part situates and discusses the emergence of the alignment discourse and its articulation. The focus in the final part is on whether the new discourse became dominant in the subsequent official documentation and related parliamentary debates. Three key findings are highlighted here. First, it is suggested that a new discourse was being articulated by the mid-1990s. Although this drew on historical discourses of the Finnish state it was intrinsically linked to developments in foreign and security policy in post-Cold War Europe. Significantly, the identity it endorsed was more symptomatic of alignment with Western Europe than of neutrality. Second, the development of the CFSP and the CSDP was crucial in the articulation of this new discourse. These twin polices signified a break with the past, and clarified Finland's policy and position vis-à-vis other actors and alliances in Europe. Third, the new alignment discourse largely replaced the neutrality discourse. It had become dominant by the early 2000s, propelling a rapid and fundamental shift from neutrality to alignment in the Finnish state identity.

The Finnish neutrality

An initial survey of the empirical material showed that the dominant theme in the articulations of Finnish foreign and security policy prior to EU membership in 1995 was Finland's neutrality.[2] Given the wide use of the concept in political statements and documents as well as in scholarly literature, a brief overview is warranted in order to establish its application in Finland. The term is closely associated with modern states and the relations among them, and draws on centuries of European military and political history (Goetschel 1999: 118). Legal codes of neutrality are usually traced back to the Hague Conventions of 1907 (Ojanen, Herolf and Lindahl 2000: 11). These conventions on sea and land war defined neutrality mainly in military terms. Neutral states cannot participate in wars directly or indirectly. Neither should they support or favour warring parties militarily, nor make their territory available to them, supply them with weapons or credits, or restrict private armaments exports in a one-sided way. Neutrals are also required to defend themselves against violations of their neutrality.

Although the concept of neutrality has a long history, most scholarly understanding of it is linked to the Cold War – namely to the neutral positions adopted by some countries towards the two superpowers and their alliances. In this context, scholars have found it useful to distinguish between permanent and temporary neutrality, also referred to as *de jure* and *de facto* neutrality (Ojanen, Herolf and Lindahl 2000: 12). Whereas permanent or *de jure* neutrality is based on a binding law or treaty, as in the cases of Austria and Switzerland, temporary or *de facto* neutrality refers to the political practices of countries such as Ireland, Finland and Sweden, which have claimed or sought a neutral status (Ojanen, Herolf and Lindahl 2000: 12, see also Luif 1995, Cramér 1998). The assumption underpinning this distinction is that permanently neutral states often extend neutrality to areas of (foreign) policy other than defence (Ojanen, Herolf and Lindahl 2000: 11–12), such as participation in inclusive and non-military international organizations. However, and in practice, the distinction has proven to be problematic. For instance, permanently neutral Austria participated in Western economic organizations such as the European Free Trade Area (EFTA) prior to the end of East–West confrontation, and temporarily neutral Finland adopted an extremely cautious policy towards Western European economic integration.[3] Moreover, and against the logic of permanent and temporary neutrality, the general foreign policy of both *de jure* neutral Finland and *de facto* neutral Austria has been equated with 'an "activist" neutral policy', in other words a broad policy aimed at maintaining or changing the given structural and operational principles of the larger regional or world system in order to lessen international tension (Carlsnaes 1993: 77).

Given its elusive nature, some scholars suggest that there are as many 'neutralities' as there are states claiming neutral status, and that any adequate understanding of the term must be able to account for 'variations of the theme' in different national contexts (Ojanen, Herolf and Lindahl 2000: 10). On account of the difficulty in establishing a general criterion, its political nature and context-specific meaning have been emphasized in analyses of neutrality policy (Väyrynen 1990: 13).

In the case of Finland it should be noted that the country did not claim neutrality immediately after the Second World War. The immediate post-war years were rather characterized by appeasement with regard to the Soviet Union and acceptance of Soviet security interests in Finland, including joint security arrangements and the presence of a Soviet naval base on Finnish territory (Möttölä 1993: 67–69, see also Kalela and Turtola 1975, Apunen 1977). The Soviet withdrawal from the naval base, located just outside of Helsinki, in 1956 consolidated Finnish sovereignty and enabled the country's entry into the United Nations; the initial articulation of a policy of neutrality soon followed. Significantly, consolidating sovereignty and claiming neutrality were largely considered a positive outcome of Finland's immediate post-war foreign and security policy, the aim of which was to build mutual trust with the Soviet Union.[4] The distinctness of the Finnish neutrality policy is evident in the initial articulations in scholarly accounts, which adopted terms such as 'a particular kind of neutrality' (Jakobson 1968) and 'coloured neutrality' (Apunen 1977, my translation).[5] In legalistic and military terms Finland's neutrality would appear to have been rather spurious throughout the post-war period, however. Some writers have even argued that the country was neutral for only a five-month period of its post-war history, from January 1992 when the bilateral Treaty of Friendship, Cooperation and Mutual Assistance (FCMA) with the Soviet Union, including the military articles, lapsed until June 1992 when Finland became an associate member of the NATO-led North Atlantic Cooperation Council (NACC) (Häikiö cited in Arter 1996: 615).[6] Nevertheless, its neutrality policy and aspirations were essential aspects of Finland's post-war foreign and security policy. Indeed, scholars have suggested that both the Cold War division of Europe and the political content of neutrality were consolidated in Finland at the Conference for Security and Cooperation in Europe (CSCE) in 1975. As Fierke and Wiener (2001) point out, prior to the period of *détente* in Europe there was some hope that the two Germanys could be reunified. However, the Helsinki Final Act, signed by states from the East and the West, established common principles for the peaceful co-existence of both in Europe and thus consolidated its division.

The West recognized the communist regimes of the East and granted them the legitimacy they had not previously enjoyed (Fierke and Wiener 2001: 126–127). Significantly, the status of the neutral European states was also laid out at the CSCE, as the three main parties of the Final Act were (i) the NATO states, (ii) the Neutral and Non-Aligned states, and (iii) the Warsaw Treaty Organization (or the Soviet bloc) states (Nolan 2001: 300). However, it was only in 1989 that Moscow unreservedly recognized Finland's neutral status. Before this recognition Soviet leaders had been equivocal on Finland's neutrality, suggesting that the country owed special deference to the Soviet Union.

Finnish neutrality, then, appears to have been a political process that came to maturity in the 1970s, and finally achieved one of its key aims – Soviet recognition – by the end of the 1980s. In order to elucidate the meaning of neutrality in Finland, the chapter continues with an analysis of its re-articulation in the field of foreign and security policy.

Re-articulating the neutrality discourse

There is no shortage of empirical material on neutrality articulation. Given the focus of the study on the impact of the CFSP and the CSDP on Finnish foreign and security policy discourse, it is feasible to turn to the key re-articulations made prior to the establishment of the CFSP and the CSDP, such as the security and defence policy review in 1990. The representations generated in this document are weighed against some seminal texts on Finland's neutrality policy, including a collection of President Urho Kekkonen's speeches from 1943–1969 (Vilkuna 1970) and his monograph (1982) laying out the policy.[7] The examination of the representations generated in the articulations of these texts generates a portrait of Finnish neutrality discourse.

Predication. The key states and other actors referred to in the texts, and the key virtues assigned to them are listed in Table 4.1. Two significant observations arise from this analytical exercise. First, given the rather lengthy time period involved, there is only one coherent discourse. Although the numerous representations related to each actor are not identical across the columns, there is enough evidence of coherence among them. In other words, the predicates, adverbs and adjectives (i.e. predication) linked to particular subjects and objects in the texts 'hang together' in a certain way (Doty 1993: 310). None of the virtues listed in relation to a particular actor seem radically out of place, and there is rather a kind of 'family resemblance'. For example, representations of Finland as 'a small state' and 'a relatively powerless country' (Table 4.1) resonate with each other in a meaningful way. Second and significantly, the virtues articulated also make sense in relation to the other actors constructed in the texts. Apart from Finland, the main actors are the Soviet Union and the other Eastern European states, the Nordic countries, the Western European states, Europe and some international organizations such as the CSCE and the United Nations.

Through predication Finland is construed as a small state with a geopolitically challenging location on the rim of Europe. The country had limited resources and, as a small state, was a relatively powerless subject. As such it had to take into account the political and security interests of the great powers. Several other representations of Finland are generated in the texts: it is a 'democracy' with a 'market economy'; it is also a 'Northern' and 'Western European country', yet has some ties with 'the Eastern cultures' as well. It is also given the qualities of an 'international broker' and a 'builder of mutual understanding', which could reduce tension between the East and the West. This, in turn, is constructed to enhance Finnish security and its international position.

The Nordic countries are largely assigned the same textual qualifiers as those attributed to Finland. By means of predication they are also construed as 'small states', 'democratic states' and 'strategically important for the superpowers'. The following extract from President Kekkonen's memoirs is illustrative. He wrote:

> Being Nordic is more than a matter of will to us: it is an inseparable part of our history, our background, our culture, our social and economic system, our customs, our laws and our religion. It used to be customary to say that we Finns were linked to the other Nordic countries by our shared conception of freedom. Now I understand that the ties that bind us are stronger than that.
> It is a question of the whole profound nature of being.
>
> (Kekkonen 1982: 82)

However, a representation that marked a difference among the Nordic countries was their 'basic arrangement for security'. Whereas Finland and Sweden adopted neutrality, Denmark, Iceland and Norway joined NATO. This difference in the field of foreign and security policy is explicable in the neutrality discourse however: it relates to the small-state character of these states and their different geopolitical locations in the bi-polar world.

The representations of the West share significant similarities and dissimilarities with those of Finland. The similar aspect includes the predication of Western powers as 'democratic' states 'with a political tradition based on parliamentarianism' and a 'market economy'. On the other hand, the differences relate to the construction of key Western powers such as the United States and Britain as 'great powers' (Table 4.1) with significant military might. These subjects and objects are made more meaningful in presupposing a certain kind of knowledge about the world out there, which is elucidated below. However and interestingly, the major Western subject, the United States, is rarely explicitly addressed in the texts, and NATO is straightforwardly constructed as the Western 'military alliance' with 'automatic defence guarantees'. As such, Finland's relationship with it is constructed in terms of opposition. Moreover, Western organizations such as the European Community and the European Free Trade Area do not occupy a central position in the texts. The predication assigns them economic importance, and Finland's loose relations with the Community and membership in EFTA are constructed to 'support the neutrality policy'. However, full membership of the European Community is constructed as detrimental to neutrality.

Table 4.1 Predication of the neutrality discourse

Finland	The East	The West	The North	Other
A small state (1, 2, 5, 7)	*The Soviet Union:*	*The EC and EFTA:*	*Nordic Community/ Nordic Countries:*	*Europe:*
An independent state (1, 11–13)	A great power (11)	Have economic importance (10)	Comprise a special and privileged group of states (10)	Is divided (10)
A democratic state (2, 12)	Has allies (9)	Have networks and relations with Finland (10)	Are small countries (3)	Is more than the European Economic Community (10)
A Nordic state (part of the Nordic Community) (3)	Has substantial military power (9, 10)	Support Finland's neutrality (10)	Are European states (10)	Is more than Western European countries (10)
An inseparable part of the Western culture of Europe (7)	Has a different cultural heritage and social system (1, 5)	Are not synonymous with Europe (10)	Have a strong sense of kinship with Finland (10)	Includes Eastern and Western states (10)
A market economy (2, 12)	Was the hereditary enemy (1, 10)	*Britain:*	Have shared memories, customs, traditions (10)	Reaches from the Atlantic to the Urals (10)
Relatively powerless (1, 7, 12, 13)	Is a suspicious state (1)	Home of Western democracy (8)	Are strategically important for the superpowers (10)	Has disputes (10)
Has to adapt to international changes (1, 7, 12, 13)	Has not forced Finland to adopt the communist system (5)	Home of parliamentarianism (2)	Are mainly objects of international politics (3)	*The UN:*
Practises a cautious foreign policy (12)	Pursues a friendly and understanding policy towards Finland (1)	Model for the Finnish Parliament (8)	Have different basic arrangements for security (10)	Is a cornerstone of common shared rules in international politics (7, 10)
A geographically peripheral state (12, 13)	A European power (10)	Understands, accepts and tolerates differences between peoples and nations (40)	*Sweden:*	Is a security organization (7)
Is important for the Soviet Union (1, 4, 6, 7, 11)	*The Warsaw Pact:*	Has been at war with Finland (8)	Is a neutral country (10)	Can work for world peace (7)
Has links with Occidental cultural circles (12)	Is a military alliance (9)	A European country (8)	*Norway, Denmark and Iceland:*	*The CSCE:*
Is a builder of international understanding (8, 12)	Has automatic defence guarantees (9)	*The US:*	Are NATO members (10)	Can ease tensions between East and West (10)
Understands, accepts and tolerates differences between peoples and nations (10)	*The FCMA Treaty:*	Is a democracy (6)		Is an inclusive organization, includes Eastern and Western states (10)
Has good neighbour relations (10)	Is for building friendship and mutual trust (4, 10)	Has nuclear weapons (6)		Has an important role in European security (10, 11)
A relatively secure state (10, 11)	Is for security (4, 10)	*NATO:*		Is the main achievement of Finnish foreign policy (10)
Has some influence in international politics (10)	Has had a major impact (4, 10)	Is a military alliance (9)		*The Developing World:*
	Is different from a military pact in that it does not contain an automatic mechanism (9)	Has automatic defence guarantees (9)		Has illiterate and hungry people (10)
	Is in line with the policy of neutrality (10)			Has overpopulation (10)
				Has human rights problems (10)

Note: The numbers in the brackets refer to the source documents as follows: (1) Parlamentaarinen puolustuspoliittinen neuvottelukunta 1990, (2) Kekkonen 1943, (3) Kekkonen 1949, (4) Kekkonen 1951, (5) Kekkonen 1952, (6) Kekkonen 1955, (7) Kekkonen 1957, (8) Kekkonen 1961a, (9) Kekkonen 1961b, (10) Kekkonen 1963, (11) Kekkonen 1965, (12) Kekkonen 1970, (13) Kekkonen 1982.

Although the main Eastern subject, the Soviet Union, shares the great-power representation with the key Western powers, several other representations highlight the difference between the Eastern subjects and the West, the North and Finland: their predication constructs them as having 'a different cultural heritage and social system' than the Western states. Moreover, predication generates representations of the Soviet Union as a 'suspicious' subject that could use coercive measures and 'military might' in its search for security in a bi-polar world. In this the representation of gaining Soviet 'trust' is crucial in constructing Finland's relationship with the East. The East had political and security interests in Finland but, as a result of trust and good-neighbour relations, Finland was not forced to adopt the communist system. Rather, the Soviet Union pursued 'a friendly and understanding policy towards Finland'. The predication of Finland as having links with 'Occidental cultures' is important in the construction of Soviet trust. Although Finland is constructed as a different kind of subject, it could understand Eastern concerns and mentality. The FCMA Treaty, which represented friendship and mutual trust with the East, was the symbol of Soviet trust in the field of foreign and security policy.

Presupposition. Discourse analysis suggests that foreign and security policy documents and statements rarely speak for themselves, but are rather loaded with different kinds of presuppositions that construct background knowledge about the subject field. This often operates through certain binary oppositions that are crucial for the meanings generated in the documents (Doty 1993: 312; Torfing 2005). The core opposition that structures the construction of actors and their environment in the texts is that of *minor* and *great* powers. Several other binaries, such as *idealism/realism, periphery/centre and strength/weakness* are also significant in the logic of neutrality discourse. In particular, the background knowledge constructs a certain kind of geopolitical environment within which the representations of Finland, the East and the West appear commonsensical.

The neutrality discourse presupposes that the world is inhabited by great and minor powers. This binary is essential to the re-articulation of Finland's engagement in the Second World War, namely the Winter War (1939–1940) and the Continuation War (1941–1944) against the Soviet Union, and the War of Lapland (1944) against Germany, for instance.[8] It thereby structures the meanings generated and makes certain policies, such as appeasement with the Soviet Union, meaningful. War Marshal and then President Mannerheim's letter to Adolf Hitler in August 1944, when Finland sought to withdraw from the Continuation War, is illustrative of this. Mannerheim said, 'Germany is such a mighty nation that it shall live on even if it loses the war.' According to Mannerheim, Finland, however, was such a small nation that 'it could be evicted from its dwelling place and destroyed.' (Mannerheim cited in Jakobson 2004, my translation). The binary is also essential to the construction of the events leading up to the outbreak of war in 1939 on the one hand, and the end game of the war on the other. In both cases Finland emerges as a minor power 'trapped between great powers' – the Soviet Union and Germany (ibid.). Although the outbreak of war is seen as a direct result of the 1939 Molotov–Ribbentrop Pact, with secret protocols dividing Europe into

Soviet and German spheres of influence, the ending of hostilities with the Soviet Union led to war against Germany in 1944.

These representations are re-articulated in the neutrality discourse in terms of the bi-polar world order. As the 1990 security and defence paper argues: 'Since the Second World War the international system has been characterized by the United States and the Soviet Union superpowers, the NATO military alliance and the Warsaw Pact in Europe, and confrontation and power-political rivalry' (Parlamentaarinen puolustuspoliittinen neuvottelukunta 1990: 5, my translation). It was within this (great-)power rivalry that small Finland had to navigate. Although there were competing views in the immediate post-war period they were discredited and made unintelligible within the neutrality discourse. As President Kekkonen wrote in 1982:

> During his term as Prime Minister after the war, Paasikivi had to endure a speech in which a certain Member of Parliament sharply criticized the Government's foreign policy. When Paasikivi managed to get a word in, he urged the deputy to go home, take out a map and look where Finland was situated. That advice remains useful to one and all this very day.
>
> (Kekkonen 1982: 16–17)

The background knowledge constructed in these extracts is also linked to another binary, namely idealism/realism. Significantly, as the predication of the neutrality discourse suggests, neither the ideological differences nor the normative judgements between the superpowers feature very highly in the discourse. The rationality behind this largely lies in the interplay between the binary oppositions of great/minor and idealism/realism. As Kekkonen argued:

> Since the task of a foreign policy should be to cherish and promote, by all means available, the interests of the country in question, there is no justification for allowing ideological likes or dislikes to influence the general guidelines which this foreign policy follows – nor can this be afforded. A small country, in particular, must observe this rule, because the stances it takes and their reflection in the country's foreign policy will assuredly not count for very much in world history, stamped as it is by the major nations' struggle for power. By contrast, inestimable harm could be caused . . .
>
> (Kekkonen 1982: 20–21)

Instead of ideological difference and normative judgements, the presupposition of Finland's geopolitical environment underlines great-power rivalry and prag-matism. Against this background the binary opposition of centre and periphery assumes importance. This is particularly evident in the military and strategic environment constructed in the neutrality discourse, within which Finland emerges as more important with regard to the security interests of the Soviet Union than of the US and other Western powers. This construction draws on historical evidence of the lack of material support from Western powers during the Winter

War, and is reflected in catchphrases of the neutrality discourse such as 'there is nothing we can do about our geographical location' and 'we must accept the realities'. The periphery/centre binary was therefore essential to the construction of Finland on the rim of Europe and therefore doomed to be left alone should it once again be invaded by this superpower. Thus, in military terms Finland could only rely on self-help and not, for instance, on security guarantees provided by military alliances.

Standing alone in this geopolitically challenging environment presupposed a certain kind of Finnishness, which was also projected onto the state. The experienced insecurity, the difficulties of the war and the reconstruction constructed Finns and their state in terms of persistence and determination. As Kekkonen argued in 1952: 'The Finnish people did not stand to look back. They set their hands to the plough to draw a new furrow in a new strip of land' (Kekkonen 1952: 58). This representation of the Finns and Finland as strong is arrived at through re-articulation of the perseverance of the Finnish people in building their state. On the other hand, the opposition of wise/foolish highlighted the enlightened character of a small state and its officials. As Kekkonen suggested: '. . . in order to save its position a small people must be able to produce clever initiatives to ward off dangers before they become too great' (Kekkonen 1982: 20). The consolidation of Finland's sovereignty and its international position in the deteriorating East–West relations in the neutrality discourse rests on the presupposition of a steadfast and smart Finnish state and state officials.

Subject positioning. The predication and the presupposition contribute to the creation of particular subject positions available to states and other actors articulated within the neutrality discourse. The availability of a subject position for a particular actor reflects the degree of agency assigned to it in the hierarchical arrangement(s) of the discourse. In the neutrality discourse this is the bi-polar world order. Two subject positions are of particular importance here: those of (i) small and relatively powerless peripheral state(s) (in the North) and (ii) powerful and central power(s) (in the West and East).

The central subject position created in any foreign and security policy discourse is that of the relevant state (Weldes 1996: 287). This specific subject position was arrived at by positioning Finland in relation to other major subjects made meaningful within the neutrality discourse in light of predication and presupposition. The Soviet Union and the major Western powers were endowed with significant degrees of agency. The representations of the East and West constructed them as subjects with significant security interests. They had both the political will and the capability to influence world politics, and to interfere militarily if needed. On the other hand, the subject position available to Finland – that of a small and relatively powerless peripheral state – assigned it a significantly limited degree of agency. As Kekkonen wrote:

> One of the lessons which history teaches us is that a small people like the Finns can not coerce its neighbours into the kind of settlements which it would like. Our own resources are not adequate for that and relying on outside

support would mean throwing oneself on the mercy of the unknown as well as sowing the seeds of discord.

(Kekkonen 1982: 17–18)

Due to its limited capabilities Finland was subject to great-power politics, and because of its peripheral location it could only rely on self-help. In so doing it had to adapt to the external environment and follow a cautious foreign and security policy. As Kekkonen continued: 'caution has been and will always be the essence of the Finnish foreign policy' (Kekkonen 1982: 19). Similarly, the neutrality discourse suggested that Finland was not in a position to address normative questions or to follow a value-based foreign policy. Kekkonen argued:

> ... if we look around us, we can see in every quarter things which ought to be protested at in the name of humanity. But we do not do it ... Here, too, our conduct is dictated by our policy of neutrality. There is a great difference between it and a policy of protest.
>
> (Kekkonen 1982: 20–21)

The hierarchical arrangement of the bi-polar world granted Finland a significantly limited degree of agency. Hence, turning a blind eye to ideological and moral questions in world politics was accepted. Finland could egoistically pursue its own interests through policies and relations with countries that could be considered detrimental to its values and those of the Nordic states, for instance. Indeed, allowing moral judgements to affect foreign and security policy was constructed as a privilege of the great powers and states located in less challenging and more secure environments.

However, the construction highlighting the need to adapt to the international environment indicates a degree of agency by definition. In other words, Finland had some statutory rights based on its status as a sovereign state, and a high international standing as one of the Nordic countries. As Kekkonen argued in a speech given at the National Press Club in Washington in 1961:

> I have heard it said that neutrality has been imposed upon us. This is not so. It is a way of solving our problem of security that has its roots in our history, and it reflects, I believe, a realistic appraisal of our national interests and possibilities and a true understanding of our position in the world today.
>
> (Kekkonen 1961b: 87)

The Soviet Union did not determine Finnish policy, and Finland played a significant role in deciding how to adapt to the external constraints. Finnish policy was not decided by the Western superpowers either. Indeed, the need to explain Finnish neutrality suggests a certain misfit between Finnish and Western aspirations, which needed to be addressed.

Significantly, the Finnish way of manoeuvring in the challenging external environment – namely the adoption of a neutral position and smart policies – was also constructed in order to empower the small state. In relation to the normative aspects of foreign and security policy, Kekkonen argued in 1961 that '[w]e see ourselves as physicians rather than judges; it is not for us to pass judgement nor to condemn, it is rather to diagnose and to try to cure' (Kekkonen 1961a: 94). The Finnish state could diagnose and try to resolve challenging international problems, in other words ease the confrontation among the superpowers. Within this judge–physician allegory Finland emerges as a potential initiator of action, a formulator of policies, and an assessor of situations. Specifically, it could build mutual trust among the superpowers.

However, Finland's subject position in the neutrality discourse also constitutes clear boundaries for its degree of agency. It was not in a position to take sides or make normative judgements. This was reflected in the strict rejection of any kind of military cooperation with Western powers and their alliances. Neutrality also cast a shadow over Finnish participation in Western European economic integration, even if this was seen to be in its interests. The neutrality discourse made it very difficult, if not impossible, for Finnish state officials to articulate Finnish membership aspirations in the EU in the context of the diminishing power and the eventual collapse of the Soviet Union.

The dominance of the neutrality discourse and the CFSP and the CSDP

Although discourses, and the identities they construct, are always open-ended, and complete interpellation is merely a theoretical possibility, it is suggested here that the neutrality discourse acquired a dominant position in Finland and thus temporarily fixed the state identity in the realm of foreign and security policy. This dominance could be discussed in terms of Finlandization, for instance. Although the term refers to the broad idea of small states attempting to secure their sovereignty through appeasement to great-power interests (Kennan 1974), in Finland it also carries some negative connotations. It is linked to external criticism of developments in Finland during the post-war period, in particular in the 1970s and 1980s, as well as to the post-neutrality internal Finnish debates in the 1990s. Although it is largely seen resulting from pragmatic *realpolitik*, it has been suggested that the Finns' willingness to appease the Soviet Union was at times too great given the consolidated status of Finland, and that it continued even when Soviet pressure on Finland eased. The term is also related to the argument that Soviet appeasement deeply influenced Finnish society – its politics, economics, media, culture and science (Vihavainen 1991: 15). Significantly, it is suggested that the initial censorship with regard to the Soviet Union's internal and external affairs and to communism in general developed over time into a Finnish self-censorship system (Salminen 2000: 152).

The fact that these rather profound arguments related to Finlandization were initially raised aboard suggests the successful interpellation of the neutrality discourse. Moreover, the criticism did not result in significant political debate in Finland before the end of Finnish neutrality. This is not to argue that there were no competing views or political debates on Soviet appeasement or neutrality: it is merely suggested that the dominant discourse was able to accommodate the rather profound criticism in a way that was largely acceptable to Finnish state officials and the broader political elite. In other words, the subject position available to Finland as well as the construction of the external environment were considered accurate and were accepted as true representations of the reality.

The dominance of the neutrality discourse is also apparent in the Finnish state officials' (and institutions') responses to the large-scale transformation related to the closing stages of the Cold War that resulted in the disintegration of Eastern Europe and increasing integration in Western Europe. Significantly in the midst of Soviet military and political withdrawal from Eastern Europe and the joint Soviet–US declaration of the end of the Cold War in 1989, the Finnish security and defence policy review in 1990 emphasized continuity rather than change. It concluded:

Finland's position on security is unchanged. With its independent foreign policy, systematic neutrality and active participation in the CSCE Finland has had a positive influence on the security environment in the North as well as more broadly in Europe. The Treaty of Friendship, Cooperation and Mutual Assistance has had a positive impact on the stability in the North, and continues to do so.

> ... the neutrality of Finland and Sweden and the credible independent defence capability of these states have been widely seen to enhance stability in the North ... It is important that in the changing international environment Finland's defence policy remains predictable.
>
> (Parlamentaarinen puolustuspoliittinen neuvottelukunta
> 1990: 24, my translation)

It is true that the key foreign and security policy documents tend to highlight continuity. Moreover, it was logical for Finland to highlight its own policy's predictability in an increasingly unpredictable environment. However, it is worth emphasizing the continuing relevance to Finland of the subject position established in the neutrality discourse given the ongoing profound changes in its environment.

Significantly, the neutrality discourse also structured the meaning given to the expanding Western European integration and possible Finnish EU membership. Although integration was mostly advancing in the economic sphere, the key problem with membership for Finland was the modest attempts within the EU to strengthen foreign policy cooperation and gradually establish a security and defence policy.[9] Prime Minister Harri Holkeri's response to the claims, which originated within the leadership of his own right-leaning National Coalition Party in 1990, is illustrative. He said: 'Finland's neutrality constitutes the corner stone in the protection of our living, our independence, our sovereignty and our national existence' (cited in Joenniemi 2001: 183). He continued: 'Submitting to the EC's foreign policy and giving in to the demands of a joint defence would imply that Finland voluntarily abandons its independence and becomes part of a major power' (ibid.). He further emphasized the impossibility of EC membership by comparing it with a puzzle posed by ancient geometers called 'squaring the circle', which in 1882 was proven to be unsolvable (Ojanen, Herolf and Lindahl 2000: 95).[10] Even if some of the historical accounts of the events that eventually led to Finland's EU accession suggest that the president and some ministers adopted a more positive position towards membership in private discussions, it is worth noting the extremely strong expressions suggesting the end of Finnish sovereignty and independence in the event of EU membership. Moreover, a prime minister representing a Pro-European party that emphasized its role in initiating and concluding Finnish EU membership gave the statement. However, and in the context of this study, these representations continued to make sense in the official state discourse in 1990. They were not publicly refuted, but rather accepted as adequate and true. In the prime minister's re-articulation this is highlighted by the fact that Finland was still constructed as subjected to the politics of the great powers. Although Soviet influence was clearly diminishing, it was not about to 'submit' itself or 'give in' to Western European pressures. Significantly, the neutrality discourse still structured the meaning given to the changing environment in the state officials' re-articulations of Finnish foreign and security policy in 1990.

The Europeanization of the Finnish foreign and security policy discourse

> When the Cold War system broke down it was natural that Finland's foreign policy changed.
>
> (Forsberg and Vogt 2003, my translation)

The discussion in the first section of this chapter focused on the dominance of the neutrality discourse in Finland. The aim in the second section is to analyse the EU security dimension as it was initially articulated within the official foreign and security policy. It is suggested that the Finnish foreign and security policy was re-articulated in a radically different way in 1995 when Finland joined the EU. Consequently, a new alignment discourse emerged that structured the meaning of Finland and its security milieu fundamentally differently than the neutrality discourse. Significantly in this context, the developing CFSP, with the prospect of the CSDP, had a major role in the new articulations and in the discourse.

EU membership in Finland largely represented a break with the past in terms of the country's foreign and security policy. Prior to the negotiations, which started in 1992, Finland was seen as a neutral state. However, it joined the EU in 1995 as a previously neutral state. Although remaining militarily non-aligned, it aligned with Western Europe politically, economically and culturally. Although cultural ties with the Nordic and other Western European states were emphasized throughout the post-war period, political and economic integration gained momentum after the collapse of the Soviet Union. State officials' articulations of Finland and its place in the world also gradually changed during this period of dramatic upheaval. Although still emphasizing its neutrality in 1990 after the reunification of Germany, Finland unilaterally announced that the military restrictions (with the exception of the ban on nuclear weapons) imposed under the Paris Peace Treaty that was signed in 1948 were no longer applicable.[11] At the same time the military articles included in the bilateral treaty for Friendship, Cooperation and Mutual Assistance with the Soviet Union were 'reconsidered'. In January 1992, after the break up of the Soviet Union, the Finnish foreign policy leadership announced the end of the FCMA treaty. A new treaty governing relations between Finland and the Russian Federation was signed soon after, in which no mention was made of military issues. Interestingly, the decision to apply for EU membership in 1992 is often portrayed as a sudden and profound change in Finnish post-war foreign policy,[12] and has been linked to joining the NATO North Atlantic Cooperation Council (NACC) during the same year. A year later Finland joined NATO's Partnership for Peace programme (PfP). Although the foreign policy leadership emphasized several continuities and later argued that membership was a logical continuation of Finnish neutrality (Council of State 1995), it did not deny the fundamental transformation of its foreign and security policy. Moreover, even if the more recent scholarly literature has also recognized some significant continuities in the Finnish policy (Tiilikainen 2001: 68), analyses published around the period leading to membership mainly noted the changes.[13]

Significantly in the context of this study, state officials have explicitly argued that 'security-policy considerations were the most important factors behind Finland's membership and that economic factors were, after all, secondary' (Koivisto 1995: 554, my translation). Several scholars have reached the same conclusion. Even if some policy-makers and scholars believed the rationale for membership was economic (Redmond 1997, Ingebritsen 1998), the debate was about security (Arter 1995, Tiilikainen 1998) and identity (Arter 1995, Tiilikainen 1998, Browning 1999, 2003, Joenniemi 2001, Moisio 2003). Indeed, Moisio argues that, given the 'massive economic decline in the early 1990s with increasing unemployment rates, decreasing GDP, collapsing financial markets, the crisis of the welfare state and rising social insecurity' one would have expected the EU membership debate to be based on rational economic argumentation (Moisio 2003: 13). However, although the economic dimension existed, it was over-shadowed by the seemingly irrational argumentation related to the Finnish identity, geopolitics and security (ibid.).

Given that EU membership was generally understood as a matter of foreign and security policy, the EU's developing policy had a particularly strong impact on the official Finnish articulations. In 1992 the European Commission explicitly expressed its concern about the level of Finland's commitment to the CFSP and, in particular, to the possibly evolving CSDP.[14] It highlighted, for instance, the fact that the European military alliance, the Western European Union, had broader political aspirations than the crisis-management tasks welcomed by the Finnish Government (Rehn 1993: 208). Due to these pressures the CFSP and the CSDP underpinned the re-articulation of the Finnish foreign and security policy, and in 1992 President Koivisto indicated that 'he did not have anything against redefining neutrality in terms of non-alignment and independent defence'

(Koivisto 1995: 548, my translation). Membership negotiations with the EU were closed in 1994, and on 1 January 1995 Finland became a full member of the Union and an observer member of the WEU. The government report of June 1995 re-articulated and clarified the new Finnish foreign and security policy. Crucially, it states that neutrality was no longer an option:

> Since the end of the East–West division, the policy of neutrality that Finland followed in the Cold War is no longer a viable line of action. During the Cold War, Finland tried to avoid making political, and especially military, commitments that might have drawn it into conflicts between the great powers. In the new situation, Finland's strategy is an active participation in international political and security cooperation for prevention and resolution of security problems.
>
> In acceding to the Union, Finland has not made any security policy reservations concerning its obligations under its founding treaties or the Maastricht Treaty. Finland has joined the Union as a militarily non-aligned country which wishes to play an active and constructive role in creating and implementing a common foreign and security policy. A capable EU is in Finland's interests.
>
> (Council of State 1995: 58)

Whereas the code word for independence was still neutrality in 1990, and EU membership was seen as endangering Finnish independence, the 1995 report argued that 'membership of the European Union (EU) will reinforce the foundations of Finnish security and provide a significant channel through which Finland can pursue its interests and carry its responsibility in international relations (Council of State 1995: 5). Accordingly, the European Union became a new code word for Finland's sovereignty.

Several other changes in the re-articulation deserve attention. The 1995 report on Finland's foreign and security policy addressed a wide range of security questions.[15] It was based on a 'comprehensive conceptualisation of security' that highlighted the so-called 'new' and 'soft' issues such as development, economic cooperation and environmental degradation (Council of State 1995). Although the large-scale social, political and economic transformation set up the wider context in which Finland's new position in the world was made meaningful, the EU and its 'developing security dimension' were pivotal in the re-articulation of its foreign and security policy discourse, in other words in the articulation of a radically different discourse than before (Council of State 1995: 5–6, 9–10, 58–62). The report also addressed the approaching EU summit in Amsterdam in 1996, which was set out to clarify the future development and decision-making mechanisms of the CFSP (Council of State 1995: 61–62). As Ms O. Ojala, a senior Member of Parliament (MP) of the Left Alliance, suggested in the Parliamentary debate on the document '. . . we are here to discuss how the decision accepted by the Finnish people to join the European Union will affect Finland's security policy (Eduskunta 1995b, my translation).

Articulation of the alignment discourse

The 1995 report re-articulated Finland and its position in the world differently in comparison with the neutrality discourse. In other words, the predication, presupposition and subject positioning of the major subjects and objects were significantly different from the earlier re-articulations, thereby articulating a new discourse. I call this the alignment discourse. The expression illustrates its key feature: economic and political alignment and military non-alignment with the West. In terms of the official foreign and security discourse the former represented continuity and the latter signified change. Moreover, the emerging EU foreign and security policy played a key role in the political struggle between the discourses, and state officials constructed it as a middle way between neutrality and full alignment.

Predication. Table 4.2 lists the main subjects and objects in the 1995 report, as well as their predication. Although some of the representations generated in the texts hang together in a familiar way, others form a novel and distinct story line. I suggest that the table is indicative of two discourses. Moreover, in the 1995 report the Finnish state identity emerges at the intersection of the two discourses, thereby reflecting continuity (neutrality) and change (alignment).

It is clear from the table that some of the key representations of Finland indicate continuity of the neutrality discourse. For instance, in 1995 Finland was considered a 'small' and 'militarily non-aligned state' that 'has to adapt to international changes' (Table 4.2). On the other hand the predication suggests that its geo-political location had changed. Finland was 'no longer located between the East and the West' and had joined the 'core group of European democracies'. Further, although still identified as a Nordic country, the explicit predication of Finland as a welfare state, with respect for human rights, is also somewhat at odds with the neutrality discourse. Moreover, whereas the normative aspects of foreign and security policy were marginal in the neutrality discourse, in 1995 several international organizations such as the United Nations, the OSCE and the Council of Europe (CoE) were constructed as bodies that could enhance 'human rights', 'democracy and freedom' and 'shared rules'.

In relation to the representations of the West, the role of the European Union became dominant and Western European states assumed increasing significance within this context. Several attributes that were previously associated with Western states, such as 'democracy', 'influence' in world politics and international 'security', were now explicitly attached to the European Union. Through predication it emerged as a 'developing organization', 'a union of independent democratic states', 'a major market area', and 'a major political actor in international politics'. As such it had a crucial role in European and international security, and could 'promote stability' and Finnish national interests, for instance. On the other hand, the number of representations of particular Western states, such as Britain, decreased.

Significantly, and contrary to the neutrality discourse, the relationship between Finland and the West with reference to the European Union was based on similar and complementary aspects. As the report argues, EU membership 're-enforced the

Table 4.2 Predication of the alignment discourse

Finland	The East	The North	The West	The Globe
An independent state	*Russia:*	*Nordic Community/ Nordic Countries:*	*The EU:*	*OSCE:*
A member of the international community	Is a great power	Are democratic states	Is the core group of European democracies	Is a security organization
A small state	Has substantial military power	Have respect for human rights	Is a developing organization	Has an important role in European security
A democratic state	Has nuclear capability	Are just states	Has a crucial role in European security	Is an inclusive organization
Has stable defence	Can shape the world and European politics	Are welfare states	Is a union of independent democratic states	Can build mutual trust and enhance human rights
Has to adapt to its environment/international changes	Has a great culture	Have a prestigious international status	Is a major political actor in international politics	Cannot guarantee security or enforce peace
Has a stable international position	*The Former Eastern European States and Commonwealth of Independent States:*	Can contribute to international crisis management	Has a vital role in international security	*The UN:*
Is no longer placed between the East and the West/ Has broken free from its Cold War international position	Are independent states	*Sweden:*	Can promote stability	Is the cornerstone of common shared rules in international politics
The only EU member that shares a common border with Russia	Are European states	Has a special historical relationship with Finland	Can promote (Finnish) national interests	Has respect for human rights
Is a member of the core group of European democracies	Are unstable and unpredictable states		Re-enforces the foundations of Finnish security	Is democratic
A Nordic state (part of the Nordic Community)	Have violent conflicts		*NATO:*	Can promote security
Has a market economy	Are moving towards democracy		Is a military alliance	Cannot enforce peace
Supports international cooperation	Are moving towards a market economy		Has substantial military might	*CoE:*
Can influence arrangements concerning its international standing and national security	Have several internal problems		Can promote stability	Is a human-rights organization
Has played an active role in international organizations	Have crime		Can threaten Russia	Promotes the values of democracy and freedom
Has respect for human rights	Have environmental problems		Can create new dividing lines in Europe	Has a vital role in Europe
Is a welfare state	Are a source of transnational diseases		Has a crucial role in European security	*The South:*
Is militarily non-aligned	Are nationalistic		Can enforce peace	Has several regional and local wars and crises (in central America, southern Africa and Southeast Asia)
Can defend itself	Have problems with minorities		Is credible in peacekeeping	
			The US:	
			Is a superpower	
			Has nuclear weapons	

Note: Table is based on the *Report by the Council of State to the Government* in 1995 (Council of State 1995).

foundations of Finnish security' and offered 'a channel of influence' to enhance Finnish interests in world politics. Within the West, NATO's role in European security was also highlighted, for instance in relation to 'crisis management'. Moreover, whereas NATO was constructed in terms of difference and otherness in the neutrality discourse, the alignment discourse indicated a more positive relationship. Accordingly, the previously unimaginable NATO membership became an option that merited discussion.

The representations of the East also changed significantly. Whereas the Soviet Union largely disappeared from the discourse, Russia inherited some of its great-power status and characteristics. The predication of the Eastern states also changed. They were simply construed as great powers in the neutrality discourse, their allies or satellites endowed with distinct values and norms that reflected their economic and political systems, whereas in the alignment discourse they were seen as moving towards Western values and systems. However, and in so doing, they were construed as unstable and as a source of insecurity. The representations of the East highlighted 'political instability', 'poverty', 'uncontrollable migratory movements' and 'regional and internal disputes', as well as 'nationality conflicts' (Table 4.2). Whereas the West was constructed as a source of security, the East was rendered a source of insecurity. Accordingly, the number of oppositional features between Finland and the East increased.

Presupposition. The presupposition that established a particular kind of knowledge about the world out there and, in so doing, constituted the operational logic of a discourse, changed in Finland in 1995.[16] According to the analysis, although the *minor/great* opposition retained some of its significance, the new core *unstable/stable* opposition underpinned the re-articulation of the Finnish discourse on foreign and security policy. Several other binary oppositions can be subsumed under this core opposition – *democratic/undemocratic, economically developed/underdeveloped, reason/passion and order/disorder* – which informed the presupposition of the radically different 'security environment' in which Finland found itself.

The core opposition – unstable/stable – was clearly stated in several parts of the 1995 report, such as in the section describing the European security order:

> Managing stability has come to be the main task of Europe's security policy. If the opportunity for change is to be seized, every state in Europe must be involved. The challenge facing European security policy is simultaneously to support change promoting stability and balanced development, and to manage the new kinds of conflict.
>
> (Council of State 1995: 19)

Accordingly, 'stability policy' was articulated as the underlying feature of Finnish foreign and security policy. As the report stated: 'Finland's central goal in the post-Cold War situation has been to maintain and strengthen the stability that has long existed in northern Europe' (Council of State 1995: 65). Significantly, the EU was given a key role:

> In the area of stability policy, Finland is broadly committed to international
> cooperation and has plenty of institutional channels for exerting influence ...
>   The primary channel for Finland's stability policy is to exert effective
> influence on the European Union's common foreign and security policy.
>
> (Council of State 1995: 68)

However, the articulation associated with managing instability and creating
stability presupposed a certain world in which Russia and the former communist
states were articulated as fundamentally different from the Western European
states. The markers of difference were the binary oppositions of *democratic/
undemocratic, developed/undeveloped, rational/irrational* and *order/disorder*.

Within the official discourse the identities of the Eastern state were characterized
in terms of non-democratic or quasi-democratic regimes and underdeveloped
economies and poverty. The predication of the subjects was embedded in the large-
scale political, economic and social transition from communism and a command
economy to liberal democracy and a market economy. However, the process of
transition was in its early stages, and the democratic political systems as well
as the market economies in these states were, at best, developing. Significantly,
the concept of transformation and development was extended to other former communist states in Finland's near abroad and beyond in the 1995 report. The
following extract from the government's report is illustrative:

> The transition to democracy and a market economy has advanced farthest in
> Central Europe, including the Baltic countries. Profound social and economic
> change is also under way in Russia and the other countries of the
> Commonwealth of the Independent States (CIS), and in parts of the former
> Yugoslavia ...
>
> (Council of State 1995: 18)

The process of transition also presupposed insecurity. In other words, the process
of change was so far-reaching and rapid that it sometimes led to worsening living
conditions, disputes and violence. The report states:

> Political and economic reform is an uncertain, irregular sequence of events
> over a long period. Change since the end of the Cold War has brought with
> it several new problems: political instability, regional and internal disputes,
> uncontrollable migratory movements, nationality disputes and other problems.
> At worst these escalate into armed conflict and, subsequently, streams of
> refugees.
>
> (Ibid.)

Similarly, the unstable/stable core opposition drew on the binaries of *violence/non-
violence* and *order/disorder*. The period of transition, as articulated above, was
characterized by potential conflicts:

The number of armed conflicts has not decreased, and they are increasingly connected with internal or historical ethnic or religious disputes or nationality issues. Conflicts sometimes lead to the collapse of state structures, making it even more difficult for the international community to help manage and resolve them. The forms violence takes include violations of human rights, ethnic cleansing, war crimes and terrorism. The result of conflicts is often a wave of refugees in nearby regions and elsewhere.

(Council of State 1995: 14)

Another opposition encompassed in the above extract is order/disorder, which presupposed a particular kind of Western identity. The West was an orderly space based on democratic political systems with functioning economies that could deliver welfare. The poor and undemocratic or quasi-democratic states of the East, with internal problems that could potentially lead to violence might, in turn, collapse and produce chaos.

This presupposition of the East and the West, and Finland's location in between, resonates with the historical constructions predating but significantly shaped by the 1917 communist revolution in Russia. As Harle and Moisio note, Finnish geopolitical reasoning traditionally incorporated two directions in the world's political map, the East and the West. Historically, both have acquired rather different political meanings (Harle and Moisio 2000, Moisio 2003). In the historical discourse the East is typically reduced to Russia, which functioned mostly as the negative other in Finnish identity politics. Russia represented difference in terms of culture and political tradition. Moreover, it constituted the 'hereditary enemy' of Finland (Kekkonen 1943, Harle and Moisio 2000, Moisio 2003), the Finnish nation and people, their society and the state. It signified a clear threat to Finland's very existence.

Conversely, the West, in particular the Nordic countries and Western Europe, is represented as a highly valued societal, political and economic space. In the historical discourse it functions as the ideological 'home' (Browning 1999), and a model for development. It represents the political, economic, societal and cultural values with which Finland and the Finns wanted to be identified (Harle and Moisio 2000, Browning 2003, Moisio 2003). Despite the periods of anxiety, the West is largely constructed as a friend rather than a foe.[17]

Interestingly, the core opposition underpinning the construction of the East and the West in the 1995 report is significantly different from that in the neutrality discourse. Whereas the latter construed a specific Eastern and Western identity in terms of the minor-/great-power and periphery/centre oppositions in the bi-polar world, and downplayed cultural and ideological difference in the superpower confrontation, the 1995 discourse articulated Eastern and Western subjects in terms of instability in the post-Cold War world. Moreover, cultural differences between the East and the West gained dominance in the official Finnish discourse on foreign and security policy, the East being construed as a source of insecurity and the West as a source of security.

Subject positioning. The 1995 re-articulation of the Finnish foreign and security policy discourse positioned Finland differently in relation to the East and the West than the neutrality discourse. The subject positions constructed in 1995 included: (i) a stable, developed and potentially influential Finland; (ii) a stable, developed and powerful West; and (iii) an unstable, developing and potentially powerful East. The analysis suggests that a significant factor that postulated the change was the articulation of Finland's relationship with the European Union and, in particular, with its developing foreign and security policy. The initial phases of the CFSP and the CSDP were constructed as complementary and in terms of similarity in the Finnish discourse.

Although the representations of Finland still reflected a small-state identity, its potential to shape its external environment increased. In 1995 it was constructed as a more pro-active, 'responsible' and 'influential' subject. Moreover and significantly, it 'had broken free from its Cold War international position' (Table 4.2). It was no longer located between the East and the West and was a member of an 'influential core group of European democratic states'. As such, Finland had more influence on the 'arrangements concerning its international standing and national security'.

Whereas the Finnish subject position in the neutrality discourse was arrived at in relation to two rather similar, although ideologically different great-power subjects, the East and the West, in the 1995 discourse the positioning was in relation to significantly different Eastern and Western identities. Despite the degree of agency attributed to Russia, its internal problems rendered it a developing subject. Although all the states in the new Europe were argued to be committed to the shared values of 'democracy, human rights and fundamental freedoms, minority rights, the rule of law, social justice, as well as economic liberty and responsibility for the environment' (Council of State 1995: 10), some were constructed as more advanced in practising these ideals. As the 1995 report argues:

> Following the end of the division of Europe, Finland is no longer placed between East and West . . . In terms of security policy the world and Europe are living through the post-Cold War era, a period that could be described as a new transition.
>
> (Council of State 1995: 65)

On the other hand:

> Developments in Russia have a major impact on Finnish security . . . Finland will support democratic reform in Russia and its commitment to European unification and compliance with international norms.
>
> (Council of State 1995: 6)

In addition to the linkage in the neutrality discourse with realist ideas of world politics reflected in the minor-/great-power opposition, the new security discourse correlated with liberal ideas of a modern state and development manifested in the unstable/stable binary. In other words, whereas the representation of the East in the neutrality discourse highlighted the insecurities related to possible superpower conflict and their strategic interests, the new representations drew from different premises of insecurity. The insecurity was based on problems associated with 'political instability' and the underdevelopment that was constitutive of 'new security issues' such as 'regional and internal disputes, uncontrollable migratory movements, nationality disputes' and 'environmental problems' (Council of State 1995: 18). However, internal disputes could escalate to regional conflicts, which in turn could develop into conflicts between the great powers.

In contrast, the subject position available to the West and the EU was characterized by increasing influence and fully developed political and economic systems. Implicit in both is an extensive and complex identity and they were endowed with a significant degree of agency. As the 1995 report argues: 'The EU is a key force for change and stability in the new Europe. It is also a global actor with evolving economic and political relationships of cooperation with states and groups of states on all continents' (Council of State 1995: 10). Finland's relationship with the West and its subject position were constructed as similar and complementary with the West and the European Union, which constituted a highly valued political space and was providing Finland with opportunities and influence. Moreover, the European Union was seen to empower Finland as a small state. As the report states:

Membership in the European Union (EU) has clarified and strengthened Finland's international position. Finland has joined a community of similar democratic states. Finland's foreign and security policy rests on national security assessment and decision-making. EU membership gives Finland the chance to pursue its aims as a member of an influential and evolutionary association of states. It has become part of Finland's international identity.

EU membership has increased Finland's chances of influencing arrangements concerning its international standing and national security. It also gives it more responsibility with regard to European security and the future of the whole world.

(Council of State 1995: 10)

Accordingly, the 1995 discourse positioned Finland differently in relation to the East and the West than the neutrality discourse, assigning the country a considerably greater degree of agency. It assumed a more complex and wide-ranging identity than before, and was a more powerful initiator of action, formulator of Europe-wide policies, and assessor of the European security environment. Whereas the neutrality discourse endowed it with a significantly limited ability to influence its environment and to engage in international cooperation, the 1995 discourse re-articulated the Finnish identity as an influential and pro-active actor in Europe and beyond. As the Report states:

Ever since its independence Finland has believed that effective international collaboration on the basis of equality promotes the security of small states.

Finland has played an active role in the work of international organizations, seeking in particular opportunities for influence through cooperation with the other Nordic countries; this has shaped its international identity.

(Council of State 1995: 9)

Significantly, the European Union's developing foreign and security policy was argued to reflect Finnish and Nordic values and norms. The government's report stated that the values of democracy, human rights and the rule of law, which were 'already long cherished in Nordic countries', were the 'foundation for the common foreign and security policy of the European Union' (Council of State 1995: 10). All in all, both the empowering aspects of Finland's relationship with the European Union and the construction of similarity and commensurability in the EU and the Finnish foreign and security policies enabled a radically different re-articulation of the Finnish discourse: in other words, 'membership of the European Union (EU) will reinforce the foundations of Finnish security . . .' (Council of State 1995: 5).

Interpellation of the alignment discourse

The interplay between the neutrality and alignment discourses in the report suggests that the latter was not the dominant discourse in 1995. Accordingly, the Finnish state identity was in flux in the field of foreign and security policy. Findings based on an analysis of the parliamentary debate on the report substantiate this. The analysis is based on the representations that were generated in the speeches, questions and other interventions, remarks and proposals (hereafter remarks) by MPs in the parliamentary hearings. The official records of the debate were read through bearing in mind the predication of the subjects and objects featuring in the texts, the presupposition of a certain kind of knowledge and the subject positions available. Through careful analysis it was determined whether a particular remark belonged to the alignment or the neutrality discourse, or both, or to some other discourse.[18] The data collected is presented in Table 4.3 and Figure 4.1.

It appears from the data that although a new discourse was clearly articulated in 1995, it had not become dominant, and competing views drawing largely on the neutrality discourse were articulated. Moreover, the remarks introducing and defending the government's report included representations structured within the neutrality discourse. Prime Minister Lipponen's opening speech in the parliamentary hearings on the report serves as an example:

In a world of rapid change, security policy must be coherent and flexible. It must keep up with the change. We Finns are accustomed to the idea that Finland's basic line of policy is adaptation to the international environment. This is a natural approach for a small state with a challenging geopolitical position.

(Eduskunta 1995a, my translation)

Table 4.3 The neutrality and alignment discourses in the 1995 parliamentary debate

Remarks and speeches	Neutrality discourse	Neutrality and alignment discourse	Alignment discourse	n/a	Total
First Hearing	44	12	31	4	91
Second Hearing	68	73	36	7	184
Overall Debate	108	84	67	11	270

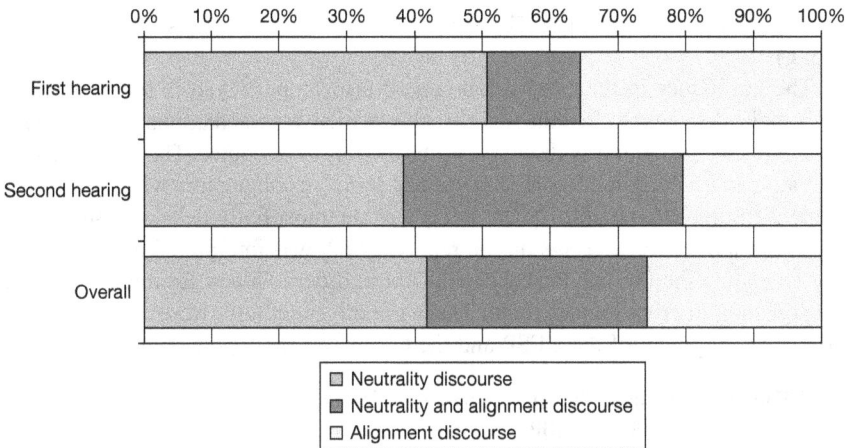

Figure 4.1 The neutrality and alignment discourses in the 1995 parliamentary debate.

This excerpt creates several representations that are typical of the neutrality discourse. The predication constructs Finland as a small state located next to a great power. It presupposes a realist world-view highlighting great-power interests and also Finland's peripheral existence. The subject position available to Finland is characterized by a significantly limited degree of agency, and adaptation is articulated as a key feature of Finnish identity. However, the prime minister continued:

> Since the end of the Cold War conditions [of Finnish security] have changed in many ways. The international field has opened up and agendas have broadened. Security is no longer seen merely in political or military terms but as a comprehensive and broad question. It is improved when human rights are respected and democracy strengthened. International crime, environmental crisis and uncontrollable population movements require closer international cooperation.
>
> Membership of the European Union enhances the foundations of Finland's security. It offers an effective channel of influence to advance Finland's interests and enable it to meet its international responsibilities. EU membership has brought Finland into a union of states with a central role in international relations.
>
> (Ibid.)

The alignment discourse clearly governed the representations articulated in this extract. For instance, through predication the object of Finland's actions, security, is seen as a broad concept. The presupposed world-view was very different from that in the previous extract. Moreover, EU membership was seen to empower Finland. Its new subject position assigned it more influence, but also more responsibilities. Both are suggestive of an increased degree of agency. Both of these representations that were indicative of the different discourses were often identifiable in the remarks made during the 1995 parliamentary hearings. As Prime Minister Lipponen said: 'At the same time as we, as a small state, have to adapt, we also want to be influential. This is the core question for today's security policy' (ibid.).

The key issues in the 1995 debate could also be portrayed in terms of these two main discourses. In other words, the related representations were largely structured by the neutrality discourse or the alignment discourse. The government's initiative to establish the Rapid Deployment Force in conjunction with the Finnish Defence Forces (Council of State 1995) was the most hotly debated issue in the 1995 parliamentary hearings on the report, which was interpreted as a blueprint for amending the Finnish Peacekeeping Act in order to allow for more extensive engagement in crisis management. These initiatives, in turn, were closely related to the development of the CFSP and the CSDP. As the report states:

> The main emphasis [in EU security and defence issues] will be on developing the Union's own capabilities, and the combined capabilities of the Union and the WEU, in humanitarian and other peacekeeping operations in the field of crisis management. Finland supports consolidation of the European Union's crisis-management capacity.
>
> (Council of State 1995: 62)

The majority of the representations generated in the remarks opposing the government's plans drew on the neutrality discourse. As MP Kääriäinen, representing the main opposition party, argued:

> The difference between traditional peacekeeping and the development and deployment of the Rapid Deployment Force is a not minor, it is fundamental. If the troops are produced we have to be ready to take on a new kind of responsibility and accept unfortunate consequences. Depending on the mission, casualties are possible. Lives would be given for a purpose other than defending Finland's independence. Are the Finnish people and parliament ready for this?
>
> (Eduskunta 1995a, my translation)

In the second hearing, former Prime Minister Aho, from the same party, clarified this position:

> The fact that the responsibility in crisis management is different is self-evident. We cannot be asked to fulfil the same requirements as countries belonging

to a military alliance ... Our basic starting point is that a country that is member of a military alliance has a different responsibility than a non-aligned country.

(Eduskunta 1995b, my translation)

Although the opposition pointed out that Finnish peacekeeping capabilities should be strengthened, it emphasized the fact that Finland did not have the same moral obligations, responsibilities or crisis-management resources as the major powers and other more secure states. The representations created in these statements clearly draw on the neutrality discourse, whereas those generated in the government's defence mainly reflect the alignment discourse. As the prime minister responded:

Mr Aho said that we do not have the same responsibility as others. Yes we do. In participating in peacekeeping missions we have responsibility for the whole mission. We only limit our engagement to a suitable level, which reflects our foreign policy line and our resources.

(Ibid.)

MP Paasio explicitly highlighted the moral dimension of the initiative. He said: 'the committee suggests that there are no reasons why Finland should not carry out its international responsibilities' (ibid.). Moreover, the foreign minister noted that if Finland declined, others involved in the Nordic peacekeeping alliance could take its place:

It is possible that Finland could be involved in Bosnia if the mandate, peace accord, and all the other requirements have been fulfilled. It is obvious that it is not a problem to find enough troops for Bosnia without Finland being involved. It is possible that Polish troops could replace Finnish troops in the Nordic group.

(Ibid.)

What is implicit in this argument is that the European foreign and security policy environment was in flux and Finland could not take its standing for granted even in the context of Nordic cooperation. Therefore it had to become more active player in order to consolidate its place in the rapidly changing world. Accordingly, the representations generated in these articulations are clearly governed by the alignment discourse. Finland had responsibilities and it was in a position to address normative questions. Moreover, the Finnish state identity in the realm of foreign and security policy was increasingly constructed in terms of similarity with rather than difference from the Nordic countries. The neutrality discourse assigned the Nordic countries a different geopolitical situation and different security interests and arrangements.

After EU membership

The final section in this chapter analyses the re-articulation of the alignment discourse. The focus is on the security and defence policy reports published in 1997 and 2001, and on the parliamentary debates on these documents. Special attention is devoted to the role of the CFSP and the CSDP in the relevant documents and debates, and well as to the interplay between the neutrality and alignment discourses. The analysis suggests that the alignment discourse had become dominant by 2001 in terms of structuring the meaning of statements and debates concerning the Finnish foreign and security policy, and that the role of the EU's policy was pivotal in this transition. Significantly, towards the end of the 1990s there was a stronger emphasis on traditional military aspects related to the development of the CSDP and NATO enlargement in the Finnish re-articulations. Accordingly, both the possibility and the feasibility of military non-alignment were increasingly being called into question.

The aim of the 1997 and 2001 security and defence reports was to review the development of the Finnish foreign and security policy in light of the 1995 report, which laid out a 'broad and sturdy foundation for the development of a comprehensive security policy' (Council of State 1997: 6). Although the two later reports clearly focus more on defence and military issues, both give a comprehensive (re)assessment of the developments in Finland's external security environment after the publication of the 1995 report.[19] Therefore, these reports and the related parliamentary debates constitute interesting material in terms of analysing the development and impact of the 1995 articulation of the alignment discourse, in which the European Union and its developing foreign, security and defence policies played a central role.

The introductory sections of both reports discuss the 'constant change' that was 'put in motion after the end of the Cold War' and that was both 'profound and lasting' (Council of State 1997: 11, 2001: 6–8). The 1997 paper notes that the threat of large-scale military conflict in Europe remained low. On the other hand, Finland was facing new kinds of security threats such as 'political instability, regional and international conflicts, ethnic disputes and other security problems that could erupt as armed conflicts and associated refugee flows' as well as extensive 'environmental problems' (Council of State 1997: 8). The 2001 report added to these issues threats and risks concerning human-rights violations, damage to the infrastructure, information-related threats, disasters, terrorism, international crime and epidemics (Council of State 2001: 17). The proliferation of weapons of mass destruction and the uncontrolled spread and use of conventional weapons are explicitly mentioned in both reports.

Significantly for this study, both reports highlight the increasing importance of the European Union as a security actor (Council of State 1997: 18–19, 2001: 22). According to the 2001 report:

> The importance of the European Union in relation to Finland's security interests and goals has continued to increase. A strong Union based on

solidarity will enhance security, prevent crisis from emerging and improve Finland's ability to cope with such situations should they arise.

(Council of State 2001: 8)

Finland's first EU initiative, the European Union's Northern Dimension, the aim of which was to increase regional stability in the North of Europe, was influential in the construction of Finland's increasing international influence as an EU member.[20] The 2001 report notes that the 'implementation of the EU's common policy on the Northern Dimension will provide a long-term approach for promoting sustainable development' (Council of State 2001: 8). Indeed, with the initiative of the Northern Dimension Finland emerged as a regional security provider. Significantly for the Finns, it showed that a small EU member state could play an important and constructive role in shaping the Union's policies (Arter 2000). The development of the CFSP, and specifically of the CSDP, was also highlighted in both reports. The significance of the approaching EU summit in Amsterdam is explicitly addressed in the 1997 report (Council of State 1997: 19). It suggests, for example, that the 'EU has a central task in countering the security problems arising from economic and societal instability in the countries of Central and Eastern Europe' (Council of State 1997: 13). Significantly, the 2001 report highlights the European Union's responsibility in the field of crisis management and the importance of its military capabilities:

The Amsterdam Treaty, which was signed in 1997 and came into force in 1999, has made EU decision-making more effective and given it new tools for pursuing its common foreign and security policy. The Treaty expanded the scope of the EU's common foreign and security policy by adding crisis management to EU competence.

(Council of State 2001: 22)

Moreover, the 2001 paper affirms that further 'improvement in the European Union's ability to take action will remain a fundamental principle of Finland's policy on Europe (Council of State 2001: 8).

The subsequent sections of both reports outline the future development of Finland's defence policy and defence forces in accordance with the policies of military non-alignment and credible independent defence (Council of State 1997: 54, 2001: 47). In other words, Finland was to stay outside of any military alliances and the Finnish policy would be based on a territorial defence system. This system would remain anchored in general conscription, which was considered necessary in order to ensure the capacity to defend the entire country (Council of State 1997: 59, 2001: 47). In order to keep the defence up-to-date, however, the Government introduced several structural changes in the forces that would 'meet the demands of the early parts of the next millennium' (Council of State 1997: 54). These changes were based largely on new perceptions of warfare and strategy suggesting that the defence of core areas of the country had to be strengthened (Council of State 1997: 71, 2001: 45–46). Another key theme in the reports is the interoperability of Finnish troops with international forces, mainly through NATO's PfP programme and participation in the European Union's developing military structures (Council of State 1997: 65–66). It is argued that this would serve Finland's defence forces and the country's international crisis-management capabilities. The development of crisis-management troops and of Finland's defence is constructed as 'mutually beneficial' (Council of State 1997: 52, 2001: 46, 69).

Re-articulation of the alignment discourse

According to the analysis of the reports, the representations of Finland and the environment in which it found itself were progressively structured by the alignment discourse, which is increasingly reflected in the predication of the actors, the knowledge presupposed and the subject positions available to them. On the other hand, and although still identifiable, the neutrality discourse was clearly getting weaker in these re-articulations. The importance of this finding is highlighted by the fact that the 1997 and 2001 reports explicitly deal with the traditional 'hard security' question of military defence, in which the legacy of neutrality is argued to prevail in the form of military non-alignment.

The main subjects covered in the 1997 and 2001 reports are broadly the same as in the 1995 report, although the West is increasingly constructed in terms of the European Union and NATO and the East is increasingly reduced to Russia. According to the 1997 report: 'From the perspective of Finland, the European Union, Russia and NATO are the most central actors in security developments in Europe' (Council of State 1997: 6). The North is still considered significant, but it is increasingly addressed in relation to the EU. For instance, the reports explicitly refer to the joint Finnish–Swedish proposal in 1997 related to the European Union's defence dimension (Council of State 1997: 19). Significantly too, they increasingly discuss Finland's relations with the rest of the world in terms of the European Union. In particular, they both highlight Finland's role in EU relations with the East and Russia (Council of State 1997: 23, 2001: 31–32), NATO (Council of State 1997: 22–23, 2001: 23–24, 41), and the West and the United States (Council of State 1997: 25, 2001: 41).

The West, the North and Finland

As mentioned above, the main theme of the 1997 report is the changing European security arrangements. It is argued that European security was 'seeking a shape', that it was 'in a state of flux' and that the institutions were 'adjusting to new challenges' (Council of State 1997: 11). Significantly, it suggests the representation of the West was changing and that its role in the construction of Finland's place in the world was increasing. The CFSP is increasingly prominent in the Finnish re-articulations: it is constructed as a developing policy in the 1995 report, whereas in the 1997 document it is construed as a pivotal factor shaping the defence policy:

The EU's importance as a player in the field of security will grow as integration proceeds. The Treaty on European Union (the Maastricht Treaty, which came into force in 1993) broadened the scope of the Union's competence to encompass the development and implementation of a Common Foreign and Security Policy (CFSP). The Maastricht Treaty provides for a security and defence dimension to be part of development of the CFSP. This dimension includes the eventual framing of common defence.

(Council of State 1997: 18)

Moreover, whereas the link between the CFSP and the national defence policies was considered insignificant in 1995, in 1997 the government articulated a relationship between the two. Moreover, Finland's engagement in military-crisis-management is re-articulated as non-contradictory with the policy of military non-alignment and independent defence with reference to another Nordic and previously neutral country, Sweden:

The joint Finnish–Swedish proposal was made on the basis of the defence dimension provided in the Maastricht Treaty ... Under the proposal, humanitarian and crisis-management tasks involving the use of military organisations would be included in the Union's competence ... The proposal would further provide for all EU member states contributing to crisis-management operations, including those not participating in military alliances, to have an equal opportunity to take part in planning and decision-making within the WEU in relation to those operations.

(Council of State 1997: 19)

Significantly, it was not participation in the military missions but exclusion from them that constituted a problem for the militarily non-aligned Finland in 1997. This representation clearly related to the new Finnish subject position established by the alignment discourse. In other words, the European Union gave Finland not only security but also influence. In this context participation in EU crisis-management was considered significant. These representations are linked to Finland's overall European policy as articulated by Prime Minister Lipponen following entry into the Union: the best way forward was to 'be, as much as possible, within the circles in which the future of the Union is decided' (Lipponen 2001: 166). Therefore, close participation in the CSDP was assumed to guarantee 'the effectiveness of its [Finland's] foreign and security policy' (Council of State 2001: 7) and to empower Finland within the EU. Within this context the closer integration and full CSDP participation are constructed as complementary rather than detrimental to a Finnish defence policy based on military non-alignment. Significantly, the credibility of the Finnish defence forces is linked to their 'interoperability' in the 2001 report (Council of State 2001: 73). Further:

By improving its security cooperation and operational capacity in line with UN and OSCE principles within the EU, within NATO Partnership

Cooperation and with other Nordic countries in international crisis management, Finland will improve its own capacity to manage crises and threats affecting the country. Engaging in international cooperation will also support Finland's precautionary measures aimed at securing key societal functions in exceptional circumstances.

(Council of State 2001: 39)

Similarly, NATO is clearly more prominent in the re-articulation of the alignment discourse in both reports although, mainly in relation to the CFSP and the CSDP. More specifically, it is largely discussed in the context of EU-led crisis management, for instance with regard to EU access to NATO resources and its military infrastructure (Council of State 2001: 23), and NATO enlargement is linked to the EU. As the 1997 report states:

Although enlargement in the EU and NATO are independent of each other and apply to different spheres, they are mutually influential because they are parallel and both have security linkages. The stability effects of EU enlargement could be accentuated as NATO gradually expands. Several EU member states would like all members to be in both the WEU and NATO before long.

(Council of State 1997: 20–21)

The change is significant in that the 1995 report generates representations that highlight a clear distinction between NATO and the EU. Another major shift is the emphasis on NATO's 'open-door policy' (Council of State 2001: 24) and the reaffirmation of the policy of military non-alignment 'under prevailing conditions' (Council of State 2001: 7). Crucially, the so-called 'NATO option policy' suggests that the alignment discourse penetrated into the field of defence policy, which was largely considered the field within which the previously dominant neutrality discourse was still being re-articulated.

The East

The East retains its importance in the construction of Finland's foreign and security policy in the 1997 and 2001 reports. Although the Eastern subjects were moving towards the West in terms of their developing political and economic values and norms, they are still substantial markers of difference in the documents' re-articulation of the alignment discourse. For one thing, the East connoted significant insecurity in terms of both the traditional and the new and broader conceptualizations of the term. For instance, it is suggested in the 2001 paper that 'Russia was continuing its transition towards democracy, rule of law, and a functioning market economy. However, there were still uncertainties surrounding the country's future development.' (Council of State 2001: 31) These uncertainties included political and economic instability and adjustment to Russia's declining international position (Council of State 2001: 16–19, 31–32). Accordingly, the background knowledge in which the representations of Finland's place in the world are largely generated was based on the unstable/stable core opposition.

Interestingly, the 1997 and 2001 reports assign a bigger role to the EU in Finland's relations with the East:

> The importance of cooperation between the EU and Russia for the future of Europe is continually growing. Security in the Baltic Sea region will improve as a result of regional cooperation within Europe. This will be shaped by the enlargement of the EU and of NATO and developments in relations between Russia and the Baltic States.
>
> (Council of State 2001: 7)

Finland's EU membership and full participation in the CFSP and the CSDP are also noted in this respect: 'The key aim of the political and economic integration process that began in Western Europe is to improve European stability, security and prosperity' (Council of State 2001: 22). Moreover, 'although the EU is primarily a political and economic entity, its Member States have wished to strengthen their ability to manage crises in Europe and its environs, including by military means, following experiences in Bosnia and Kosovo' (Council of State 2001: 23). Here the presupposition of the unstable East and the stable West is taken as given, and the EU is imperative in the constitution of the specific kind of East in the Finnish foreign and security policy discourse.

The representations of Finland in the face of these threats also changed. Whereas the 1995 report states that 'Finland has never enjoyed protected security status' and 'neither will it have a privileged status amid the present changes in Europe, or in the conceivable future' (Council of State 1995: 66), the 1997 and 2001 reports argue that Finland will not be left alone to address its security challenges. Indeed, according to the 1997 report, 'membership of the European Union has added clarity and strengthened Finland's international position. Although membership does not entail security guarantees, it does include the protection that is founded on mutual solidarity' (Council of State 1997: 6). The 2001 report goes further, affirming that 'a strong Union based on solidarity will also benefit Finland's security situation and help to prevent the eruption of crises that may affect the country, as well as improve its ability to deal with them. (Council of State 2001: 40) Accordingly, the alignment discourse was increasingly structuring the construction of Finland and its geopolitical and security milieu. The country was no longer isolated between the East and the West, it was located firmly in the West and could rely on the solidarity of the Western powers.

Interpellation of the alignment discourse

Analysis of the parliamentary debates on the 1997 and 2001 security and defence policy reports supports the claims made above. The number of remarks that were structured by the neutrality discourse decreased in the 1997 and 2001 parliamentary hearings, which suggests that over time state officials and MPs were increasingly influenced by the alignment discourse. In other words, the representations created by state officials increasingly drawing on this discourse were largely accepted as adequate and true reflections of reality. The data collected following a careful reading and analysis of the 1997 and 2001 parliamentary debates is presented in Tables 4.4 and 4.5 and Figures 4.2 and 4.3.

It is clear from the data that whereas several of the remarks made in 1995 by both state officials in charge of the foreign and security policy and MPs drew from both the neutrality and alignment discourses, in 1997 they were increasingly structured by the alignment discourse and in 2001 they were predominantly governed by it. Prime Minister Lipponen's opening speeches in 1995 and 1997 serve as good exemplars. He argued in 1995 that adaptation to the external environment was natural for a small state like Finland. However, in 1997 he also noted that Finland wanted to have influence:

> EU membership is of key importance in Finland's overall security policy. It has stabilized Finland's position in the new Europe, and in so doing has security value for our country. We carry joint responsibility in the Union, and we influence the strengthening of security.
>
> (Eduskunta 1997a, my translation)

Table 4.4 The neutrality and alignment discourses in the 1997 parliamentary debate

Remarks and speeches	Neutrality discourse	Neutrality and alignment discourse	Alignment discourse	n/a	Total
First Hearing	20	18	51	15	104
Second Hearing	7	30	55	56	148
Overall Debate	27	48	106	71	252

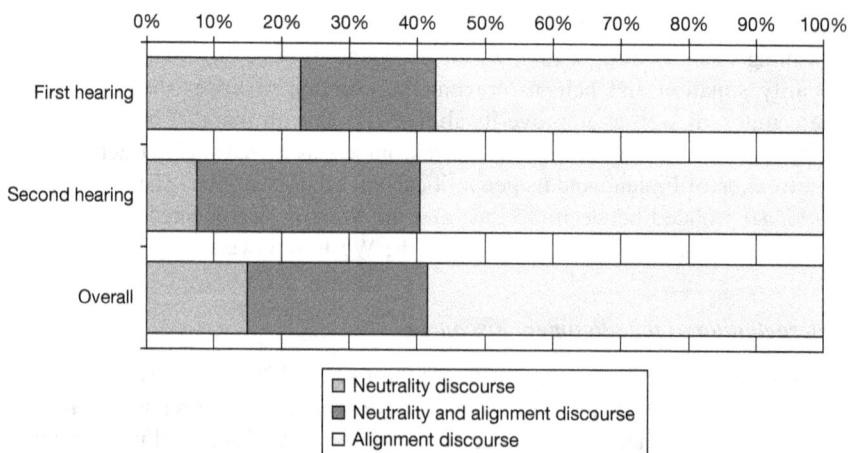

Figure 4.2 The neutrality and alignment discourses in the 1997 parliamentary debate.

Finland clearly emerges in this excerpt as an increasingly influential actor, with power in terms of adapting to the external environment. Moreover, the increased degree of agency vested in the country is progressively taken as given. It was no longer merely seeking to carry responsibilities or have influence – it was already doing so.

The neutrality discourse does not disappear, however. Its structuring of meaning was still clearly present in the key disagreement aired in the 1997 parliamentary debate linked to the reform of the Finnish peacekeeping legislation. Peacekeeping operations were previously conducted directly under the Ministry of Defence, and as such the missions were not directly linked to the operability or operations of the Finnish Defence Forces. In practice the links were strong, however, for instance in the recruitment and training of personnel as well as in many practical management matters. The distinction nevertheless mattered in terms of the Finnish post-war defence policy of neutrality and military non-alignment. In short, the Finnish Defence Forces could not operate outside of Finnish territory.

However, the 1997 review proposes that peacekeeping and crisis-management activities abroad should be fully taken over by the Finnish Defence Forces. Opposing views emerged, which were largely articulated in terms of the neutrality discourse. Esko Aho, representing the main opposition party, argued thus in 1997:

Table 4.5 The neutrality and alignment discourses in the 2001 parliamentary debate

Remarks and speeches	Neutrality discourse	Neutrality and alignment discourse	Alignment discourse	n/a	Total
First Hearing	9	5	101	26	141
Second Hearing	4	6	100	65	175
Overall Debate	13	11	201	91	316

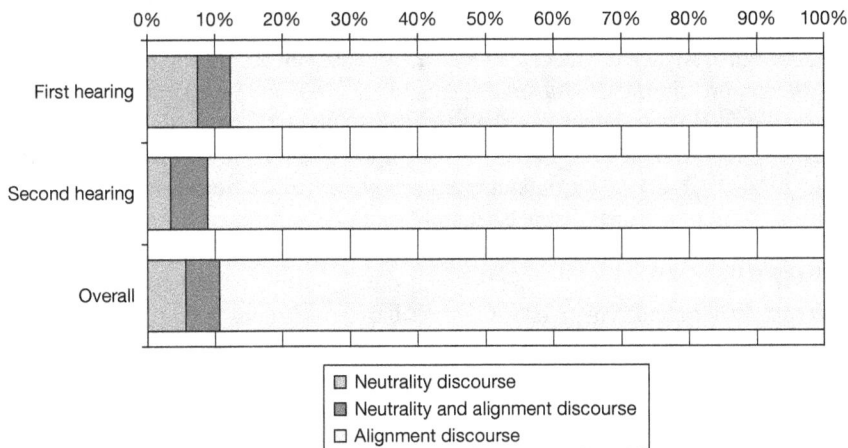

Figure 4.3 The neutrality and alignment discourses in the 2001 parliamentary debate.

> We have not opposed Finland's participation in the Bosnian peace-keeping operation at any stage. However, we have insisted that it is not wise to include peacekeeping training and Rapid Deployment Forces destined for peacekeeping operations within the peacetime organisation of the Defence Forces.
>
> (Ibid.)

The logic behind this remark relates to the special character of the Finnish Defence Forces within the neutrality discourse. 'Left alone' in a geopolitically challenging environment to take care of its defence, an independent defence capability was essential for Finland's survival. This capability referred not merely to material factors but also and largely to ideational factors such as the Finnish people's willingness to defend their country by all available means. An essential element in the construction of such willingness was the mobilization of the whole society for defence purposes (Rainio-Niemi 2008), and the defensive nature of the Defence Forces. The Finnish army was thereby meant to operate only on Finnish soil. As MP Aho continued, 'Finland's strength lies in our strong will to defend our country. This can only last if citizens have a clear vision of the national policy and the tasks of the Defence Forces'. Moreover, Aho stressed that it was important for every Finn to be able to relate to the Defence Forces and, 'if needed, to be willing to participate in defending our country' (Eduskunta 1997a, my translation). This debate provoked strong reactions in 1997, but it was resolved in 1998 when the new Peacekeeping Act brought peacekeeping and crisis-management into the remit of the Defence Forces. This new arrangement was largely accepted by 2001, and the neutrality discourse lost ground in the debate on the 2001 report.

On the other hand, calls for Finland to join NATO grew stronger, and were explicitly voiced in the parliamentary debates in both 1997 and 2001. Significantly, it appears from the analysis that the CSDP and NATO membership were clearly connected. Although the government re-articulated the policy of military non-alignment, MPs argued that the increased interoperability among Finnish troops and EU and NATO crisis management were a preamble for full NATO membership. As MP Vistbacka stated: '. . . we cannot accept the hidden agenda of the report aiming to subsume Finland in NATO' (Eduskunta 2001a, my translation). He also noted that the same 'slow but sure strategy' that had been used to take Finland into the EU was being applied again to take the country into NATO (ibid.). MPs defending the government's view insisted that the development of national defence capabilities and EU military crisis-management ability were not mutually exclusive, as they were under the neutrality policy. As MP Kekkonen argued: 'Quite the opposite! Finland's military contribution to international peacekeeping operations is based on troops whose main task is national defence' (ibid.).

In fact, the analysis suggests that both EU membership and the EU foreign and security policy were significant in the emerging consensus among the majority of parliamentarians. More specifically, in the 1997 and 2001 reports the European Union's developing crisis-management capabilities, which Finland had been 'planning and building' (ibid.) constituted the key rationale behind the claimed Europeanization of foreign and security policy in Finland. The shift in the debates on the foreign, security and defence policy reviews from 1995 to 2001 from EU membership towards NATO membership is indicative of the successful inter-pellation of the alignment discourse. It reflects a series of successful re-articulations and debates in which the impossible became possible. By 2001 the prefix 'non' was being called into question in the Finnish policy of military non-alignment. Data collected in opinion polls conducted between 1998 and 2001 is also highly interesting in this regard: support for military non-alignment remained high (60 per cent in 1998 and 68 per cent in 2001), whereas support for military alignment was low (29 per cent in 1998 and 21 per cent in 2001) (Puolustusministeriö 2004). However, the opinion polls also revealed that more than half of Finns thought that Finland was moving towards and committing itself to full membership of NATO (66 per cent in 1998 and 53 per cent in 2001) given the increasing cooperation on different levels (Puolustusministeriö 2001). The increasing support for military non-alignment and the lowered expectations from NATO membership could be attributed to the election of the new president, Tarja Halonen, in 2000. She was known for her support of non-alignment under the then current security environment, and as president was still in charge of the Finnish foreign and security policy, although her powers were significantly reduced in the constitutional reform approved in 1999. However, prior to her election Tarja Halonen had served as Foreign Minister from 1995, and was thus one of the key state officials articulating the new policy and discourse. Moreover, these opinion polls suggest that the population, by and large, believed that that many key state officials in the field of foreign and security policy, and MPs, were increasingly leaning towards military alignment.

Conclusion

This chapter analysed the Europeanization of foreign and security policy in Finland. It seems that EU membership and the European Union's developing foreign and security policy had a significant impact upon the Finnish official discourse. They had a major role in the post-Cold War re-articulation of the official line in terms of alignment rather than neutrality. Moreover, the development of the EU's foreign and security policy, specifically the creation of crisis-management capabilities, had a significant effect on the subsequent re-articulations of the official discourse and its successful interpellation. EU membership and participation in the CFSP and the CSDP facilitated the transition from neutrality to alignment in the realm of foreign and security policy, and shaped the state identity of Finland.

5 The Europeanization of British foreign and security policy discourse

Re-articulating the great-power identity

Introduction

Throughout the 1990s Britain was widely viewed as having a problematic relationship with the European integration project. This view drew on representations suggesting that it was declining as a great power. After refusing to participate in the initial phases of the project in the 1950s Britain decided to join it in the1960s, largely on account of the worsening economic situation. However, France blocked its entry into the European Community until 1971.[1] As a member, Britain was soon constructed as a reluctant and 'awkward partner', both at home and in Europe (Allen 1988: 171, Wallace, W. 1992, Forster 1998, George 1998, White 2001). It was perceived as opposing any development that could undermine its sovereignty, and thus as holding back Western European integration. In the field of foreign and security policy Britain considered itself the key ally of the US in the Cold War world. As such it highlighted the importance of US commitment to European security and NATO, and was reluctant to accept or support the enlargement of independent European capabilities.

British policy towards European integration did not change amid the developments in European foreign and security policy – such as the establishment of the CFSP potentially leading to common defence in 1992. Indeed there appears to be strikingly little discussion or debate among British state officials on the significant economic, political and security changes in the post-Cold War world. It is suggested that, indeed, the most remarkable aspect of the British foreign policy debate in the 1990s was how little it appeared to be affected by the transformation of the international system (Forster 2000: 47). Similarly, the Europeanization of foreign and security policies in the wake of the CFSP and the CSDP inspired only modest debate until the late 1990s. The Labour party's entry into government and the Strategic Defence Review (SDR) in 1997, followed by the joint British–French declaration on European defence at St Malo in December 1998, are thus often considered to mark a dramatic change in British policy towards Europe. As such they provoked lively discussion concerning British reorientation and Britain's place in the world in the twenty-first century. The government argued that Britain needed a fresh start with Europe, and a more positive policy towards the European Union. Significantly, the major factor propelling the change was British engagement with the CFSP and the CSDP.

The aim in this case study is to establish what impact, if any, the CFSP and the CSDP had on the seemingly rigid British state identity in the field of foreign and security policy.[2] The first step was thus to analyse some of the key British documents on foreign and security policy from the 1990s, prior to the publication of the SDR in 1997. The analysis reveals the existence of a dominant discourse in which the CFSP and the CSDP had a significantly marginal role. In order to assess the impact of the increasing weight given to the CFSP and the CSDP in the official policy, the second section focuses on the foreign, security and defence policy documents and the parliamentary debates concerning the joint British–French declaration on European defence in St Malo in 1998. According to the analysis, the increasing Europeanization of foreign and security policy was important for the 1998 re-articulation(s) of the British policy. However, this re-articulation represented a twist rather than a turn in the discourse, in other words the key elements structuring the meaning given to the key actors and their environment were largely unchanged. Finally, in order to establish how this re-articulation developed in light of the intensifying Europeanization the third section analyses the subsequent white papers and parliamentary debates concerning these documents. It is suggested that the traditional British great-power discourse and identity prevailed in the documentation as well as in the parliamentary debates.

Britain as a great power

This section lays out the discursive context within which the EU foreign and security policy were first articulated and made meaningful in Britain. In so doing it maps out the dominant foreign and security policy discourse(s) in Britain until 1998, when a policy turn in relation to the CFSP and the CSDP became evident in the empirical material. I suggest that the dominant discourse in which these policies were made meaningful was the traditional Britain-as-a-great-power discourse. The main elements of this are: (i) Britain as a great power with a global reach; (ii) Britain as a leading member of several international organizations, most importantly the (iii) European Union and (iv) NATO, in which it emerged as the (v) closest ally to the United States. Analysis of the official documentation from 1989 to 1997 is preceded by a brief descriptive discussion based on scholarly literature on Britain's foreign and security policy.

It was apparent from an initial survey of the empirical material that the dominant theme in the official foreign and security policy debates in the 1990s was Britain's position and influence in the world.[3] The documents examined highlight its aspirations to retain and increase its influence in the world economy, international institutions and military affairs in the post-Cold War period. In short, the British foreign and security policy was discussed in terms of capabilities, influence and leadership. Two themes stand out in the scholarly literature with regard to claims concerning the Europeanization of the British foreign policy: (i) the so-called three-circle doctrine and (ii) Britain's suggested declining influence in world politics. Macleod's comprehensive study on perceptions of Britain's foreign policy role from 1989 to 1993 identifies three dominant themes in the academic debate on British foreign policy in the post-war era (Macleod 1997: 165): (i) the nature of Britain's position in the world; (ii) the relevance of the special relationship with the US; and (iii) Britain's link with Europe (see also Hill 1988, M. Smith, S. Smith and White 1988). Churchill initially articulated this doctrine in the Conservative Party Conference in 1948. He located Britain at the intersection of three spheres of influence embracing the Commonwealth, the United States and Europe.

A review of other sources suggests that the doctrine indeed constituted 'a most significant conceptual framework to have influenced the making of the postwar British foreign policy' (Allen 1988: 169, Hill 1988: 44, Tugendhat and Wallace 1988: 13–14, White 2001:120). As such, it was integral for the British state identity in this policy field. Indeed, within the three-circle doctrine a particular kind of British identity emerged, labelled the great-power identity in this book. White's analysis of the three key assumptions behind the doctrine is illustrative. First, the doctrine portrays Britain as a global power with global interests rather than a middle-range state pursuing mostly regional interests. Second, it establishes pragmatism and flexibility as the key principles of the British foreign and security policy, the aim being to play a leading role in all three dimensions and not to become committed to any particular 'circle' at the expense of the others. Consequently and third, Britain is seen as a central and powerful player. As White suggests: 'Churchill's notion that the British 'have the opportunity of joining them [the three circles] all together' provided a rationale for a bridge-builder's role for Britain, which has continued to be a powerful self-image throughout the post-war period' (Macleod 1997: 165–167, White 2001: 120).

The other common theme in the accounts dealing with the Europeanization of Britain's foreign and security policy concerns Britain's declining international status.[4] It is argued in several of them that Britain had lost its dominant position in world politics by the time the Suez Crisis erupted in 1956.[5] This argument is linked to the loss of the Empire and, more recently, to the diminishing role of the Commonwealth. However, several other international and domestic developments are noted in the literature. Macleod suggest that rise of the bi-polar world, the loss of empire, and the birth of a European Union, to which Britain applied three times before being finally admitted, were enough to shake the country's self-confidence in its international status. In addition Britain had to contend with domestic economic decline and the country gradually fall behind its two major West European rivals, France and Germany. This loss of political, economic, techno- logical, and military power was 'accompanied by a crisis of national identity and status as Britain has striven to define its place in Europe and adjust to qualitative change in its 'special relationship' with the United States'(Macleod 1997: 161).

Characteristic of the decline theme is the representation of Britain as a state that was searching for a new international identity. As Dean Acheson put it in 1962, 'Britain had lost an empire but had not yet found a role' (cited in ibid.).

Alternative analyses suggest that some of the decline claims are overstatements. According to Hill, for instance, one of the 'apparent geohistorical continuities' or 'givens' in the British foreign policy has been its global reach, which should not be underestimated 'in the closing years of the twentieth century' (Hill 1988: 31–32). Hill further argues that British diplomatic influence was still considerable and certainly beyond the country's economic ranking. Moreover, British culture was capable of exerting a formative influence on millions of people in many different kinds of societies, independent of the British military capability, in connection with which the country maintained its formal nuclear-weapon status. In the 1980s Margaret Thatcher's assertive rhetoric inspired some scholars to conclude that Britain's influence in the world was increasing rather than diminishing. Britain is seen as one of the most influential states in the Cold War world, and as the closest ally of the US it also had a key post-Cold War role (Macleod 1997: 165).

Nevertheless, there is broad scholarly consensus that, although Thatcher restored a certain sense of national self-assurance (Tugendhat and Wallace 1988: 22), her time in office did not indicate the return of British dominance in world politics (Sanders 1990: 291–294, Macleod 1997: 165). On the contrary, as Macleod notes, instead of increasing British influence, the collapse of communism aggravated Britain's identity crisis by removing the foundations of one of the vital pillars of its special place in the world, namely its contribution to the Western defence network. Her influential identity 'could no longer depend on being perceived as one of the principal European ideological and military bulwarks against any possible show of the Soviet strength' (Macleod 1997: 162).

The decline thesis and the three-circles doctrine are both crucial to a scholarly understanding(s) of the Europeanization of foreign and security policy in Britain. For instance, Britain is widely seen to have valued its special relationship with the United States over participation in Western European integration (Sanders 1990, George 1998, White 2001). In the 1950s it endorsed transatlantic defence cooperation over European cooperation and highlighted NATO's role in European defence. The explicit aim of British policy makers was to safeguard US commitment to post-war European security and defence. On the one hand the policy was based on the assumption that there was no credible European alternative to the US security guarantees and Britain's favourable position in this arrangement, and on the other it reflected the continuing British otherness as well as supremacy over Europe. Former Prime Minister Margaret Thatcher's 2002 reasoning concerning Europe and the US–British relationship is illuminating. With reference to Nazism and Communism she argued: 'During my lifetime most of the problems the world has faced have come, in one fashion or other, from mainland Europe, and the solutions from outside it.' (Thatcher 2002: 320).

Britain's decision to opt out of the initial stages of economic integration also signalled an autonomous or detached relationship with Europe (Sanders 1990, George 1998; White 2001). Reconsideration of this decision in the 1960s could be interpreted as reflecting British pragmatism in terms of rational calculation of the economic costs of detachment. Accordingly, and as scholars have noted, the membership application did not represent any special commitment to Western European integration (Larsen 1997: 53, George 1998: 40, White 2001: 121).

Britain's aim was rather to consolidate its special relationship with the United States (Sanders 1990) and safeguard its trade interests in Europe, and in so doing retain some of its international ranking following the demise of the Empire. Following its eventual entry into the EEC in 1973 Britain quickly gained a reputation as a reluctant partner. British efforts to renegotiate its entry conditions and to retain full autonomy in several policy areas signalled the continuing salience of the three-circles doctrine. In the 1970s prominent observers defined Britain's relationship with Europe in terms of 'semi-detachment' from the Community (Jenkins cited in White 2001: 121), and by the late 1980s it was suggested that Britain had become 'an awkward partner' (George 1998).

However, and as White notes, in the 1990s the Major and Blair governments increasingly insisted that they were determined to 'locate Britain in the heart of Europe' (White 2001: 121). Nevertheless, as the empirical material of this study and the scholarly literature suggest, Britain was still seen as an outsider and a reluctant partner. Successive negative descriptions of Britain's relationship with Europe as detached, semi-detached and awkward still underpinned the policy statements of these governments. Significantly for this study, Forster suggests that the political debates related to British autonomy and the reluctance to integrate obscured significant concessions of substance, including the incremental introduction of majority voting and developing the linkage between community and intergovernmental pillars. It is suggested in the scholarly literature on foreign and security policy that this so-called 'ratchet effect' indicated that Britain was being drawn into integration based on the development of the CFSP and the CSDP without ever 'admitting to a domestic audience how far integration in this policy sector has proceeded' (Forster 2000: 47).

Re-articulating the great-power discourse

Against this background it would be interesting to bring to light how British state officials marginalized the Europeanization of foreign and security policy in the official re-articulations of British policy until 1998, when the more engaged articulations of the EU policy emerged. Tools of discourse analysis are therefore used in scrutinizing key official documents such as policy papers, election manifestos and prime ministers' speeches formulated prior to the British–French declaration on European Defence in 1998.

Predication. The main subjects and objects and their predication in the documents are presented in Table 5.1. There is evidence of a dominant foreign and security policy discourse. In other words, the representations arrived at by assigning predicates, adverbs and adjectives to the subjects and objects (i.e. predication) in the texts correspond and none seem to be radically out of place. For instance, the predications of Britain as a 'major participant in world affairs,' a 'leading member' of several international organisations' and a 'responsible nuclear power' that 'promotes democracy, liberal capitalism and the rule of law' (Table 5.1) make sense within the particular discursive context of the official

British foreign and security policy. They establish a particular kind of British subject characterized by greatness, influence and leadership ability. This is labelled the great-power discourse in this study.

The table also indicates that the official discourse was euro-centric, and although the dramatic changes related to the end of the Cold War are noted in the texts, it largely reflects a bi-polar world order and an East–West division. For instance, the main actors are Western subjects such as NATO (also cited as the Alliance), the European Union, the WEU, the United States and Western European states, or Eastern subjects including the Soviet Union, its successor the Russian Federation and the former Eastern European states. However, other influential actors such as Israel in relation to the Palestine question, Iraq and other Gulf states in relation to the Gulf crisis in 1990, and several international organizations such as the UN, the CSCE, Group of 7 (G7), the World Trade Organization (WTO) and the Commonwealth also appear.

The adjectives, attributes and predicates assigned to the subjects hang together in a certain way in the great-power discourse. The representations generated indicate distinct political spaces. Three geopolitical dimensions appear to dominate the discourse and the British state identity in the field of foreign and security policy, namely the West, the East and the Globe. Moreover, Britain is clearly located within the West and the Globe.

The representations of Western actors highlight similarity, particularly in terms of political tradition reflecting a set of values. Whereas Britain 'promotes democracy, liberal capitalism and the rule of law,' NATO is 'committed to peace, democracy and the rule of law', and the European Union, including the majority of the Western European states, can build 'democratic systems and enhance liberal democracy and the rule of law' (Table 5.1). However, and significantly for this study, within the realm of security and defence the predication of Western actors, NATO and the European Union in particular, differs. Whereas NATO is seen as the 'only credible' defence organization in Europe, the European Union is construed mainly as 'an economic organization' with 'a developing foreign and security policy'. Whereas the credibility of NATO is based on its military supremacy guaranteed by the United States and its member states' full 'commitment to the common defence', the European Union lacks capability and political will in this field. For instance, it 'includes four neutral member states' with distinct security and defence policies. Accordingly, whereas more cooperation is considered feasible within the CFSP, a common defence policy is construed as 'not credible' and 'not feasible'. The official discourse suggests that the CFSP clearly 'distinguishes between security and defence'. Further, it has a 'long history'. As such, it does not mark a break with the past, but rather relates to the longer-term development of intergovernmental European Political Cooperation. Interestingly, given the continuing salience of NATO and the increasing importance of the European Union, Britain emerges as a pivotal actor. The British initiative of the 'Atlantic assembly' re-articulated the country as a 'bridge' between Western Europe and North America, as well as between the European Union and NATO.

Table 5.1 Predication of the great-power discourse in Britain

The UK	The West	The East	The Globe
A major participant in world affairs (4)	*NATO:* A unique political and military alliance (2)	*The Soviet Union:* Is a threat (2)	*Iraq:* Is an enemy (3)
A leading member of several international organizations such as NATO, the EU, the WEU, the Commonwealth and G7 (9)	Committed to peace, democracy and the rule of law (2)	Is going through dramatic changes (2)	Is ruled by a brutal dictator (3)
A permanent member of the UN Security Council (9)	A primary instrument of Western security (2, 8)	Has massive military superiority in Europe (2)	Is a threat to regional peace and stability (9)
A nation that lives by trade and investment (8)	An essential framework for safeguarding freedom and security (1, 2)	Was under totalitarian control (2)	Is a threat to international peace (3)
Has global interests and responsibilities (8)	Can ensure a full US and Canadian role in the defence of Europe (3)	Is becoming freer and more democratic (2)	Has oil (9)
Is a mature democracy (1)	Has a political dimension (4)	Was a menace (4)	Iraqi people are oppressed (3)
Promotes democracy, liberal capitalism and the rule of law (8)	Is getting bigger (9)	*Russia:* Is still the largest single military power in Europe (4)	*Africa:* Is a troubled continent (7)
Is a source of international ideas and can spread them (1)	*The US:* Is the cornerstone of NATO's military forces (2) Is essential for European security (3)	Is undergoing a process of political and economic reform (4, 8), which will take decades (6)	Comprises third-world countries (7)
Cannot be everywhere or do everything (5)	*The EC/EU:* Provides a basis for growing economic interdependence (6)	Is facing several security-related problems (8)	Is in debt (7) Is underdeveloped (7)
Is a formidable military power (6)	Is an arena for foreign-policy coordination (6)	*Eastern European States:* Are emerging from forty years of political stagnation (3)	*The UN:* Maintains international security and peace (5)
Has nuclear weapons (2, 3)	Has economic and trade relations (9)	Are going through dramatic changes (2)	Is a growing influence (6)
Can defend its territory (2, 3)	Can resolve conflicts and disputes (9)	Are unstable (4)	Can authorize operations (1, 5)
Can defend the European mainland (2, 3)	Can build democratic systems and enhance liberal democracy and the rule of law (9)	Are experiencing a rise in nationalism, extremism and ethnocentrism (6)	Is transforming (6)
	Has neutral member states (1)	Have environmental problems (8)	*CSCE/OSCE:* Is an essential element of the new European security architecture (4)
	The CFSP: Represents intergovernmental cooperation (4, 9)	*Balkans and Yugoslavia:* Have tragic and dangerous conflicts (6)	Provides a forum for a dialogue on arms control and confidence-building measures (9)
	Distinguishes between security and defence (4)		Can assess and prevent conflicts (4)
	Is becoming more important (6)		Is developing (3)
	Has a long history (6)		Is inclusive (3)
	The EU's Common Defence: Not feasible and not credible (8, 9)		Is becoming more important (9)
	WEU: Has a central role in building the European pillar within NATO (3)		Has links with NATO (peacekeeping) (5)
	Has a peacekeeping role (5)		
	Should be able to operate when NATO as whole will not (8)		
	Should not be incorporated into the EU (8)		

Note: The numbers in the brackets refer to the source document as follows: (1) Thatcher 1990, (2) Ministry of Defence 1990, (3) Ministry of Defence 1991, (4) Ministry of Defence 1992, (5) Ministry of Defence 1993, (6) Ministry of Defence 1994, (7) Major 1994, (8) Ministry of Defence 1995, (9) Ministry of Defence 1996.

The representations of the Eastern actors also construe a particular kind of political space. Russia has a dominant role, largely inheriting the Soviet Union's 'military might' and thereby constituting 'a great power'. However, following the end of the Cold War, 'Russia is not a menace' and does not pose a clear or current 'military threat' to the West. Nevertheless, it retains the potential to do so. Several predicates, adjectives and attributes assigned to the Eastern subjects highlight the ongoing process of 'political, economic and social transformation'. Although this process is endowed with some positive features, the predication of some subjects, such as the (former) Yugoslavia, generates representations of unpredictability and instability in the ongoing transition. The general representation of the East as an 'unstable' region is arrived at through the predication of its subjects in terms of 'political instability,' 'nationality disputes' and 'environmental degradation', although some positive developments are acknowledged. Nevertheless, the East is largely constructed in terms of difference from the West.[6]

The other key actors constructed in the discourse do not represent a definable geopolitical region, but rather relate to Britain's global presence. The predication of subjects such as Iraq generates representations of enmity. Iraq is directly construed as an 'enemy' and a 'threat' to regional and international peace and British interests in a strategically important region. Moreover, its leader is described as a 'brutal dictator' who could acquire 'weapons of mass destruction'. On the one hand the representations of Africa and the African states highlight the 'problems' and 'instability' of the continent related to 'underdevelopment'. Then again, the predication of several international organizations, such as the United Nations (UN), the Group of eight (G8) – including leading industrial economies and Russia – and the WTO, generate representations that emphasize the importance of these subjects in enhancing British interests in the world.

Presupposition. The above representations make sense given certain background knowledge. Within the theoretical and methodological context of this study, the knowledge presupposed in the articulation and re-articulation of a discourse simultaneously positions the subjects and objects it creates. The positioning, in turn, usually takes place along the binaries established by certain core oppositions. Therefore, the identification and discussion of these oppositions shed light on the identity construction related to a particular discourse. It is suggested that, although the Britain-as-a-great-power discourse incorporates the core opposition of *great/minor*, several other oppositions such as *global/local, liberator/oppressor, stable/unstable* and *developed/underdeveloped* can be subsumed under it. Taken together, these oppositions enable the construction of a particular kind of British state identity.

Britain is still straightforwardly construed as a great power. The ruling Conservative Party's general election manifesto from 1992 is illustrative:

The respect with which Britain is regarded in the world has rarely been higher. We play a central part in world affairs as a member of the European Community, NATO, the Commonwealth and the Group of 7 leading industrial countries, and as a Permanent Member of the UN Security Council. No other country holds all these positions.

(Conservative Party 1992)

Even if the scholarly literature on Britain's post-war foreign and security policy is preoccupied with decline, Britain's pre-eminence in world politics is clearly re-articulated in the official discourse. However, the overwhelming emphasis on its great-power status could be interpreted as a response to representations suggesting decline. For instance, Thatcher argues that 'we re-establish respect for Britain abroad', suggesting in a defensive manner how Britain's economic achievements 'are not measured just in statistics, but in changing attitudes and in our much greater influence in the greater world' (cited in Macleod 1997: 178). Even if Thatcher's successor, John Major, was more willing to accept Britain as a European power, he also insisted that it was a power 'with continuing responsibilities in many parts of the world.' (Major 1991, cited in Macleod 1997: 178).

The essence of Britain's greatness lay in its global rather than its local interests and responsibilities. The great-power discourse suggests that its wellbeing, prosperity and greatness were distinctively tied to its global reach as an island state depending on sea and air transportation. As the 1996 Statement on the Defence Estimate (SDE) puts it:

... our well-being depends to a greater degree than most other developed economies on international trade and investment. We are as a consequence reliant on the secure transport of goods by sea and on the supply of raw materials from overseas.

(Ministry of Defence 1996: 3)

This presupposition underpins one of the core aspects of Britain's greatness, its global military reach. The first paragraph of the first chapter of the 1994 SDE states:

The United Kingdom remains one of the world's most formidable military powers. Only the United States, Russia and France can deploy as broad a range of capabilities as the armed forces of the United Kingdom who, in terms of their experience, training, leadership and spirit, are the match of any in the world.

(Ministry of Defence 1994: 7)

The focus on military power is also indicative of a realist world-view according to which states seek to maximize their power in world politics and to safeguard their interests. On the other hand, in the great-power discourse Britain's global responsibilities reflect its historical role in several regions around the world. This presupposition positions it along the binary opposition of *liberator/oppressor*. Interestingly, this opposition informed the representation of the ongoing transition in Eastern Europe in the mid 1990s. As Prime Minister Major argued in 1994:

... the challenge now is to catch the tide of events that have flown in recent years so very strongly in our favour, to draw the nations of eastern Europe – historic, vivid nation states: Poland, Hungary, the Czech lands, and others – back into the European camera, to make democratic Russia an ally and not a threat, to help the democracies in the third world escape the excessive debt that cripples their development – and time after time it has been British initiatives that have led the way in achieving this, to use our age-old links with Africa to help prepare that troubled continent for a better future.

These are historic roles; historic roles for which Britain and the Conservative Party are marked out by history and by experience. We will use that experience.

(Major 1994)

At the heart of the great-power discourse, then, is Britain's ability 'to lead the way' in post-Cold War Europe. This representation, in turn, assumes a particular British role in the world, that of a liberator. Although this 'historical role' draws on specific and rather positive representations of Britain's colonial rule and its role in the Second World War, in the 1990s its historical role was re-articulated in terms of the end of the Cold War.

The 1992 SDE states that the 'lowering of the Red Flag over the Kremlin on Christmas Day last year brought to an end the menace of the discredited ideology with its struggle for global dominance by every means available . . .' (Ministry of Defence 1992: 5). Further, when the communist rule collapsed 'nations in Central and Eastern Europe have elected democratic governments . . .' and Britain in turn is 'helping the former communist countries to achieve the unprecedented transition . . .' (Ministry of Defence 1992: 7). Furthermore, Britain's major role as a liberator is re-articulated in relation to the Gulf crisis in 1990. The 1991 SDE states:

The British forces from all three Services made the largest European contribution to deterring further aggression and defending Saudi Arabia and the Gulf States; to enforcing the embargo against Iraq; and eventually to the military operations that liberated Kuwait.

(Ministry of Defence 1991: 7)

Here British greatness derives from combining representations of its material global reach with its normative responsibilities in the world. One of Thatcher's speeches is illustrative:

My Lord Mayor, I can't remember a time when the demands upon us – upon Britain and the Western countries – have been greater: calls for help to sustain democracy and reform in the Soviet Union and in the countries of Eastern Europe; the call to help defend countries outside Europe threatened by aggression. Thank goodness we kept our defences strong so that we could respond to the crisis in the Gulf with our Tornados and our Royal Navy ships and the Desert Rats!

(Thatcher 1990)

Britain thus emerges in the great-power discourse as a particular kind of great power – a power with a global reach and a normative commitment to liberate peoples from oppression. On the other hand, the representation of specific and rather great British responsibilities presupposes and generates knowledge that was familiar, for instance, in the academic study of post-Cold War security and development. The binary oppositions of stable/unstable and developed/underdeveloped are of key importance here. The 1995 SDE states:

> The removal of the constraints imposed by the structure of ideological confrontation has resulted in civil war, cross-border conflict and the collapse of economic links in Europe and elsewhere. The previous low risk of global war has as a result been replaced by a greater risk of smaller-scale conflict and suffering, spawned by the instability present in many parts of the world, exacerbated in many cases by resource and economic pressures. The consequences of the rise of nationalism, extremism and ethnocentrism are nowhere more apparent than in some of the newly independent states of eastern Europe and in the former Yugoslavia, where we have seen how quickly regional instability can erupt into violence and how quickly conflict in one state can spill over into a neighbour.
>
> (Ministry of Defence 1995: 23)

The presupposition relating to the core opposition of stable/unstable constructs particular kinds of subjects: stable and developed or unstable and underdeveloped. For instance, the great-power discourse constitutes former communist states, and African and Middle Eastern states as a particular kind of subject, as developing and unstable. The following short extract from the 1996 SDE is illustrative of how the core opposition of stable/unstable establishes certain knowledge about the world in which a particular British identity emerges.

> The United Kingdom has interests and responsibilities across the globe. We have a commitment to the security of our 14 Dependent Territories. Our trading history has resulted in a large expatriate population, with significant numbers of British nationals living in areas of potential instability such as Africa and the Middle East, to whom we have obligations.
>
> (Ministry of Defence 1996: 3)

In essence, this world constitutes certain kinds of subjects: global and stable powers and regional developing and unstable nations. The presupposition is that Britain was an influential global and stable power with significant international responsibilities.

Subject positioning. The construction of subjects along the oppositional dimensions discussed above simultaneously position them in a hierarchical order, which is evident in the degree of agency assigned to them in the discourse. It is suggested that the force that positioned subjects in relation to others was the anarchical international society. In light of the increasing interdependence, however, the emphasis on common interests and shared norms became more visible towards the end of the 1990s. Against this background it could be said that the great-power discourse incorporated four major subject positions: (i) a powerful, global and transatlantic Britain; (ii) a credible and transatlantic NATO; (iii) an increasingly powerful but unreliable European Union; and (iv) the dependent and developing countries in the East, the Middle East and Africa. The relationships among the positioned subjects reproduced a particular kind of British state identity.

Britain as the key actor in the discourse is attributed a significant degree of agency. Specifically, its global reach and ability to safeguard its interests is emphasized. As the extracts in the previous sections suggest, it had the material capacity to defend itself and its interests in bilateral relations and international organizations as well as militarily. Moreover, the historical constructions of Britain as a 'former maritime empire', one of the oldest 'democracies', the 'founder of industrial development and technological innovation' and the 'victorious power of the two world wars' (Table 5.1) underline its moral right as well as responsibility as an international subject. Britain could and should 'shape the world'.

These aspects of British leadership and power were particularly pertinent in Britain's position in relation to the former communist states in Europe and to the developing states in the third world, for instance. Britain had responsibilities based on its history, society and economics to 'lead' and 'show the way' within the Commonwealth and in Africa, as well as in Asia and former Eastern Europe. Although the representation(s) of Russia also indicate significant agency in terms of capabilities and resources, the subject position available to Russia in the hierarchical arrangement of the great-power discourse is that of a collapsed great power. As such, it is re-articulated as an unstable and developing subject in need of guidance and assistance.

The other Western subjects mainly constitute NATO, the United States and the Western European states. Whereas the United States is associated with NATO, the other Western European states are largely increasingly linked to the European Community and, after 1993, to the European Union. The most significant difference between NATO and the European Union in the field of foreign and security policy reflects the degree of agency assigned to them: NATO's supremacy derives from the allotting of a greater degree of agency to the US than to Britain or other states in Western Europe. Although the United States is rarely explicitly mentioned in the documents, it clearly underpins the agency of NATO. As the 1994 SDE states:

> NATO is the only security organisation with the military to back up its security guarantees. It secures the vital link between Europe and North America: vital in political terms because of our shared fundamental values and common interests, and in military terms because no other European country or group of counties is likely to be able to field the intelligence capabilities, sophisticated firepower or strategic lift supplied by the United States.
>
> (Ministry of Defence 1994: 9)

Here the United States is depicted as empowering the West. The US military power invested in NATO, which constituted the cornerstone of Western European defence and military arrangements against traditional large-scale military attack as well as new post-Cold War security issues and threats. Moreover, NATO's increasing political role in Europe is directly referred to: NATO was 'enlarging' and due to its cooperation and partnership programmes it was becoming a more political and inclusive organization (Table 5.1). Moreover, notwithstanding Britain's own nuclear capabilities, the United States largely reinforced the United Kingdom's nuclear deterrence. Significantly, in the great-power discourse Britain's special relationship with the United States signifies an influential role within NATO. In other words, the close political and cultural ties with the United States, 'who share our belief in freedom, democracy, the rule of law and the non-violent mechanisms for political change' (Ministry of Defence 1994: 9) politically empowered Britain within NATO and, consequently, in Europe. On the other hand, Britain's relationship with Western Europe and the European Union was also significant in terms of British influence in the world economy.

Accordingly, and although the role of the European Union in foreign and security policy was noted in the early 1990s, it did not translate into a powerful subject position in this policy field. As the capabilities-expectations gap argument suggests, the CFSP seemed to lack the institutional structure and political will required in building a strong and decisive policy. On the other hand, the development of a common defence strategy is constructed as an unfeasible project. Nevertheless, Britain 'endorsed a development of European security and defence identity, which will strengthen the European pillar of the Alliance . . .' (Ministry of Defence 1994: 15), in other words a more prominent European and British role within NATO. A significant representation that is constitutive of the British great-power identity highlights Britain's ability to shape European developments. As Prime Minister Major put it, he was 'to carve out a right position for Britain in the right sort of Europe' (Major 1994). On the other hand, none of the major representations generated in the discourse highlight the impact of the European Union upon Britain. In light of the Europeanization of the foreign and security policy, the 'right sort of Europe' had the more effective CFSP, but not the CSDP. Thus the relationships among the subject positions established in the great-power discourse highlight NATO's and the United States' continuing significance in Europe and for the British foreign and security policy. Moreover, whereas the CFSP is constructed as potentially beneficial and as developing EU policy, the CSDP is dismissed as neither credible nor feasible for the near future.

The dominance of the great-power discourse and the CFSP and the CSDP

Notwithstanding the debate in the discursive field, and the continuous need for the reproduction of identities, it seems that the re-articulation of the British discourse on foreign and security policy proceeded in a rather familiar way until 1998. In other words, officials continued to identify their state with the above-mentioned subject position and the foreign and security policy embedded in the great-power discourse. This suggests that the discursive space for alternative re-articulations that would have highlighted the significance of EU developments in foreign and security policy, for instance, was rather limited. The predication, presupposition and subject positioning of the great-power discourse nevertheless indicated that the development of the EU foreign and security policy was not beyond reason. The CFSP and the CSDP could be intelligibly articulated. Indeed, these policies were articulated in a seemingly radical way in the official discourse as early as in 1994. As the SDE states:

> There is a long tradition of co-operation with our European partners on foreign and security policy issues. The growing interdependence of our economies and in increasing coincidence of foreign policy concerns and goals will mean that our foreign and security policies will to a greater degree be co-ordinated and implemented at European level. We have declared through our signature of the Maastricht Treaty our intention to contribute to work towards a common European defence policy which may, in time, lead the European Union to a common defence.
>
> (Ministry of Defence 1994: 15).

However, it is striking how little this official articulation of the CFSP, with the prospect of common defence, was discussed and elaborated given Britain's attitude to European integration. Hill's observation is illuminating. He notes that John Major did not mention the CFSP even once in the prime minister's address to the British government conference on British foreign policy at the Royal Institute of International Affairs in 1995 (Hill 1996a: 89, endnote 28). It is suggested here that the lack of reflection or debate on the development of the CFSP and the CSDP in Britain in the mid-1990s is indicative of the dominance of the great-power discourse discussed above. Within it the CFSP and the CSDP were seen largely as passages describing European political aspirations rather than reality affecting Britain. Thus the state officials did not see the need – nor were they pushed by the opposition or certain observers, for instance – to defend British engagement in the emerging EU foreign and security policy. In this sense they and the audiences they addressed were largely interpellated by the great-power discourse. In other words, the cynical constructions of the CFSP and the CSDP generated in the re-articulations of the great-power discourse made sense and were largely accepted as true representations of the reality.

In this context the CFSP is explicitly linked with the notion of the 'long tradition of the European foreign policy cooperation' (Ministry of Defence 1994: 15). This highlights the incremental nature of the ongoing developments. In other words, the development of the CFSP did not represent a break with the past in European foreign and security policy. Given the failure of European efforts to gain a more independent role in both the immediate post-war and the Cold War security environments, and the continuing salience of NATO and the United States in Europe, a particular construction of the CFSP emerges. Within the British great-power discourse the policy is rendered deeply suspect and is constructed as indecisive and weak. The 1994 SDE specifically mentions the weaknesses of the CFSP thus: 'the United Kingdom wishes to ensure an effective CFSP, and to preserve its intergovernmental status. The CFSP should be more active, less declaratory than previous foreign policy co-operation . . .' (Ministry of Defence 1994: 15).

These representations were put under scrutiny in the lead-up to the 1997 general election, however. At the same time the Conservative Government was engaged in the Amsterdam Treaty negotiations, which heralded a new phase in the development of the CFSP and the CSDP. While the EU's foreign policy-making institutions and procedures were being developed the common European defence policy was clearly fast-tracked, and British state officials had to respond to this. Within the great-power discourse the development of a common European Union defence capability and the absorption of the WEU into the EU were seen as deeply problematic and unfeasible. The representations highlighted the lack of capabilities and of political will in the EU to act in the field of defence, referring to the three neutral states of Austria, Finland and Sweden that joined the Union in 1995. The 1996 SDE states:

> ... common decisions and actions in the defence field – most sensitive area of policy – must proceed by consent . . . Here we are particularly conscious of the way in which the Inter-Governmentalism and the principle of consensus have served the Atlantic Alliance and WEU well over nearly 50 years . . . The European Union contains at present four neutral countries which do not share obligations to mutual defence. Against that background, we do not believe it realistic for the European Council to take decisions in the area of defence – nor is it equipped to do so.
>
> (Ministry of Defence 1996: 13)

The structuring role of the great-power discourse is clearly present in the representation of difference between the EU and NATO. Whereas the diversity among European Union members is considered indicative of the breaking down of consensus and commitment in the sensitive area of defence, NATO is constructed as a unitary and credible defence organization Accordingly, the 1996 SDE, which was published prior to the concluding phases of the Amsterdam Treaty negotiations in 1997 in which issues related to the CFSP and the CSDP were high on the agenda, argues thus:

> We believe that the European Union can achieve the extension of security and prosperity we enjoy by helping to embed liberal democracy, freedom and prosperity in the countries of central and Eastern Europe, without any need for it to emerge from the IGC as an organisation with a defence component.
>
> (Ministry of Defence 1996: 13)

The great-power discourse, then, constructs the CSDP as an unfeasible development in European foreign and security policy, a construction that was still being re-articulated by the ruling Conservative Party on the eve of the 1997 general election. Although the 1997 Conservative Party manifesto stated that 'we will seek more co-operation between national governments on areas of common interest – defence, foreign policy and the fight against international crime and drugs' (Conservative Party 1997), the nature of the cooperation was very limited. The manifesto continued: 'We will retain Britain's veto and oppose further extension of qualified majority voting in order to ensure we can prevent policies that would be harmful to the national interest' (ibid.). In terms of the European Union's defence capabilities it was emphasized that 'NATO will remain the cornerstone of our security. We will resist attempts to bring the Western European Union under the control of the European Union, and ensure that defence policy remains a matter for sovereign nations' (ibid.). However, the Conservative Party was voted out of office after 18 years in power, and the Labour Party took over with a seemingly more engaging policy towards the EU's foreign and security policy. Whether this represented a break with the past or the Europeanization of British discourse is the question addressed in the remainder of this chapter.

The Europeanization of the British foreign and security policy discourse

In the view of many the election of the Labour government in 1997, the new Strategic Defence Review and the British–French declaration on European defence at St Malo in 1998 marked a turning point in the British foreign, security and defence policy of the 1990s. A key feature of this turn was Britain's seemingly new and more engaged approach to European integration. Whether this reflected, or postulated, a change in the dominant discourse on foreign and security policy is the key question addressed here.

Part of the novelty of New Labour was its allegedly more positive and engaged stance towards European integration (Driver and Martell 1998: 145–146). Prime Minister Tony Blair clarified the British position on Europe in his speech at the French National Assembly in 1998 thus:

> Yet it is these same fundamental changes which call for new ways of working and organising our society that impel us to cooperate ever more closely between nations. Just over half a century ago, Europe was at war. Then for 40 years or more, the Iron Curtain descended. Now we are members of the European Union, and clamouring to enter are the former East European communist dictatorships. It is on any basis a remarkable achievement.
>
> Yet here too the challenge of change confronts us. Let me first clear away any remaining doubts about the new British Government's position. Britain's future lies in being full partners in Europe. At Amsterdam, we played a constructive part in bringing about a new European Treaty. Now, as EU President, we are launching the enlargement negotiations and doing our best to ensure the Euro starts successfully.
>
> (Blair 1998a)

He also highlighted his personal commitment to integration:

> I believe in a Europe of enlightened self-interest. Without chauvinism. It is the nation-state's rational response to the modern world. If globalisation of the world economy is a reality; if peace and security can only be guaranteed collectively; if the world is moving to larger blocs of trade and cooperation and look at ASEAN or Latin America: if all this is so, then the EU is a practical necessity. I happen to share the European idealism. I am by instinct internationalist. But even if I weren't, I should be internationalist through realism. The forces of necessity, even of survival are driving us to cooperation. In the United Nations, in Bosnia, no less than in international trade.
>
> (Ibid.)

The traditional British argument that integration was about the economy and that the political aspects, including foreign and security policy, should be kept on a minimum level was clearly revised. Conversely, Blair embraced a 'political vision' of the EU. Nevertheless, he acknowledged that the Europeans felt strongly about their states and that integration must consider public opinion. He implied that the political vision of Europe was not easy to realize. However, in addition to the obvious benefits of economic integration, he identified another increasingly important field in which Britain could take part. As he argued, in the field of defence Britain and France were particularly qualified to cooperate with each other:

> Now is the time for a new initiative on the military side. We are in the final stages of conducting a major Defence Review. You are in the middle of the complex process of professionalising and restructuring your armed forces. When our review is complete, I am asking the Defence Secretary and Chiefs of Staff to report to me urgently on the scope for future Anglo–French cooperation. How we can create a capacity to deploy forces rapidly on a joint basis in future crises, where both countries agree.
>
> (Ibid.)

Launched on 28 May 1997, the Strategic Defence Review (SDR) set out to determine the future direction of the British defence policy. The main objective was to respond to the challenges of the post-Cold War world, and in so doing to address both traditional and so-called new security threats and issues. The new threats largely arose from political instability and increasing transnationalism. As the review states:

> Instability inside Europe as in Bosnia, and now Kosovo, threatens our security. Instability elsewhere – for example in Africa – may not always appear to threaten us directly. But it can do indirectly, and we cannot stand aside when it leads to massive human suffering.
>
> ... There are also new risks which threaten our security by attacking our way of life. Drugs and organized crime are today powerful enough to threaten

the entire fabric of some societies. They certainly pose a serious threat to the well-being of our own society. We have seen new and horrifying forms of terrorism and how serious environmental degradation can cause not only immediate suffering but also dangerous instabilities. And the benefits of the information technology revolution that has swept the world are accompanied by potential new vulnerabilities.

(Ministry of Defence 1998)

Although the review allots a minor role to the CFSP and the CSDP, it lays out the wider context in which they are re-articulated. It argues that 'the European Union has a vital role in helping to preserve and extend economic prosperity and political stability, including through the Common Foreign and Security Policy' (ibid.).

In St Malo the British prime minister and the French president issued a joint declaration covering several issues aimed at strengthening the CFSP and the CSDP. First (i), 'the European Union needs to be in a position to play its full role on the international stage'. This would involve enforcement of the Treaty of Amsterdam, which reformulated the decision-making process of the CFSP; (ii) to this end, the Union should develop 'the capacity for autonomous action, backed up by credible military forces, the means to decide to use them, and a readiness to do so, in order to respond to international crises.' (iii) Britain and France's commitment to NATO was reiterated, and in order for the European Union to 'take decisions and to approve military action, where the Alliance [NATO] as a whole is not engaged, the Union must be given appropriate structures and a capacity for analysis of situations, sources of intelligence, and a capability for relevant strategic planning, without unnecessary duplication, taking account of the existing assets of the WEU and the evolution of its relations with the EU'. In this regard, the European Union needed access to suitable military means (European capabilities pre-designated within NATO's European pillar, or national or multinational European means outside the NATO framework). (iv) Europe needed strengthened armed forces that could react rapidly to the new risks, and that were supported by a strong and competitive European defence industry and technology; finally (v), the United Kingdom and France were united in their efforts to enable the European Union to give concrete expression to these objectives (British–French Summit 1998).

The St Malo Declaration is of high significance in this study because it is widely considered to represent a major shift in the United Kingdom's official discourse on foreign and security policy. Significantly, the CFSP and the CSDP are seen as the key features of this change, which produced an increase in the number of studies advocating the Europeanization of the British foreign and security policy. Rutten (2001), for instance, suggests that Britain lifted its decades-long objections to the EU acquiring an autonomous military capacity in St Malo, and Howorth argues that in so doing the British foreign and security policy elite constructed a radically new discourse on European security (Howorth 2004). The SDR is also significant for this study in that it constructed the foreign and security policy context in which the re-articulation of this new discourse took place.

Re-articulation of the great-power discourse

A discourse analysis of the official documentation on foreign and security policy was conducted in order to establish what, if anything, had changed in the British discourse, and whether the re-articulations indicated the emergence of a new discourse in 1998. The empirical material includes the SDR, speeches made by Prime Minister Tony Blair and the St Malo Declaration. The analysis suggests that, rather than articulating a radically new discourse, the traditional Britain-as-a-great-power discourse was largely re-articulated. However, there were some significant changes related to Britain's position among the other major Western subjects, namely the European Union and the United States. The 1998 re-articulation of the great-power discourse is thus labelled the Europeanized great-power discourse.

Predication. Analysis of the adjectives, attributes and predicates assigned to the subjects and objects constructed in the documents indicates that the key subjects are constructed somewhat differently than previously (see Table 5.2). Significantly, these changes relate mainly to the predication within the West, in other words Britain, the European Union, NATO and the United States. However, continuity is also evident. In the documents in question predication generates representations that emphasize Britain's status and leadership in the world. It is referred to as 'a leader in the world' and is articulated to have 'immense importance to the international community as a whole'. Britain is also seen as a 'major' and 'leading' power in several international organizations. Its global reach is underlined in the representations generated in the texts: it has 'overseas territories', it is 'a major global economic power' and the British people are 'international people'. In this respect not much has changed in comparison to the earlier foreign and security policy articulations. However, there are more references emphasizing British leadership and power in military affairs, and an increase in the number of textual qualifiers accentuating normative leadership in the world. Moreover and significantly, the adjective 'European' is directly attached to Britain: for instance, the UK is a 'major European state' and 'a leading European member of the Alliance'.

The predication of NATO in 1998 also reflects significant continuity in comparison to the pre-St Malo re-articulations: it is re-articulated as the 'corner stone of the UK security and defence'. Significantly, the representations generated in the official documentation suggest that NATO's role was increasing and its purpose was widening. It was 'engaged with peacekeeping operations' in Kosovo and Bosnia, and was 'enlarging' to the former communist states. As the SDR states: 'Politically, it [NATO] has responded positively and imaginatively to the aspirations of the new European democracies' (Ministry of Defence 1998). Thus the predication of the official discourse also highlights NATO's political role in Europe. Through enlargement, embracing former Eastern Europe and cooperation with Russia and the Ukraine, for instance, it is constructed as strengthening the 'political and security relationships in Europe' and bringing about 'stability' (Table 5.2).

Table 5.2 Predication of the 1998 re-articulation of the great-power discourse

The UK	NATO and the US	The EU	Russia and Eastern Europe	The Globe
Is a major European State (1) Is a leading member of the EU (1) Is the leading European member of the Alliance (NATO) (1) Is strong in Europe (2) Is strong with the US (2) The British are international people (1) Is a global player (3) Is a world leader (1) Is of immense importance to the international community as a whole (1) Is a force for good (1) Has international responsibilities (1) Is a major global economic power (1) Is an influential member of several international organizations (1) Has 13 overseas territories spread around the globe (1) Has 10 million citizens living overseas (1) Is an open society (1) Is vulnerable (1) Has a value-based foreign policy (1) Does not aspire to be the world's policeman (1) Has armed forces with valuable skills and capabilities (1)	*NATO:* Is a cornerstone of UK security and defence (1) Has been militarily reinvigorated and has shown its continuing value (1) Is highly relevant in Europe today (1) Is positive and imaginative (1) Is getting bigger (1) Is engaged in peacekeeping and crisis-management missions (1) *The US:* Has strong bonds with the UK in terms of history and heritage, language, political pluralism and freedom (2) Is different from the UK (2) Has defended free and open markets (2) Has helped the UK and Europe to preserve democracy and freedom (2) Is willing to stand up for what it believes (2) Its armed forces are under review (1)	*The EU:* Is a partner and an ally (1) Has a common foreign and security policy (1) Is about to have a defence policy (1) Can preserve and strengthen economic prosperity (1) Needs to be in a position to play its full role on the international stage (4) Must have the capacity for autonomous action (4) Must have credible military forces (4) *The CFSP:* Enhances political stability (1) *The CSDP:* Is not a European Army (1) It is for the EU to undertake crisis-management operations (1) *France:* Has similar defence interests (4, 5) *The WEU:* Has an important role in fostering defence coordination among its members (1)	Does not threaten the West militarily (1) Is operating under the NATO umbrella (1) Has moved in a positive direction (1) Has instabilities, in particular in former Yugoslavia (1)	*Middle East:* Is an important region (1) Faces increasing risks (1) Confrontation in the Middle East can potentially escalate (for instance to North Africa) (1) *Iraq and Saddam Hussein:* A powerful reminder of the threat of conventional war (1) May acquire ballistic missiles, biological and chemical weapons (1) Has oil *Afghanistan:* Exports drugs (1) *OSCE:* Has an important role in building confidence and preventing conflict (1)

Note: The numbers in brackets refer to the source documents as follows: (1) Ministry of Defence 1998, (2) Blair 1998d, (3) Blair 1997a, (4) British–French Summit 1998, (5) Blair 1998a.

In relation to the pre-1998 articulations the United States retaines a minor role in the 1998 SDR and the St Malo Declaration. However, and implicitly, its dominant role in NATO is re-articulated. The SDR notes that the 'partnership between Europe and North America has been a uniquely effective' (Ministry of Defence 1998). On the other hand, Britain's relationship with the United States is increasingly addressed directly in the prime minister's speeches from 1997 and 1998. This change in the official discourse could have been partly attributable to the new British Government's aspiration to re-articulate its continuing transatlantic commitment. However, British–US relations are mostly addressed in conjunction with Britain's relations with Europe and the European Union. An extract taken from Prime Minister Blair's key foreign policy speech in 1998 is illustrative:

> ... Britain does not have to choose between being strong with the US, or strong with Europe; it means having the confidence to see that Britain can be both. Indeed, that Britain must be both; that we are stronger with the US because of our strength in Europe; that we are stronger in Europe because of our strength with the US.
>
> (Blair 1998d)

Accordingly, in 1998 the British–US relationship became a key issue in the official discourse. Although the difference between the United States and the United Kingdom is noted, the representations of similarity are arrived at through the predication of a shared culture, politics, economics and security. The US had 'strong bonds with the UK in history and heritage' as well as through 'language', 'political pluralism' and 'freedom' (Table 5.2). In terms of the world economy, the United States and Britain have 'defended free and open markets'. In addition, the predication of the United States as the 'mightiest military and economic power' in the world generates representations of the country's importance for the world order and peace. It is 'able and willing to provide assistance' to others. For example, it had 'helped the UK and Europe preserve democracy and freedom' and it was 'willing to stand for what it believes'. However, representations of unwished for isolationism also emerge. Blair's speech in Washington is evocative. He said: 'We [Britain] are back as a country engaged and constructive in Europe. Internationalist not isolationist in perspective. There is no future in isolationism in today's world.' (Blair 1998c). Here, Britain's increasing engagement in Europe is made meaningful in relation to increasing internationalism. Simultaneously and implicitly, the United States is construed as a potentially isolationist superpower.

In 1998 the predication of the European Union generated the representation of its increasing economic and political significance. Although the emphasis is still on the 'intergovernmental' and state-based 'international organization' (Table 5.2), the representation of the EU as a more autonomous and distinct political entity emerges, specifically in relation to the world economy. As Blair argued in 1998:

> We have an economic framework for the EU. We now need a political framework that is dramatically more relevant, more in touch than the present

one. I say this quite apart from the pressure of enlargement. The next step for Europe is to match its vision of its economic role with one for its political and social role.

(Blair 1998a)

In addition to the increasing pressure since the late 1980s to 'preserve and extend economic prosperity,' the predication of the European Union in the above extract is rather different from the pre-1998 discourse. For one thing, its role to 'enhance political stability' in the former Eastern Europe, for instance through cooperation programmes and enlargement, is stressed. Significantly, its political dimension is underlined in the representations of its increasing importance in the field of foreign and security policy.

Prior to 1998, representations of the CFSP and the CSDP were few in number and tended to emphasize the initial steps taken in this policy field. There were more in 1998, and the official discourse suggests that the European Union had 'a common foreign and security policy' and was 'about to have a defence policy' (Table 5.2). The SDR states that 'The European Union has a vital role in helping to preserve and extend economic prosperity and political stability, including through the Common Foreign and Security Policy' (Ministry of Defence 1998), but the St Malo Declaration goes further. Whereas the former merely notes that the EU could develop its defence policy in the future, in the latter Britain calls for an independent EU military capability:

The European Union needs to be in a position to play its full role on the international stage. This means making a reality of the Treaty of Amsterdam, which will provide the essential basis for action by the Union ...

To this end, the Union must have the capacity for autonomous action, backed up by credible military forces, the means to decide to use them, and a readiness to do so, in order to respond to international crises.

(British–French Summit 1998)

The predication of the European Union, then, changes quite dramatically. Although the developing nature of the CFSP and the CSDP is still clearly noted, these policies assume prime importance in the British foreign and security policy discourse. Moreover, establishing the CSDP has become the explicitly articulated objective of British policy towards Europe.

Several other subjects are also constructed in the 1998 re-articulation of the official discourse on foreign and security policy (Table 5.2). Significantly for this study, the predication of the East continues to highlight 'transition', 'political instability' and 'environmental degradation', for instance. The crisis in Bosnia and Kosovo are explicitly mentioned as threats to European and British security. Some positive developments are also articulated. The Eastern European states are increasingly included 'within the NATO umbrella' and hence present less of a direct military threat. The predication also notes the progress among some of the Eastern European states in the transition to democracy and a market economy.

Presupposition. Although the predication of the subjects constructed in the British foreign and security policy discourse in 1998 changed to some extent, the key binary oppositions remain very similar to those in the pre-1998 discourse. The binary opposition of *great/minor* and the related oppositions of *global/local, liberator/oppressor, stable/unstable* and *developed/ underdeveloped* largely constitute the operational logic of the texts according to which the subjects/objects are given meaning. However, there are some changes, which are related to the core opposition of great/minor and the global/local distinction presupposing an increasingly interdependent world.

The presupposition of great/minor constitutes an influential operational logic through which the subjects constructed in the discourse are given meaning and simultaneously positioned vis-à-vis each other. Several aspects of British statehood presuppose a great-power status. As Prime Minister Blair argued:

> By virtue of our geography, our history and the strengths of our people, Britain is a global player.
>
> As an island nation, Britain looks outward naturally. The British are inveterate travellers. We are the second biggest outward investors, and the second biggest recipients of inward investment, behind the US in both cases.
>
> Our task has to be to shape these strengths and give them definition within a foreign policy that is clear and stated.
>
> (Blair 1997a)

However, whereas previously Britain was presupposed to be a global rather than regional power, in 1998 it was constructed as a global *and* regional state in an increasingly interdependent world. Blair asserted:

> We live in a global economy, and an interdependent world. Nations must maximize their influence wherever they can. To be a country of our size and population, and to be a permanent member of the UN Security Council, a nuclear power, a leading player in NATO, a leading player in the Commonwealth, gives us huge advantages which we must exploit to the full.
>
> Our membership of the EU gives us huge advantages too, and we must exploit those to the full as well. It requires a new maturity in our relations with Europe. This new Government will deliver that new maturity, and Britain will be the winner from it.
>
> (Blair 1998d)

The kind of regional integration embraced in the 1998 re-articulation of the official discourse presupposes a global rather than a local world out there. Moreover, being a great power is increasingly construed in terms of having a prominent role in international organizations.

Although Britain's material and military capabilities are still highlighted, especially in the defence-policy documents, its greatness is increasingly constructed through its ability to provide leadership (global and regional). As Blair argued: 'for the first time in many years there is a growing consensus in Britain in favour of constructive engagement with Europe . . . when British people see a strong, dynamic Britain influencing Europe, they support our stance . . .' (Blair 1998b). Moreover, the emerging 'alliance of people who believe that British values of creativity, tolerance, fairness and democracy can influence the shape and destination of Europe . . . People who are in favour of Europe, but in favour of a reformed Europe' (ibid.). Consequently, Britain's more positive role in EU politics largely makes sense in light of its ability to lead. Here the binary opposition of global/local provides important background knowledge for the re-articulation of British leadership in the contemporary world and Europe. Although British autonomy still features in the discourse, it is presupposed that the world is increasingly interdependent. In so doing it suggests that the aim of the British foreign and security policy is not full autonomy (i.e. sovereignty). Rather, Britain's interests and its status in an increasingly interdependent world could be secured and enhanced through interaction, cooperation and integration. Britain should 'exploit' its political and economic relationships around the globe. As the prime minister argued:

> We live in a multilateral world where influence comes from working with others. We willingly pay the price of pooled sovereignty in defence, for the greater prize of collective security through NATO. We should be ready to pay a similar price in the European Union for the prizes of political security and stability, liberal and open markets, higher incomes and more jobs. Security used to come from self-reliance and defensive barriers. Today, it comes increasingly from openness and the removal of barriers.
>
> (Ibid.)

In the interdependent world, greatness is associated with leadership in institutions representing emerging global or regional governance. Prime Minister Blair's reasoning is illustrative:

> On External Policy, the EU must be both effective and seen to be effective internationally. Political will, not hot air. We need to project our values on the world stage, to be open, outward-looking, supportive of free trade, human rights and democracy, and playing a major role in the great international issues of the day. We must equip Europe with better machinery. This means the right candidate to be the EU's voice on common foreign and security policy issues, and the right back-up. It also means enabling Europe to act in a sensible and co-ordinated way both politically and economically . . .
>
> (Ibid.)

The presupposition of interdependence is thus fundamental to the construction of Britain's more engaged relationship with the EU's foreign and security policy. Simultaneously, the CFSP and CSDP acronyms assume particular and greater significance in the discourse. They become vehicles for advancing certain values and norms such as openness, free trade, human rights and democracy.

Subject positioning. The analysis reveals that the re-articulation of the great-power discourse in 1998 included five key subject positions: (i) an influential, global and transatlantic Britain; (ii) a powerful and credible NATO, supported by an (iii) influential and global United States; (iv) an increasingly influential European Union with a developing foreign and security policy; and (v) developing and unstable states in Eastern Europe and elsewhere.[7] In comparison to the earlier re-articulations, the European Union is given a more prominent role in world politics. Nevertheless, the key subject positions and their availability to the subjects construed in the discourse indicate significant continuity. Moreover, although the hierarchical order of 1988 the discourse is increasingly shaped by ideas of interdependence, the subject positioning still corresponds with the traditional views of power and security in an anarchical international society.

Britain is still assigned a great degree of agency in the re-articulations of the great-power discourse in terms of its influence in world politics. Given the traditional views on foreign and security policy, it undoubtedly possessed a great-power identity, arrived at through its construction as the key player in combating the dangers of the contemporary world. For instance, it is re-articulated as the key US ally: in 1998 Prime Minister Blair argued that Britain was 'absolutely together [with the US] in our analysis of the continuing dangers posed by Saddam Hussein and our determination not to allow him Weapons of Mass Destruction' (Blair 1998d).

Similarly, the defence-policy documentation argues that Britain must prepare itself for possible military interventions around the globe in order to secure its interests and to help others to resolve conflicts. As Defence Secretary Robertson argued in the foreword to the SDR:

> The Government is committed to strong defence, and sound defence is sound foreign policy. As Kofi Annan, the UN Secretary General, said 'You can do a lot with diplomacy but, of course, you can do a lot more with diplomacy backed up with firmness and force'. It is my strong belief that the Strategic Defence Review will deliver Modern Forces for the Modern World which will enable Britain to achieve a 'lot more' in the Twenty-first century.
>
> (Ministry of Defence 1998)

The re-articulation of the great-power discourse explicitly restates the link between foreign policy and military capabilities as a constitutive feature of the great-power identity. Moreover, and as the above extracts suggests, the United Stated had a central role in the reproduction of this identity. The SDR and the prime minister's speeches from 1998 construct the United States as the most powerful international actor, the only remaining superpower with immense importance in the world economy, politics and military affairs. Moreover, Britain is still empowered by virtue of its special relationship with the United States in that their close cultural and political ties highlight its influence in the world and in Europe. Therefore, the hierarchical order positioning the subject retains several traditional features that reflect an anarchic international system or society.

Significantly for this study, the European Union is clearly assigned more agency than before, and the need to further develop its abilities to engage in world politics is highlighted. It is suggested that the availability of this more influential subject position is linked to the idea of interdependence. In other words, the representations of the increasingly interdependent world give a more prominent subject position to the European Union. However, construction of the means through which to achieve more prominence largely reflects the traditional ideas of power and influence embedded in the great-power discourse.

Britain emerges as the key advocate of, and the central player in, EU defence in the St Malo Declaration. As Prime Minister Blair said:

> In defence we [Britain and France] can and should do more together. We are both nations that are used to power. We are not frightened of it or ashamed of it. We both want to remain a power for good in the world. And we start off with great advantages. We both possess a minimum nuclear deterrent. We are both permanent members of the Security Council. We have without doubt the best equipped, most deployable, most effective military forces in Europe.
>
> (Blair 1998a)

Crucially, British engagement in the development of the CSDP reflects continuity rather than change. In other words, the traditional British subject position highlighting power and greatness is being reproduced through participation in the CSDP. Similarly, its more engaged role in the European Union is also reflected in the British–United States relationship. Significantly, Britain's role as 'a leading member of the EU' is connected with representations highlighting its pivotal role for the United States, thereby reproducing its traditional identity as the transatlantic bridge between the US and Europe. As Prime Minister Blair argued:

> I have said before that though Britain will never be the mightiest nation on earth, we can be pivotal.
>
> It means building on the strengths of our history; it means building new alliances; developing new influence; charting a new course for British foreign policy.
>
> It means realising once and for all that Britain does not have to choose between being strong with the US, or strong with Europe; it means having the confidence to see that Britain can be both. Indeed, that Britain must be both; that we are stronger with the US because of our strength in Europe; that we are stronger in Europe because of our strength with the US.
>
> (Blair 1998d)

The increasing agency assigned to the European Union through British engagement in the development of the CFSP and the CSDP emphasizes Britain's influential position in world politics. Therefore, the Europeanization of British foreign and security policy was an important element in the reproduction of its great-power status and identity.

Interpellation of the Europeanized discourse

Examination of the parliamentary debates from 1998 suggests that, although the government's re-articulation of the British foreign and security policy discourse did not mark a break with the past, the representations of the European Union's more prominent role for Britain sparked a debate and significant opposition.[8] In other words, the discursive constructions generated in the official re-articulations of the discourse were not accepted as adequate representations of the world out there and Britain's place in it. The findings of the analysis presented in Table 5.3 and Figure 5.1 confirm that the Europeanization of foreign and security policy was one of the most hotly debated issues in Britain in 1998.[9] The question of the CFSP and the CSDP was explicitly raised in the debates related to the SDR after its publication in June 1998. However, and as the further analysis indicates, the discourse did not appear to govern the majority of the speeches and remarks. Nevertheless, there was clear evidence of the emergence of a re-articulated discourse shaped by the CFSP and the CSDP, and the remarks drawing on it were put under closer scrutiny through references to the more traditional great-power discourse. Significantly, the CFSP and the CSDP assumed a substantially more prominent role in the parliamentary debates after the St Malo Declaration. The number of remarks structured by the re-articulated discourse increased, but so did the opposition drawing on the pre-1998 great-power discourse.

The predication, presupposition and subject positioning of the re-articulations of the government in parliament indicate a twist rather than a turn in the discourse. The words of Secretary of State for Defence Robertson are illustrative:

> The review will fundamentally reshape and modernize Britain's armed forces, sorting out the weaknesses, building on our strengths and providing a structure to deal with tomorrow's threats, not yesterday's enemies. Our forces will be more mobile, better manned, better supported and equipped, and better able to act as a force for good in the world, where we can and when we choose.
>
> (House of Commons 1998)

Although the increasing interdependence presupposed a world of cooperation and integration, representations created by the Labour ministers and MPs continued to highlight Britain's leadership and influence, rather than dependence, in the world. The modernization of its defence was intended to improve Britain's ability to deploy troops and use force if needed. In so doing, the re-articulation that generated representations of the feasibility of the European Union's foreign and security policy largely resonate with the traditional presuppositions of the great-power discourse re-articulated in the increasingly interdependent world.

Representations suggesting a more prominent role for the EU's foreign and security policy were explicitly questioned in the debate. For instance, the key representation of a foreign and security policy leadership that was 'strong in Europe and strong with the US' was questioned on several occasions. MP Maples' remarks are illustrative:

Table 5.3 The Europeanization of the great-power discourse (GPD) in the 1998 parliamentary debates

Remarks and speeches	GPD 1	GPD 1&2	GPD 2	n/a	Total
Defence Policy					
27 December 1997	42	4	4	46	96
SDR 8 July 1998	25	4	2	20	51
SDR 19–20 October 1998	60	6	10	182	258
EU (Defence Policy)	8	2	25	23	58
11 November 1998					
Foreign Affairs and Defence	17	2	34	37	90
27 November 1998					
European Council					
14 December 1998	13	0	31	16	60
Defence					
22 March 1999	33	0	15	31	79
Foreign and Commonwealth Affairs					
18 May 1999	70	0	23	16	108
Overall	226	14	140	325	704

Note: Great-power discourse prior 1997 (GPD1), great-power discourse (GPD2)

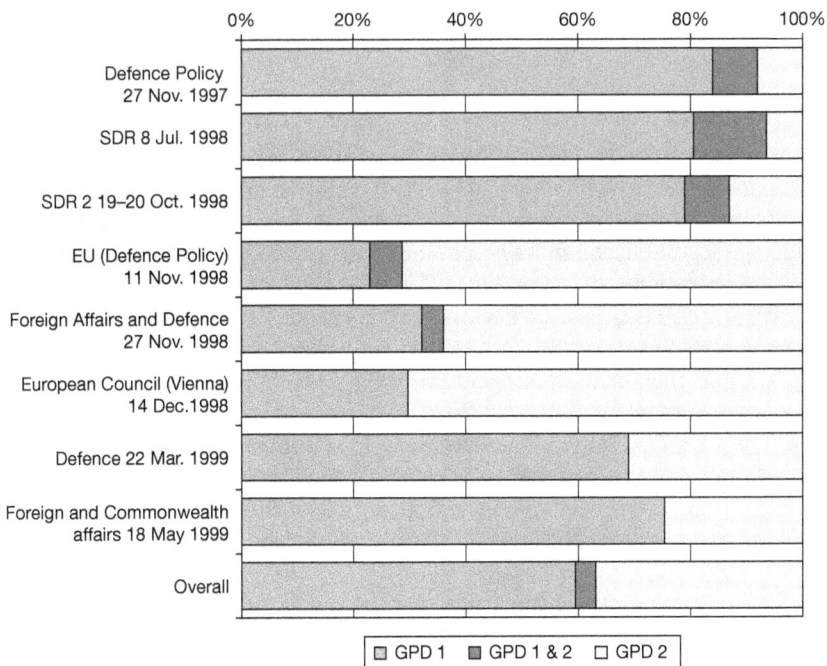

Figure 5.1 The Europeanization of the great-power discourse in the 1998 parliamentary debates.

Note: Great-power discourse prior to 1997 = GPD1; great-power discourse after 1997 = GPD2.

History teaches us that – in Henry Kissinger's memorable phrase – international stability can come only from equilibrium or domination. There is, as yet, no new world order but, if there is to be one, surely it will be American for the foreseeable future. Europe's role will be subsidiary, and should be supportive. While European co-operation at all levels is vital, the context for our defence partnership must be NATO, and cannot be the European Union.

(Ibid.)

In short, this downplays the role of the European Union in world politics. The logic structuring this representation drew on the pre-1998 great-power discourse. Whereas the 1998 re-articulation of this discourse constructed Britain's relationship with NATO and the European Union foreign and security policy as mutually beneficial, in the above extract it is constructed as mutually exclusive, presupposing a world in which order (or equilibrium) is established by hegemonic states rather than interdependence among various kinds of actors.

Therefore, and this is highly significant, the data (Table 5.3 and Figure 5.1) shows that the re-articulation of the great-power discourse did not turn into a dominant discourse among British policy-makers: in other words, they did not accept the twist in direction. Quite the opposite, the struggle within the foreign and security policy discourse intensified when the EU foreign and security policy was given a more substantial role.

After St Malo

The final part of this chapter further examines what impact, if any, the 1998 re-articulation of the British foreign and security policy discourse had on the British state identity. The analysis draws on the subsequent white papers on security and defence policy published in 1999 and the Ministry of Defence policy paper on European defence published in 2001. The 1999 Defence White Paper (Ministry of Defence 1999) is a 24-page document that sets out the progress that had been made and highlights some new issues that had arisen since the publication of the SDR. It argues that the recognition of the new post-Cold War threats and security issues in the SDR was justified, noting that since the policy framework to address these issues was made 'there has been ample confirmation of that judgement' (ibid.). Significantly, of the first two chapters, which set out the strategic context in which Britain found itself, the second specifically deals with European security in light of the institutional development of the European Union and NATO:

NATO is and must remain at the heart of our security and defence policy. But events such as those in the Balkans have shown us that Europe needs to shoulder a greater share of the burden of its own security. Britain and the other nations of the EU also wish to play an appropriate part in the response by the wider international community to crises elsewhere.

(Ibid.)

Although the commensurability of the European Union foreign and security policy and the transatlantic link is noted, Britain highlights the need to establish independent capabilities:

> Britain has consistently argued that the European defence debate should be about how to provide genuine capability improvements . . . At the Helsinki European Council, on the basis of UK proposals, EU Member States committed themselves to concrete goals for capability improvement. They specified the scale of armed forces that they should be able to deploy rapidly, with the right skills and equipment, and be able to sustain in a theatre of operations until the military job is done.
>
> (Ibid.)

Nevertheless, it is suggested that this would not be a European (federal) army. Rather, the EU forces would be under the command of the member states, as in NATO. Significantly for this study, it is argued that the defence policy would require further development in defence-related areas:

> . . . it makes real sense to create arrangements such that when EU nations decide to act together, they can act with maximum effect' . . . Thus, for the EU to undertake crisis management operations in support of its Common Foreign and Security Policy, it also needs the ability to take informed decisions in the defence field and see them through. Our approach is to establish within the EU just what is required to properly support defence decision-making and the political control and strategic direction of crisis-management operations.
>
> (Ibid.)

On the other hand, given these major developments in the European Union the 2001 policy paper (Ministry of Defence 2001) exclusively addresses the topical issue of European Defence and its evolving institutional arrangements. It outlines the development of the CFSP and the CSDP from 1992 to the present, clarifying the aims of these policies and the British government's attitude towards the future developments:

> We want to strengthen the ability of European nations to act together on foreign policy objectives. In addition to national efforts and efforts within NATO, this means strengthening the European Union's (EU) Common Foreign and Security Policy (CFSP) and enabling the EU to respond to crises, co-ordinating its civilian and humanitarian assistance with, as necessary, a military element.
>
> (Ibid.)

Both papers indicate the increasing Europeanization of the British foreign and security policy discourse in that the EU constitutes a key feature in and the rationale behind the British government's policy papers on security and defence. Moreover, both papers create representations of Britain's place in the world in relation to the European Union and NATO. As such, these policy documents form a set of artefacts that facilitate analysis of the impact of Europeanization on the discourse.

The re-articulation of the Europeanized great-power discourse

The discourse analysis reveals that the representations of the world generated in the 1999 and 2001 policy papers largely reflect the Europeanized great-power discourse as re-articulated in 1998. In short, both explicitly quote the 1998 SDR. The 1999 white paper argues that 'Britain's place in the world is determined by our interests as a nation and as a leading member of the international community. Indeed, the two are inextricably linked because our national interests have a vital international dimension' (Ministry of Defence 1999). Significantly, the 2001 paper claims that 'other European nations have also recognized the need for change and most have recently conducted defence reviews that have come to broadly similar conclusions as the SDR' (Ministry of Defence 2001). Nevertheless, given the increasing focus on the EU, the discourse is clearly more Euro-centric. Similarly, the representations of the developing and potentially unstable East and other regions continue to fuel the construction of insecurities. As the 1999 white paper suggests: 'The SDR focused attention to consequences of the break-up of states, and on ethnic and religious conflict, population and environmental pressures, competition for scarce resources, on the effects of illegal drugs, terrorism and crime' (Ministry of Defence 1999). It is stressed that nothing in the previous two years had changed that assessment. On the contrary, events in the East and around the globe had underlined the severity of these issues. It is argued: 'Indeed, events in Kosovo and East Timor and work we are undertaking on proliferation of asymmetric threats, have reinforced some of our concerns and underlined the importance of much of the defence modernization that we are undertaking' (ibid.). Significantly, the documents include no lengthy discussion or analysis of these insecurities, but rather mention them as facts and thus as largely taken as given. Moreover, the threats are assumed to be located mainly outside the boundaries of the West. Nevertheless, the insecurities in the East arose in the borderlands of the West and, as such, are constructed as highly relevant to the security of the West.

   The representations of the other key Western subjects, namely NATO, the United States and the European Union, are also re-articulated in terms of the 1998 re-articulation. First, the EU foreign and security policy is seen as increasingly important for Britain, NATO and the United States. Second, the relationships among these subjects are constructed as complementary. Moreover, the predication of the European Union highlights common values and shared interests. Hence:

   Aims to safeguard common values and fundamental interests, strengthen the security of the Union, preserve peace and international security, promote international co-operation and develop and consolidate democracy, rule of law, respect for human rights and freedoms.

(Ministry of Defence 2001)

The subject position available to the European Union increasingly resembles that of NATO, Britain and the United States. The EU is assigned a significant degree of agency in the British discourse, a representation that is arrived at through an emphasis on recent developments related to the EU foreign and security policy in the military field in particular. The paper continues:

> In short, it [the CSDP] will strengthen European military capabilities and thereby strengthen the European contribution to NATO. It will bring new responsibilities to the European Union – responsibilities which the EU is uniquely well placed to carry out. It will ensure that Europe takes a fairer share of the security burden and reinforce and sustain the relationship between Europe and North America. These aims are supported by Europeans and North Americans alike.
>
> (Ibid.)

Although the European Union is re-articulated in terms of influence and unique-ness, the presupposition of the world out there is characterized by significant continuity. The world is inhabited by states and their alliances, and the influence is tied to the traditional conceptualizations of the foreign and security policy.

Interpellation of the Europeanized great-power discourse

At the outset the interpellation of the Europeanized great-power discourse appears secondary on account of the significant continuities in relation to the more traditional great-power discourse. In other words, as the re-articulations of the official discourse represent a twist rather than a significant rupture, the discourse was likely to retain its dominance. However, examination of the parliamentary debates indicates that the Europeanization of the great-power discourse intensified the debate on foreign and security policy in Britain.[10] Significantly, the competing representations of Britain's place in the world generated in the debates correspond with the traditional and the Europeanized discourse.

It is noteworthy that according to the data presented in Table 5.4 and Figure 5.2, the Europeanized great-power discourse did not convince the parliamentarians but was increasingly questioned by MPs. Significantly, the remarks opposing the Europeanized discourse were largely drawing from the pre-1998 discourse.

The analysis of the most hotly debated issues further elucidates these arguments. The key issues in both the 1999 and the 2001 debates were the relationship between NATO and the EU foreign and security policy, and Britain's position between the EU and NATO. This was to be expected in the 2001 debate given the explicit focus on European Defence in the white papers in light of the development of the CSDP. However, it was already the subject of extensive debate in the 1999 Defence White Paper. The institutional developments in European defence were

Table 5.4 The Europeanization of the great-power discourse (GPD) in the 1999 and 2001 parliamentary debates

Remarks and Speeches	GPD 1	GPD 1&2	GPD 2	N/A	Total
Defence White Paper 22–28 February 2000	88	2	32	149	271
European Defence 19 March 2001	26	0	27	38	91
Overall	114	2	59	187	362

Note: Great-power discourse prior 1997 (GPD1), great-power discourse after 1997 (GPD2)

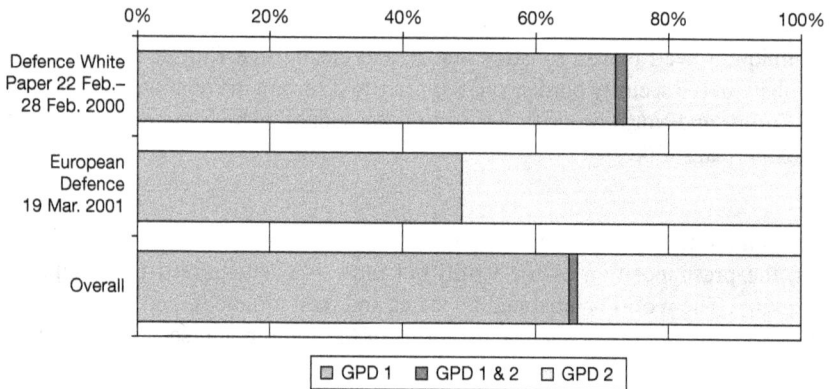

Figure 5.2 The Europeanization of the great-power discourses (GPD) in the 1999 and 2001 parliamentary debates.

Note: Great-power discourse prior to 1997 = GPD1; great-power discourse after 1997 = GPD2.

explicitly linked to events in the Balkans: the Kosovo crisis and NATO's bombing campaign in Serbia, as well as the continuing and expanding peacekeeping operations in the region (House of Commons 2000a, 2000b and 2001). Two rival positions emerged in the parliamentary debates.

First, the state officials argued that it was imperative to engage with the European Union in foreign and security policy due to the events in the Balkans in the 1990s. Secretary of State for Defence Hoon's argumentation is illustrative:

> ... it is wrong that Europe collectively can contribute such a small proportion of the total forces required to solve a problem on its doorstep [Crisis in the Balkans].
>
> ... At the Helsinki European summit in December, the European Union took an enormous step forward in the process of solving Europe's military capability problems, which were so evident in the first half of last year as we pulled together forces to go into Kosovo. We seek to improve Europe's ability to put more forces in the field and to put them there more rapidly.
>
> (House of Commons 2000a)

Moreover, through participation Britain enhanced its wider military influence in the world and its status in world politics. Hoon continued:

> We will be judged by one thing, and one only: our ability to deliver that force better than ever before. As I speak, we have men in Kosovo acting with skill and courage of which we can all be proud. We have HMS Illustrious in the Gulf at the head of a major naval deployment. We have Royal Air Force aircraft in the skies over Iraq. Those interventions show that we are acting as a force for good, day after day. All the developments that I have described are designed to increase the effectiveness of our forces. I commend them to the House.
>
> (Ibid.)

The representations of Britain's place in the world generated in these extracts clearly reflect the 1998 re-articulation of the great-power discourse. The predication of the subjects, the presupposition of knowledge about the world out there and the agency assigned to the actors are indicative of a great-power identity in an increasingly interdependent world, a world in which EU foreign and security policy was increasingly important for various subjects constructed in the discourse. The argumentation of Keith Vaz, Minister for the Armed Forces is further illustrative in this respect:

> Let me, in closing, restate the fundamental points for the benefit for of the Right Hon. Member for Wokingham. The ESDP is good news for Britain, Europe and NATO. That is why the Government developed it, why Europe supports it and why the United States and NATO have welcomed it in the statement made by President Bush and the Prime Minister on 23 February. This Government, the United States Government, our EU partners and NATO allies are engaged in making a success of the ESDP. Nice was an important step towards realising the goals of a NATO-friendly ESDP. It was a good result for NATO and a good result for Britain.
>
> (House of Commons 2000a)

In this extract the CSDP is discursively constructed as complementary to NATO and other subjects such as the United States and Britain. This complementary relationship also implies shared interests and values.

However and second, a number of MPs questioned the representations initiated by the government's re-articulation of the great-power discourse. Specifically, it was argued that St Malo was a mistake, that the CFSP and the CSDP represented imagination rather than reality and that NATO was the only credible security organization in Europe. The leader of the opposition, Duncan Smith, argued: 'I warned that, in late 1998, at St Malo, the prime minister's rushed attempt to change policy, which then moved at an alarming pace in 1999, was a big mistake' (House of Commons 2000b). Moreover, in the opposition's view the developments put in motion in St Malo were detrimental to Britain's relationship with the United States. He continued:

... Americans and others have spotted that the words in the series of agreements show up the ambitions to create a defence identity beyond NATO – outside NATO. Those are the lines and words that have been used from St Malo to Helsinki. It is a reality. That is what the Government have signed up to.

(House of Commons 2000b)

On the other hand, the credibility of the CSDP was rendered deeply suspect. MP Cash's speech is illustrative. He argued that 'the European security and defence policy is a sort of satire, reminiscent of *Gulliver's Travels* and the tales of Baron von Munchhausen. It is a myth; a voyage in time and space, which is completely at variance with judgment, experience and reality' (House of Commons 2001). Significantly, the former British Prime Minister Margaret Thatcher reappeared in the debate in relation to the credibility question. As MP Frank Cook noted:

Some of her [Thatcher] views were very reasonable. For example: 'As the Kosovo conflict showed, and as the figures for defence spending confirm, European defence capabilities are lagging dangerously far behind those of the United States.' That is eminently sensible and perfectly accurate. She added: 'This is particularly true in the vital area of military technology'. That point is as plain as the nose on one's face and it is absolutely right. However, Baroness Thatcher said that there would be a problem because the impulse towards developing a new European defence and separate European armed forces has little to do with the fact that Europe is cutting its defences while America is increasing hers . . .

(House of Commons 2001)

The remarks opposing the government's Europeanized discourse created several alternative representations of Britain's place in the world. Closer participation in EU foreign and security policy could undermine NATO's pre-eminence in European security, it could jeopardize the United States' commitment in the continent and, crucially, Britain's special relationship with the United States. It is suggested that the predication of subjects established, the knowledge presupposed and the subject positions available for the subjects of these representations are indicative of the pre-1998 British great-power discourse. Hence, the official Europeanized foreign and security policy discourse in Britain did not translate into a dominant discourse: quite the opposite, it was increasingly resisted in Parliament.

Conclusion

This chapter analysed the Europeanization of foreign and security policy in Britain. It seems that EU membership and the European Union's developing foreign and security policy were central topics in British foreign and security policy debates in 1998. However, the discourse analysis indicates that the Europeanization of the official discourse did not mark a break with the past, and that the dominant great-power discourse was re-articulated in a familiar way, highlighting Britain's great-power status, leadership and international responsibilities. Nevertheless, the analysis also shows that the European Union and its foreign and security policy became increasingly important in the reproduction of the British great-power identity. In other words, Britain emerged as a pivotal and influential state in the late 1990s and early 2000s because it 'was strong in Europe' and 'strong with the United States'. On the other hand, the re-articulation of the great-power discourse in the late 1990s did not interpellate British parliamentarians, and the traditional discourse continued to structure the representations generated by the policy-makers. Nevertheless, this struggle took place within the boundaries of the great-power discourse.

6 Comparing the reproduction of state identities in Finland and Britain

Introduction

Following the analysis of the Europeanization of the foreign and security policy discourses in Finland and Britain, this chapter focuses on the relationship between the European Union and the member-state identities in this field. Specifically, it discusses the similarities and differences between Finland and Britain in light of the increasing Europeanization of foreign and security policy, thereby elucidating the contribution of the comparative discourse analysis. It appears from the case studies that the CFSP and the CSDP were at the heart of the re-articulations of these discourses in the two countries. As such, these twin policies shaped the reproduction of these state identities. However, a comparison of the findings of the discourse analysis indicates that Europeanization had very different effects on them. Whereas in Finland it was fundamental for the rapid transformation from a neutrality identity to an alignment identity, in Britain it enabled the reproduction of the traditional British great-power identity. This chapter puts forward three key arguments. First, it seems that the Europeanization of foreign and security policy is more than intergovernmental cooperation: the case studies indicate that the identities of the states involved were shaped or even transformed. On the other hand and second, the differences between Finland and Britain are indicative of the continuing importance of the member states in the process. Significantly, both convergence and divergence are possible in this context. Finally, the differences highlight the value of context-specific discourse analysis as a tool for analysing European foreign and security policy. Crucially, comparison is imperative in explicating what, if anything, is context-specific in the analysis. In order to illustrate these arguments the first section of this chapter revisits the broader background of the book in light of two questions. Why make the comparison? Why take these cases? The second section compares and contrasts the findings of the case studies. The chapter ends with a discussion on the relevance of these findings for the analysis of European foreign policy/ies.

Europeanization and comparative discourse analysis

This book analyses how the process of European integration in the field foreign and security policy is shaping the identities of EU member states. It is argued that, despite the increasing level of coordination among European states during the 1990s and 2000s, EU institutions and policies feature increasingly significantly in European foreign and security policy. Against this background, the book calls into question the dominant modes of analysis that draw mainly on intergovernmental approaches, turning instead towards the literature on Europeanization, which acknowledges the increasing importance of EU institutions and policies in the foreign and security policy. It nevertheless promotes a novel conceptualization of Europeanization as a top-down and bottom-up process, and in so doing resists the tendency to prioritize either the national or the European level of foreign and security policy-making in the analysis. It is also claimed that discourse studies provide a way forward in terms of analysing the mutually constitutive aspects of the relationship between the EU and its members, in other words the reproduction of state identities in light of Europeanization.

Nonetheless the application of discourse analysis challenges the comparative method adopted in the majority of approaches to Europeanization. First, discourse studies approach the similarities and differences among the countries under investigation as research outcomes (dependent variables) rather than prerequisites (independent variables) of meaningful comparison. Second, the case selection favours particularity (quality) over generalization (quantity) (Keränen 2001): given that discourse analysis requires in-depth analysis of each case, the number of cases is likely to be limited rather than extensive. Accordingly, the comparison in this book is not meant to provide a general picture or to develop a general theory of Europeanization: the aim is to construct an analytical framework within which particular features of the Europeanization of foreign and security policy can be registered and analysed.

On the face of it, contrasting Finland and Britain might appear to be like comparing apples and oranges. In other words, the rationale behind the comparison may not seem meaningful given that these countries are so different. However, and as discussed in Chapter 2, both are European states and EU members, and both are actively participating in the CFSP and the CSDP. Moreover, the assumed differences in terms of geopolitical location, size, resources and history, among other factors, constituted the rationale underpinning the case selection. Finland and Britain are presumably two different cases through which to shed light on the impact of Europeanization and state identities in the field of foreign and security policy – most crucially a small and a major EU member state. The role of the major members is indeed significant for the CFSP and the CSDP. Interestingly, their traditional positions seem to be shifting. Whereas Germany has acquired a more prominent role in European foreign and security policy, partly through engagement in the CFSP and the CSDP (Lankowski 2001: 107–111), France has rekindled its traditional reluctance in participating in NATO (Sauder 1999). Moreover, the case of Britain is particularly interesting in that it is traditionally seen as the most reluctant in terms of integration.

The incorporation of a small state into the analysis is also highly relevant given that the role of such states is often downplayed in European foreign and security policy (Arter 2000, Joenniemi 2001, Hansen 2002, M. Smith 2003). However

Finland and Sweden, which are both small and militarily non-allied, have played a highly constructive and significant role in the development of the EU's military capabilities. They opposed the plans to merge the WEU – the European military alliance – and the EU, and their counterproposal was adopted as a compromise. Accordingly, only military crisis-management tasks were incorporated into the EU, and the territorial defence function of the WEU remained outside (Græger, Larsen and Ojanen 2002: 22–23). In relation to the European Union's decision to establish a Rapid Reaction Force for crisis-management missions, Finland and Sweden wished to see an explicit statement that the aim was not establish a European Army. Subsequently, the Helsinki Presidency Conclusions stated that the process 'does not imply the creation of a European Army' (Græger, Larsen and Ojanen 2002: 165).

Before presenting and analysing the findings of the case studies in a comparative framework I should pinpoint the two dimensions of comparison adopted: a strong temporal dimension complements the spatial aspect. As the case-study results indicate, comparison over time facilitated detailed analysis of the Europeanization of the discourses on foreign and security policy and state identities. The purpose of this chapter is to further elucidate the relationship between the EU and its member states through comparison over space, in other words to examine convergence or possibly divergence in preferably different states in light of increasing Europeanization. Comparison over space is also relevant to discourse studies and the analysis of state identities in that it facilitates explication of what is context-specific on the one hand and European on the other in a given country or identity.

Comparing the Finnish and British discourses

The degree and impact of the discourse on the Europeanization of foreign and security policy differed in Finland and Britain (Table 6.1): it was evident in Finland in the early and mid-1990s, but occurred in Britain in the late 1990s. On the other hand, although EU foreign and security policy had a limited impact on the re-articulation of the traditional discourse on foreign and security policy in Britain, in Finland it drove the articulation of a new discourse and identity in 1995. Moreover, whereas in Finland the new discourse was challenging parliamentarians by the early 2000s, in Britain the Europeanized re-articulation of the traditional discourse in 1998 was being increasingly scrutinized.

The discursive context of Europeanization in Finland and Britain

The Finnish policy discourse in the early 1990s generated representations of a relatively powerless neutral state located between the two political, economic and military blocks of the East and the West. As such, Finland had to adapt to its external environment and avoid involvement in international value-based considerations (Kekkonen 1982: 17–22). Until 1992 membership was considered totally incompatible with the policy of neutrality. However, the dramatic changes

Table 6.1 The Europeanization of foreign and security policy discourse in Finland and Britain

	Finland	*Britain*
Timing	Early and mid-1990s	Late 1990s
Context of the Europeanization articulated in the official discourse	The end of the Cold War and superpower rivalry Large-scale economic, political and social transformations in Europe New security threats related to the instability of the transformations Deepening Western integration EU membership application in 1992 and accession in 1995	Increasing interdependence and globalization New security threats related to the instability of the transformation Developing transatlantic relationship NATO–EU relations
Rationale for the Europeanization articulated in the official discourse	Neutrality is no longer a viable line of action The European Union is not a military alliance Participation is in line with the policy of military non-alignment Participation in the EU foreign and security policy will re-enforce Finnish security	The European Union needs to be in a position to play its full role on the international stage A more engaged relationship with the European Union is needed to safeguard British interests Europe needs strengthened armed forces that can react rapidly to the new risks Although Britain cannot be the most powerful country in the world, it can be pivotal Britain should be strong in Europe and strong with the US.

Note: The table is based on the reviews of scholarly and political discourses in Finland and Britain further discussed in Chapter 3 and Chapter 4.

in the security environment, such as the disintegration of the Soviet Union in 1991, opened up space for alternative considerations.

Accordingly, membership of the European Union and participation in the developing EU foreign and security policy became the central question in the national debate on foreign and security policy (Koivisto 1995, Lipponen 2001). Significantly, EU membership was constructed as a political question with a clear security dimension. This is not to argue that economic aspects were not significant or discussed in relation to membership: after all, the country was still struggling to overcome a deep financial and economic crisis. However, as President Koivisto noted at the time: 'security-policy considerations spoke most powerfully for the membership application. Economic considerations were secondary after all' (Koivisto 1995: 554, my translation). When Finland gained access to the European Union in 1995 it also gave up its policy of neutrality and re-articulated its foreign and security policy in terms of economic and political alignment, and military non-alignment, with the West. Therefore the CFSP, with the option of a common defence policy and also referred to as the 'EU's security dimension', played a major role in the reproduction of the Finnish state identity in the early 1990s.

Attempts in Britain to enhance cooperation among EU member states on political and security matters were noted and discussed in the early 1990s. However, it appears from the case study that it was only towards the end of the decade when the CFSP, and in particular the EU's defence policy, became one of the most hotly debated issues in British foreign and security policy. In other words, although the development of the CFSP was acknowledged and welcomed to some extent in the early and mid-1990s, it was not an essential element in the re-articulation of the traditional British great-power discourse and identity. Moreover, in Britain as opposed to Finland, the CFSP and the CSDP were initially constructed in terms of high expectations but insufficient decision-making and implementation capabilities. Scholars and policy-makers argued that a clear 'capabilities-expectations gap' (Hill 1993) existed. As such, the twin EU policies were largely marginalized within the dominant British discourse. Secretary of State for Foreign and Commonwealth Affairs Douglas Hurd's reasoning in 1994 is illustrative. He argued:

> The European Union is ambitious in foreign affairs. We feel strength in numbers and we pursue a far-reaching agenda. CFSP is still in its infancy. Entry into force of the Treaty on European Union did not overnight produce a ready-made common foreign policy ... As any builder knows, it is important to get the foundations and the framework of the structure right first.
>
> (Hurd 1994: 427)

Although some of the problems associated with the CFSP were also acknowledged in Finland, generally the representations of these policies were highly positive. Instead of showing scepticism, Finland emphasized its commitment to the on-going processes. On the other hand, the EU's foreign and security policy did not play a fundamental role in the reproduction of the British state identity. Indeed, the initial representations of the CFSP and the move towards a common defence policy suggested that the increasing EU-based cooperation was a noteworthy but not a profound development.

Nevertheless, it appears from the case study that the coming into power of the Labour Party in 1997, the 1998 Strategic Defence Review and, in particular, the joint British–French declaration on European defence in St Malo in 1998 represented a break with the past in terms of British policy towards the emerging EU foreign and security policy (Howorth 2001, Howorth 2004). The policy-makers, both for and against the Labour Party's more engaging line, argued that the traditional British position, laid out in the so-called three-circles doctrine that highlighted Britain's international location at the intersection of the Common-wealth, the United States and Europe, was changing in favour of Europe.

Accordingly, the Europeanization of foreign and security policy became one of the most hotly debated issues in the late 1990s (British–French Summit 1998, Ministry of Defence 1999).

The temporal difference in the suggested Europeanization of foreign and security policy between Finland and Britain is significant. Similarly, the rationales given for Europeanization were different. In Finland it was explicitly related to the immediate aftermath of the Cold War and the representation of neutrality as 'no longer a viable line of action' (Council of State 1995: 58), whereas in Britain it was related to its continuing internationalism and great-power status. As the 1998 SDR states:

> The British are, by instinct, an internationalist people. We believe that as well as defending our rights, we should discharge our responsibilities in the world. We do not want to stand idly by and watch humanitarian disasters or the aggression of dictators go unchecked. We want to give a lead, we want to be a force for good.
>
> (Ministry of Defence 1998)

More precisely, in Britain the developments of the CFSP and the CSDP were linked to Europe's need for 'strengthened armed forces that can react rapidly to the new risks' (British–French Summit 1998). This reflected the notion of a bigger contribution by the European states to NATO and to the developing EU foreign and security policy and crisis-management capabilities (Ministry of Defence 1998). On the other hand, international responsibilities and the CSDP, as well as the EU's crisis-management capabilities, assumed more importance in the Finnish foreign and security policy during the course of the 1990s.

The impact on the Finnish and British state identities

It appears from the discourse analysis of the Finnish case that instead of re-articulating the traditional neutrality discourse in 1995, the foreign policy leadership articulated a new discourse highlighting Finland's economic and political alignment with the West. This alignment discourse emphasized Finland's new location within the West, its increasing influence in world politics and its responsibility in international affairs. On the other hand, the country remained militarily non-aligned. Significantly, the analysis also indicates that the EU and its developing foreign and security policy played a major role in the transformation.

The case study shows how the Finnish discourse on foreign and security policy was Europeanized in conjunction with Finland's accession to the EU in 1995. From the very beginning the Finnish foreign policy leadership made it clear that Finland would engage constructively in the development of the EU foreign and security policy. The government stated that Finland did not have 'any security policy reservations' and 'wishes to play an active and constructive role in creating and implementing a common foreign and security policy' (Council of State 1995: 58). Specifically, the country wished to contribute to the EU's preventive diplomacy and civil and military crisis-management tasks. Although the foreign policy leadership re-articulated Finland's continuing commitment to military non-alignment and independent defence, its engagement towards the end of the 1990s in Western security organizations such as the WEU, NATO and the European Union in terms of the CSDP raised questions about the feasibility and credibility of the policy. After all, the new discourse emphasized alignment rather than non-alignment. (Table 6.2)

The extent of the change in the official discourse is indeed extraordinary. In 1990 the prime minister of Finland argued that EC membership was totally incompatible with Finland's long-term interest in establishing a neutral inter-national status (Joenniemi 2001). However, in 1995 the foreign policy leadership declared the 'the European Union will reinforce the foundations of Finnish security and provide a significant channel through which Finland can pursue its interests . . .' (Council of State 1995: 5). According to the case-study analysis, this radically different articulation of Finland's place in the world reflected a new discourse. In other words, the structuring of the meaning of the actors and the environment within which Finland found itself was substantially different from the earlier re-articulations. The key findings of the discourse analysis presented in Table 6.2 illustrate the differences between the traditional neutrality discourse and the new alignment discourse.

The European Union. It is clear from the analysis of the Finnish case that the representation of the European Union changed over time from that of a Western European economic organization to a European economic and political organ-ization with a 'security dimension', and later to a political entity with a full-scale foreign and security policy. In the early 1990s European integration was constructed as a process reflecting the Cold War division in Europe, whereas in the mid-1990s the European Union was articulated as an inclusive and enlarging organization enhancing Finland's aim to create regional stability and prevent the emergence of the old or new dividing lines. It was also explicitly attributed the Western values of democracy, the rule of law and a market economy, norms that had been more exclusively associated with Western states.

Significantly, the CFSP and the CSDP had a crucial role in this new articulation. In Finland these EU policies reflected a new kind of security assessment:

> As a member of the European Union, Finland is involved in a community of democratic states that have a vital role to play in international security-policy cooperation. The aim is to prevent any re-emergence of confrontation or a new division of Europe. Preconditions must be created for overcoming and managing security problems and countries' security concerns in cooperation and on the basis of equality.
>
> (Council of State 1995: 67)

According to the representations generated by the Finnish foreign policy leadership, the EU, the CFSP and the CSDP were not based on the traditional and boundary-producing security thinking that reflected the traditional security

Table 6.2 Structuring the meaning of the neutrality and alignment discourses

	Neutrality discourse	*Alignment discourse*
Predication (key representation of the discourse)	*Finland:* A small, independent and democratic state A neutral state Located between the East and the West	*Finland:* A stable and developed state A member of the core group of European democracies (the European Union) Has international responsibilities
	The West: Great powers Democratic states	*The West:* Stable, developed and influential major and minor states
	NATO: Western military alliance	*The EU:* Inclusive economic and political might with foreign and security policy Crisis management
	The EC/EU: Western economic organization	
	The East: Great power(s) with a different social-political and economic system	*NATO:* Inclusive military alliance with a political dimension Crisis management
	The Warsaw Pact: Eastern military alliance	*The East:* Unstable, developing but potentially influential major and minor states
Presupposition (knowledge created in the discourse)	Finland is a minor rather than a great power A peripheral rather than a central state	Finland is a stable rather than an unstable state Democratic rather than undemocratic Developed rather than underdeveloped Order rather than disorder
Subject position	Small and relatively powerless and peripheral state(s) in the North Powerful and central power(s) in the East Powerful and central powers in the West	Stable, developed and influential states in the North Stable, developed and powerful West Unstable, developing and potentially powerful East

Note: The table is based on the reviews of scholarly and political discourses in Finland and Britain further discussed in Chapter 3 and Chapter 4.

concerns about large-scale military confrontation and highlighted the importance of military alliances. The CFSP was rather portrayed as an inclusive policy enabling wide participation and support, for instance, in the field of preventive diplomacy. On the other hand, the CSDP was construed as facilitating military crisis-management missions based on broader international support. Moreover, the continuing enlargement of the European Union together with the entry of the three previously neutral member states and their participation in the CFSP and the CSDP were constructed in Finland as an example of EU comprehensiveness.

NATO. The representations of NATO in Finland highlighted change. It was seen as a traditional military alliance in the early 1990s, but towards the end of the decade it was constructed as a more inclusive political and security actor in Europe. This representation drew on its new partnership programmes, the NATO-led peacekeeping mission in which Finland was involved as well as its enlargement. On the other hand, its traditional role in European security was significant for the construction of a commensurable policy of military non-alignment and CSDP in Finland. The 1995 report argued: 'As the members of the European Union which are NATO countries rely on NATO for their defence, the establishment of common defence of the EU, separate from NATO, is not in sight (Council of State 1995: 48). Accordingly, it was unlikely that the EU defence policy would lead to common defence and the establishment of military-security guarantees. However, the developing relationship between the EU and NATO had a significant role in the re-articulation of NATO: the 1997 and 2001 reports on security and defence policy emphasized the increasing 'interoperability' of Finnish and NATO troops (Council of State 1997: 25, 2001: 24). NATO's military resources were seen as crucial for the European crisis-management missions agreed within the CFSP and, as such, the relationship between the EU and NATO was articulated in Finland as complementary.

The East. The construction of the East was significantly different in the alignment discourse. Although the Russian Federation inherited some of the great-power characters of the Soviet Union, the subject positions available to the eastern subjects in the new discourse highlighted instability, which was related to these states transition to democracy and a market economy. The government argued in 1997 that changes in central and eastern European countries '. . . are taking place at disparate rates. Wars, territorial disputes and minority conflicts in the countries of the former Soviet Union and Yugoslavia have affected and continue to affect the security of the entire continent . . .' (Council of State 1997: 15). Whereas the neutrality discourse constructed the East as a rather developed superpower block, in which fierce rivalry with the West constituted insecurities, the alignment discourse portrayed it as underdeveloped and therefore a source of insecurity.

It is also clear from the Finnish case study that the neutrality and alignment discourses were both present in the key foreign and security policy documents, and in the parliamentary debates on these statements in 1995. However, by 2001 the new discourse had become dominant. Finland's influence, responsibility and location within the West were increasingly highlighted in the representation generated by the official documentation. Simultaneously, references to Finland's smallness, limited agency and peripheral location faded away. MPs drew less and less on the neutrality discourse and the alignment discourse gained dominance in the parliamentary debates on the key policy papers (Figure: 6.1).

By comparison, analysis of the British official foreign and security policy dis-course indicated continuity rather than change. In other words, the re-articulation

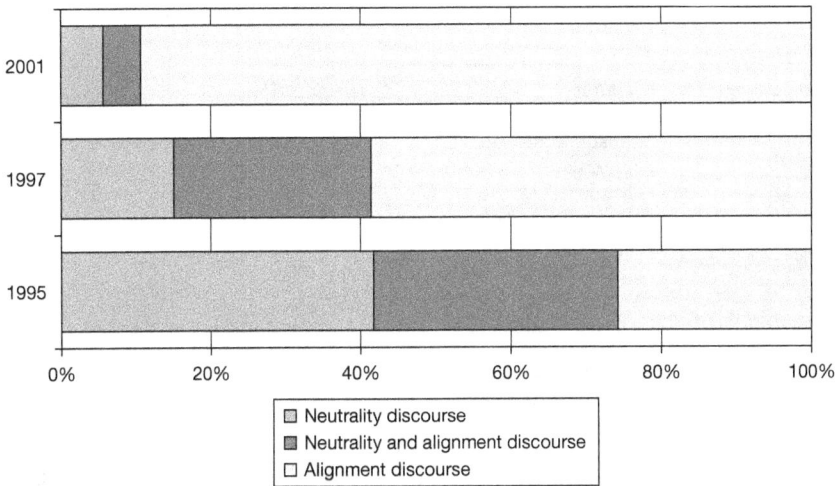

Figure 6.1 Interpellation of the alignment discourse.

of a more engaging British policy towards Europe was based largely on the traditional great-power discourse. The key features of this discourse were Britain as a great power with a global reach, a leading member of several international organizations such as the European Union and NATO, and the closest ally of the United States. Britain was also constructed to represent particular Western values and, as a great power, it had a responsibility to lead the way and shape the world. However, the 1998 re-articulation gave it a more engaged role in the development of the EU foreign and security policy.

Given the large-scale political, economic and social transition in post-Cold War Europe the continuity in the British official discourse is remarkable. Although the political rhetoric changed, there was no change in the discourse enabling and constraining what could be intelligibly said about Britain's place in the world. Indeed, the 1998 re-articulation of the great-power discourse gave Britain a very similar role as before, in other words that of a great power. As Prime Minister Blair argued in 1997, 'by virtue of our geography, our history and the strengths of our people, Britain is a global player' (Blair 1997a). Nevertheless, the European Union, and in particular its developing foreign and security policy, was given a more prominent role.

The European Union. As in Finland, the representation of the European Union in the field of foreign and security policy changed in Britain. In the early and mid-1990s the EU was seen as an economic organization with a developing political dimension. Specifically, it was seeking a more prominent role in world politics and European foreign and security policy/ies. Conversely, in the late 1990s it emerged as a global economic player and an increasingly influential foreign and security policy actor in Europe and beyond. As Prime Minister Blair argued in 1998:

Table 6.3 Structuring meaning in the pre- and post-1998 great-power discourses

	The pre-1998 re-articulation of the great-power discourse	The 1998 re-articulation of the great-power discourse
Predication	*Britain*: A major power A leading member of several international organizations The closest ally to the US A responsible great power *The West*: *NATO*: A credible and powerful military alliance A bridge between Europe and North America The cornerstone of Britain's security and defence *The EC/EU*: An increasingly influential economic organization A developing political and foreign and security policy actor An unreliable organization for common defence *The East*: Former communist states Significant military might In transition to democracy and a market economy *The Globe*: Trading partners Dependent and developing countries around the globe Hostile countries	*Britain*: A major power A leading member of several international organizations Strong in Europe, strong with the US A responsible great power with a normative foreign policy *The West*: *NATO*: A powerful and credible military alliance and political actor Crisis management Supported by the influential and global United States A transatlantic organization The basis of Britain's defence policy *The EU*: A major economic actor in world politics An increasingly influential political actor with developing foreign, security and defence policies *The East*: In transition to democracy and a market economy Unstable and developing states *The Globe*: Trading partners Dependent and developing countries around the globe Hostile countries
Presupposition	Great rather than medium-sized Global rather than regional Liberator from oppression Stable rather than unstable Developed rather than underdeveloped	Great rather than medium-sized Global rather than regional Liberator from oppression Stable rather than unstable Developed rather than underdeveloped
Subject positioning	(i) powerful, global and transatlantic Britain (ii) credible and transatlantic NATO (iii) increasingly powerful but unreliable European Union, and (iv) dependent and developing countries in the East, the Middle East and Africa	(i) influential, global and transatlantic Britain (ii) powerful and credible NATO, supported by the (iii) influential and global United States (iv) increasingly influential European Union with a developing foreign and security policy (v) developing and unstable states in Eastern Europe and elsewhere

On External Policy, the EU must be both effective and seen to be effective internationally ... We need to project our values on the world stage, to be open, outward-looking, supportive of free trade, human rights and democracy, and playing a major role in the great international issues of the day.

(Blair 1998b)

However, although the representation of the European Union changed, the British position was articulated in a rather familiar way: Britain should seek leadership in Europe. It was within this context that Britain engaged in the development of the CSDP. At St Malo in 1998 it emerged as the key player in the military and defence affairs of the European Union. However, in terms of British foreign and security policy, this marked a twist rather than turn in the discourse. In other words, the re-articulation reflected the traditional great-power discourse. As Blair noted: 'Europe wants us there as a leading player. Britain may need to be part of Europe but Europe needs Britain to be part of it. For four centuries, our destiny has been to help shape Europe. Let it be so again' (Blair 1997a).

NATO, the US. The representation of NATO in Britain was characterized by continuity and change. The uncertainty concerning its future noted in some political discussion on the European level in the immediate post-Cold War years (Fierke and Wiener 2001) never fed into the official British discourse on foreign and security policy, and it was continuously re-articulated as the only credible European security actor. As such, the government argued that 'membership of NATO will continue to provide the UK with its best insurance against all these [new and old security] risks' (Ministry of Defence 1998). On the other hand, NATO was seen to be undergoing changes. It was no longer merely a military alliance but had become a comprehensive security actor with political importance. As the SDR stated: 'Militarily, NATO has been reinvigorated and has shown its continuing value by its role in Bosnia and its response to events in Kosovo. Politically, it has responded positively and imaginatively to the aspirations of the new European democracies' (ibid.).

NATO also retained its role as a pivotal organization in terms of the transatlantic link between Europe and the United States. The 1998 SDR stated that the 'partnership between Europe and North America has been a uniquely effective' in terms of political and military security (ibid.). Moreover, the transatlantic link was essential for the construction of Britain as a particularly powerful actor in Europe and the United States. As Blair argued, Britain was 'stronger with the US because of our strength in Europe' and 'we are stronger in Europe because of our strength with the US' (Blair 1998d).

The East. The representations of Russia and other Eastern subjects changed from a powerful superpower block with significant security interests in Europe to a group of developing states that were going through political, economic and social reforms. These developments in the British discourse were very similar to those in the Finnish discourse.

The Globe. In terms of the other subjects constructed in the British discourse, the global dimension retained its importance. An extract taken form the SDR is illustrative:

> We are a major European state and a leading member of the European Union. Our economic and political future is as part of Europe. Our security is indivisible from that of our European partners and allies ... But our vital interests are not confined to Europe. Our economy is founded on international trade. Exports form a higher proportion of Gross Domestic Product than for the US, Japan, Germany or France. We invest more of our income abroad than any other major economy.
>
> (Ministry of Defence 1998)

Thus, the global dimension of the British discourse on foreign and security policy is clearly re-articulated. Britain emerges as a European great power with global interests. In short, Britain was global rather than regional, developed rather than underdeveloped, and a leader rather than a follower.

The discourse analysis of subsequent foreign and security policy documents from 1999 and 2001 indicated that the 1998 re-articulation was increasingly shaping the official statements. The eminence of the European Union and its foreign and security policy increased, and the representations generated in the policy papers largely reflected the 1998 re-articulation of the great-power discourse. Nevertheless, analysis of the parliamentary debates revealed that the 1998 re-articulation did not become hegemonic among British parliamentarians: the traditional great-power discourse prevailed and continued to structure the remarks made in the parliamentary debates (Figure 6.2).

The significant degree of change in the Finnish discourse on foreign and security policy and the lack of change in the British discourse may not seem surprising according to commonsense understanding about small and major states. Convention dictates that minor states are given a rather marginal role in world politics (Hey 2003: 1, 4) and European integration (Arter 2000). On account of

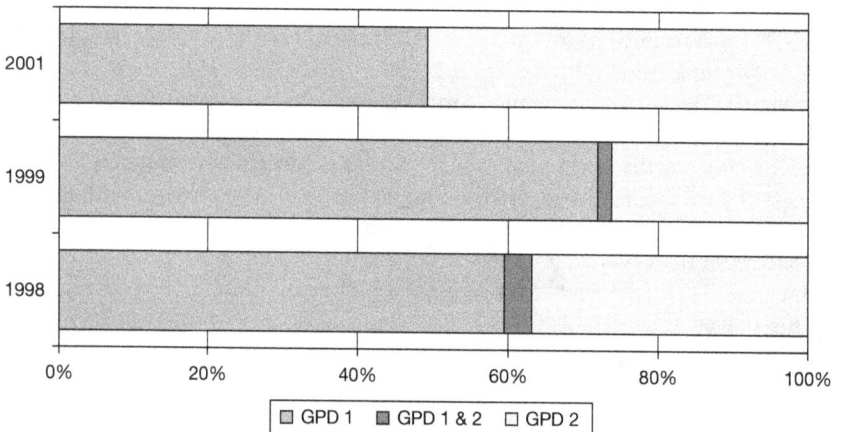

Figure 6.2 Interpellation of the 1998 re-articulation of great-power discourse (GPD).

Note: Great-power discourse prior to 1997 = GPD1; great-power discourse after 1997 = GPD2.

their size and limited resources they are expected to adapt to external changes, whereas great powers are considered more able to shape the context within which they find themselves.

However, the analysis of the Finnish and British discourses highlighted the context-specificity of these constructions. For instance, whereas Finland declared in 1995 that neutrality was a 'no longer a viable line of action' (Council of State 1995: 58), in 1996 Britain acknowledged the contribution that 'the neutral members of the European Union are able to make to building security in Europe' (Ministry of Defence 1996: 13). On the other hand, whereas the Finnish foreign policy leadership stated that 'Finland has not made any security policy reservations concerning its obligations under its founding treaties or the Maastricht Treaty' (Council of State 1995: 58), Britain argued that the neutral member states' full participation in Western cooperation on foreign and security policy was uncertain in the near future (Ministry of Defence 1995: 17, 1996: 13).

According to the British representations of European developments, Finland could have retained its neutrality and was expected to opt out of any deeper engagement in EU foreign and security policy. On the other hand, Britain was depicted in the Finnish discourse as a leading Western European power with a central role in European security (Koivisto 1995).[1] As such it was constructed as a leading actor in Europe and it was assumed to play a constructive role in the ongoing changes in European foreign and security policy. Significantly, the official Finnish foreign and security policy documentation from the 1990s did not distinguish between the major Western European powers, but given the increasing interest in EU politics the British and European constructions of Britain as a reluctant partner gained more prominence in the Finnish political discourses.

The Europeanization of state identities

The findings of the case studies support the claims and the rationale of the literature on Europeanization (Manners and Whitman 2000, Christiansen, Jørgensen and Wiener 2001, White 2001, Raunio and Tiilikainen 2003, Tonra 2003). In other words, the foreign and security policy discourses in these two member states were increasingly shaped by EU foreign and security policy. The clear 'presence' and 'interference' of the CFSP and the CSDP in the reproduction of the identities of these two different EU member states is a significant finding. The implication is that they were not merely projecting their interests on the EU level. On the contrary, their participation in the CFSP and the CSDP was also indicative of national adaptation in light of the reproduction of their identities. Nevertheless, the impact of Europeanization on the reproduction of these state identities was different (Table 6.4): it seems that this was symptomatic of the context-specific nature of the Europeanization of the foreign and security policy. The following discussion of some of the key similarities and differences illustrates the point.

In both cases the reproduction of the state identity in the sphere of foreign and security policy reflected a Euro-centric understanding of the world and of security. In terms of Finland this is hardly surprising. After all, Finland's post-war neutrality

Table 6.4 Similarities and differences in the Europeanization of the state identities of Finland and Britain

	Finland	Britain
Context of the Europeanization	Early 1990: the end of the Cold War	Late 1990s: increasing integration and new security threats in Europe
Rationale of the Europeanization	A stable and more influential international position	To exercise power and influence
Impact on state identity	Becomes a more stable and influential state	Remains a great power
Position in relation to the EU	Becomes a more central state (*Similarity*)	Remains a central state (*Complementary*)
Position in relation to the EU foreign and security policy	Constructive and responsible participation (*Complementary*)	Britain provides leadership (*Complementary*)
Position in relation to NATO	Increasing interoperability (*Complementary*)	The cornerstone of British defence (*Complementary*)
Position in relation to the East	Increasingly alienated (*Difference*)	Increasingly alienated (*Difference*)

was explicitly related to the balance of power in Europe between the two rival superpower blocks. However, in the British case it is interesting to learn that the traditional foreign and security issues of a great power with a global reach were rather exclusively debated in terms of European security. Whereas the official documents and the parliamentary debates generated representations that highlighted Britain's importance in several international organizations, as well as its ability to safeguard its global interests militarily, two largely European security organizations were assigned utmost importance: NATO and the European Union.

In both cases the EU gained prominence in the institutional arrangements related to foreign and security policy. It became the key feature of 'Finnish security' in the post-Cold War world, whereas in Britain it signified an increasingly influential political actor within which Britain should seek leadership. It also appears from the case studies that both states constructed the relationship between NATO and the EU in similar ways. Although the relationship between the EU's developing foreign and security policy and NATO was largely seen as complementary, the difference between these organizations was highlighted – but for different reasons. In Finland it was considered important to distinguish between them on account of its policy of military non-alignment, whereas in Britain the difference was linked to the priority given to transatlantic security arrangements and NATO's credibility. In both states the importance of NATO's military resources was highlighted in terms of its member states' defence as well as the crisis-management operations in Europe. Correspondingly the EU emphasized its increasing role in preventive diplomacy and civil and military crisis-management.

Consequently, the creation of the European Union's Rapid Reaction Force in Helsinki in 1999 did not constitute a 'Euro-Army' as far as Britain and Finland were concerned. It did not provoke a common EU defence either, but rather signified the EU's willingness to take greater responsibility for preventing and resolving European disputes and conflicts though preventive diplomacy and crisis management.

Broadly similar actors were articulated in the British and Finnish discourses on foreign and security policy: states, political communities desirous of becoming states, and international organizations largely constituted by the states. Significantly, there was no evidence in the official discourses of the decreasing importance of the states implied in the literature on integration, regionalization and, indeed, globalization. Instead, in both countries the EU foreign and security policy was constructed as being in the interests of the state in question. In Finland it was seen as crucial for Finnish security, providing the tools with which to address the security issues confronting the post-Cold War world. More generally, EU membership was seen to consolidate Finland's international position in the context of the large-scale political, economic and social transition. In Britain on the other hand, the construction of the CFSP and the CSDP highlighted the country's will to maintain its power in Europe and beyond. Britain was 'used to power' and intended to 'stay in power' (Blair 1998a). The foreign policy leadership constructed a more engaging policy towards the EU and participation in the CFSP and the CSDP as a strategic move to consolidate and further exploit Britain's pivotal position in world politics.

In terms of the reproduction of state identities the analysis suggests that whereas Britain retained a great-power identity, Finland acquired more influence. However, retaining and gaining influence in these two contexts was arrived at rather differently. Although the Finnish and British discourses on foreign and security policy were convergent, they also retained their specific characters. In other words, despite Europeanization, distinct Finnish and British state identities were reproduced in the realm of foreign and security policy.

Finland's EU membership and its participation in all areas of integration were central to the more influential identity constituted by the alignment discourse. The general representation of EU membership suggested that it had 'clarified and strengthened Finland's international position' (Council of State 1995: 10). As a member state Finland gained stability and influence, but on the other hand membership assigned 'Finland with more responsibility for European security and the future of the whole world community' (ibid.). In terms of its state identity, joining the EU gave Finland more substantial power in Europe and beyond.

However, by the late 1990s this very smallness was constructed to indicate influence. As the Finnish scholar Joenniemi hypothesized: 'In an international system where the very idea of sovereignty itself is under challenge and large multilateral institutions – the EU being the most obvious example – are assuming greater importance, small states could become more influential' (Joenniemi 1998: 62; see also Arter 2000: 678). He added: 'Having none of the 'hang-ups' associated with being a large power, small could indeed became a synonym for smart in the post-Cold War era' (ibid.). According to this reasoning, a state's ability to influence its external environment was no longer tied to its size but rather depended on its capacity for innovative thinking. In the world of the Cold War Finland's smartness and influence were constrained by the bi-polar world order, but in the post-Cold War context the European Union empowered it. This partly explains the remarkable speed with which the alignment discourse became hegemonic in Finland. Alignment with the EU replaced neutrality as the 'code word' for independence and also for influence. Against this background, alignment and participation in the EU foreign and security policy was considered to strengthen rather than endanger Finnish sovereignty.

On the other hand, the discourse analysis indicated that the European Union and its developing foreign and security policy were central (rather than marginal) for the re-articulation of the British great-power identity. Engagement with the CFSP and the CSDP was increasingly constructed as consolidating British influence in the world. Prime Minister Blair argued that Britain should overcome the 'hang-ups' related to its history as a great power and its independent international position. In terms of increasing 'Euro-scepticism' he argued:

> The logical conclusion of the Euro-sceptic approach that says everything that comes out of Europe is bad; that says Europe is something that is done to us, rather than something that we can shape; is to get out of Europe altogether ... But it would be a disaster for British jobs, British trade, British influence in the world. Far better is to be in there, engage in the arguments, and win the arguments.
>
> (Blair 1998d)

Accordingly, the British state identity in the late 1990s and early 2000s was increasingly reproduced in terms of the ongoing debate concerning the British relationship with the European Union and its developing foreign and security policy. The government attempted to articulate a more complementary relationship with the EU, the CFSP and the CSDP, but on the other hand the more traditional discourse highlighting the oppositional aspects of this relationship remained strong in the parliamentary debates. Nevertheless, given the seemingly intense and significant debate related to EU foreign and security policy, the findings of the discourse analysis reveal a considerable degree of continuity and consensus. In other words, the dominant discourse was not challenged in the process of Europeanization. Indeed, the Europeanization of the British discourse did not imply dislocation of the dominant discourse, and the struggle took place within the traditional discourse.

Conclusion

In terms of the questions raised in this study, the continuing salience of the state and state interests and influence in the Finnish and the British discourses on foreign and security policy did not imply the impossibility or undesirability of

Europeanization in this context. On the contrary, these very different states with their distinct historical, cultural and geopolitical backgrounds were able to construct the process of Europeanization as complementary to their interests. Within the temporal and spatial boundaries of this book, the context-specific character of Europeanization appears to be a strength rather than a weakness. In other words, the possibility of national variation makes the process more acceptable within the distinct contexts of the European Union. On the other hand, the context specificity also enables divergence. The development of the EU and its foreign and security policy is not necessarily a linear process, and in terms of pace and speed it is likely to vary over time and space.

7 Conclusion

The central argument in this book is that analyses of state identities can add to our understanding of the Europeanization of foreign and security policy because they enable and constrain the process of change or transformation embedded in the idea of Europeanization. The book starts with a critique of the dominant intergovernmental modes of conceptualizing and analysing European foreign and security policy. Notwithstanding significant variation within realism(s) and neo-liberal institutionalism(s), it is argued that these accounts share significant limitations resulting from their narrow view of integration as cooperation between states. For instance, realist-inspired analyses of European security and foreign policy in the 1990s rendered the development of the CFSP and the CSDP deeply suspect. On the other hand, given the increased interdependence that neo-liberal institutionalists emphasize, the key liberal theory of European integration – namely intergovernmentalism – has continued to highlight the role of the major states.

It is suggested that there is nothing inherently wrong in seeking to explain European foreign and security policy from the state perspective. Any social-scientific explanation is likely to be partial, and different research agendas contribute to the accumulation of knowledge in the field. However, it has been argued that the intergovernmental approach is not particularly valuable in expli-cating the complex relationships among different levels of governance in European foreign and security policy. Moreover, its overwhelming dominance on the research agendas tackling this subject field is not desirable in terms of the accumulation of knowledge, and moreover, alternative thinking has been largely marginalized. Against this background the book focuses on the recent engage-ment of theories and theorists seeking a more supranational understanding of contemporary European foreign and security policy. These accounts assume that its development has led to the emergence of a distinct European system that assigns EU institutions an increasingly significant role in the formulation of the policies. Whereas integration theorists have emphasized the usefulness of the spill-over concept, for instance, other scholars have highlighted comparative frameworks and the concept of Europeanization in accounting for the relationship between the EU and its member states and multi-level governance in Europe.

For many the recent theoretical ferment related to the concept of Europeaniza-tion indicates an analytical shift within research on European integration. There has been a change in focus from the creation and development of the very process of integration (bottom-up approach) – in terms of EU-level institution building for instance – to the process within which EU-level politics and policies feed into the member states' domestic politics (top-down approach). Notwithstanding their contribution to our understanding however, these approaches seem to offer a limited set of tools with which to inquire into EU and state-level governance. Significantly, the conceptualization of Europeanization as a top-down process fails to account for how the domestic processes feed back into integration. Similarly, Europeanization and comparative politics remain inspired by rationalism. They largely (although not exclusively) focus on causal mechanisms, which are seen to result from the increased activity on the EU level.

This book explores the feasibility of conceptualizing Europeanization in a more comprehensive manner highlighting the reciprocal features of the relationship between EU and member-state governance. It is suggested that, given the centrality of the state in any conceptualization of foreign and security policy, scholars in this specific field have approached the process more broadly. Some have high-lighted Europeanization and the national projection of state interests onto the EU level, but it is nevertheless unclear how these approaches differ from the more dominant intergovernmental modes of analysis. Others have focused on Europeanization as elite socialization and highlighted the cognitive aspects of the process, adopting more qualitative methodologies rather than concentrating on the mechanisms or quantifying the extent. Drawing on these analytical engagements this book highlights the growing contribution of social constructivism and post-structuralism to IR and EIS, which explicitly deal with mutually constitutive social relationships and political agency on various levels of analysis. Accordingly, it utilizes the concepts of identity and discourse. It is argued that the theoretical and methodological debates between and within these approaches are directly related to the analytical puzzles raised in this study.

It is also argued that the concept of state identity inherent in mainstream social constructivism appears to reproduce several of the problems associated with intergovernmental and supranational approaches. As Wæver notes, the problem with these accounts is that they operate within an ontology that assumes the pre-existence of states with a given identity. Regardless of whether the state identity is seen to reflect an international system (Wendt 1999), a particular national culture (Katzenstein 1996) or a regional system of governance such as the European Union, these approaches are unable to theorize the process of reproduction (Wæver 2002: 21). Conversely, some of the critical variants of social constructivism and the majority of those in poststructuralism embrace a radically different conceptual-ization of identity. The process of differentiating the self from others is seen as fundamental to the process of identity production. In other words, establishing a presence for oneself necessarily implies the creation of other selves. Moreover, the need to differentiate the self from others is a never-ending social process in that the identities are continuously reproduced in social and political practices. As such, socially constructed identities are inherently contingent.

In this regard, poststructuralist scholars suggest that foreign policy understood as a state-based political practice is essential for the reproduction of the state identity, and reconceptualize it as a boundary-producing political practice. As such it is reflective not of the pre-given essence of a state (self), but of a practice reinscribing the borders between the self and the other; it is also the process through which that state is continually constituted and reconstituted in inter-action with others (Doty 1996, Campbell 1998: 69–70). An essential element in poststructuralist approaches to foreign policy is the concept of discourse, which is not equivalent to language. Discourse is defined in terms of structure and practices. As a structure it comprises sociocultural resources that enable and constrain the construction of meaning, whereas as practice it constitutes struc-tures of meaning in use (Laffey and Weldes 2004: 28). As such, discourses are constitutive of identities because the meaning of the self and of others is produced and reproduced in practices enabled and constrained by them. The reconceptualization of foreign policy in light of a poststructural theory of identity takes us back to the key theme of this book, the Europeanization of foreign and security policy and the reproduction of the state identity. Thus the key *empirical* question raised concerned how the increasing Europeanization of foreign and security policy discourses shaped these state identities. Given the commitment to context specificity rather than generality, the analysis focused on two contrast-ing EU member states, Finland and Britain. The subsequent comparison of the Europeanization of the identities of these two states contributed to solving the key *analytical* puzzle posed in this book, namely the relationship between EU and state-level governance .

Empirical findings

The case-study findings suggest that although the Finnish and British foreign and security policies were Europeanized, significant national variation prevailed in the identity production of these states. In Finland Europeanization was central to the articulation of a radically different foreign and security policy discourse in post-Cold War Europe. The new alignment discourse represented a break with the neutrality discourse of the Cold War and highlighted alignment with the West. Although the new discourse was initially resisted, it had become dominant by the early 2000s. Accordingly, the Finnish state identity was transformed. Europeanization of the British discourse took place in the late 1990s in conjunction with the development of the CSDP. However, it did not translate into a radically different discourse or identity, and was rather a re-articulation. Nevertheless, the CFSP and the CSDP had a central role in this re-articulation of the conventional great-power discourse and identity.

Combined, these two findings generated a third empirical insight: that EU policies had a differential impact on the foreign and security policy discourses and national identities of these member states. Detailed examination of the similarities and differences in the Europeanization of the Finnish and British state identities revealed both convergence and divergence. In other words, given the increasing emphasis on the Europeanization of foreign and security policy the identities retained their context-specific characteristics. It is suggested that this did not merely constrain further integration, but also highlighted its importance. In other words, rather than representing a threat, Europeanization enabled the reproduction of the context-specific key characteristics of the Finnish and British state identities. It thus seems that the possibility of national variation enabled the expansion of Europeanization to policy fields that are often viewed as critical to state identity and as destined to remain in the margin of European integration. On the other hand, although the reproduction of these state identities highlighted the differences, the process of making and remaking them was increasingly taking place within the European Union context. This was somewhat expected in the case of Finland given its previous relationship with the Soviet Union and recent accession to the EU. However, the analysis suggests that the British great-power identity was becoming increasingly aligned with the European Union in the field of foreign and security policy.

One of the most significant findings of the discourse analysis in the Finnish case was the speed of change. The Finnish state identity was transformed within less than ten years. This shows how seemingly fixed identities can change rapidly and fundamentally over a short period of time, and how discourse analysis serves to explain the change. First, it seems that the Finnish discursive context enabled the transformation. In other words, the neutrality identity was intrinsically tied to the Cold War bipolar world and to Finland's special relationship with the Soviet Union. When the bipolarity ended and the Soviet Union collapsed the Finnish state identity was in flux, and this enabled radically different re-articulations. On the other hand, analysis of the neutrality identity elucidated why a particular kind of re-articulation and identity emerged in 1995, and how it had become dominant by the early 2000s.

In the British case the analysis reveals that the fierce debate on the EU's foreign and security policies did not necessarily translate into discourse and identity transformation. The CFSP and the CSDP were instrumental in the reproduction of the conventional British great-power identity, in other words it enabled continuity rather than postulated change. Moreover, the increasingly intense debate and growing opposition to the government's seemingly more Euro-centric discourse suggest that the traditional identity continued to frame British EU policy. Indeed, the importance of the EU in the reproduction of the British great-power identity increased. It could be said in light of these findings that the context-specific discourse analysis enhanced our understanding of Europeanization: rather than measuring its extent or highlighting the mechanisms of the process within a rationalism-inspired quantitative framework, it calls for further qualitative analysis of the discourse(s) of Europeanization in different contexts.

Analytical findings

The analytical findings comprise two elements: first, comparative discourse methodology offers new insights into the process of Europeanization; and second,

Europeanization should be understood as both a top-down and a bottom-up process in which state identities are transformed by EU discourses (differentially depending on prior national identities) and also, indeed, shape them.

Although there is disagreement among discourse scholars on methodological questions (Milliken 1999: 226–227), it is posited in this book that attention to method and rigor does not necessarily entail the kind of scientism against which many discourse analysts define themselves (Laffey and Weldes 2004: 28). Instead, it is suggested that discourse analysts' methodological criticism is indicative of a rather self-reflective and critical approach to the analytical frameworks and tools. In terms of methodological reflection it could be said that whereas discourse-analytical approaches can contribute to the analysis of Europeanization, the literature on Europeanization can contribute to the discourse theorization of IR.

Implicitly or explicitly, discourse analysts often employ comparative methods, but offer very little direct methodological reflection on the comparative perspective (Howarth 2005: 332). Indeed, the emergence of comparative discourse analysis (J. Kantola 2006) is a novel, although significant, theoretical development. The comparative ethos of this study draws on the Europeanization literature. The dialogue between discourse and comparative analysis identified two key features that are imperative for a comparative discourse theory. First, rather than being method-driven it must be question-and-problem driven. In other words, the practice of comparison is relative to, and should be first and foremost weighed against, the questions raised and the problems addressed. For instance, in this study the comparative method was used to explain why Europeanization produced similar and different representations of the world out there, and variation in the reproduction of the Finnish and British state identities. Second, and in so doing, it highlighted the need for comparative discourse analysis to comprise 'thick descriptive interpretations' of the historical context and concrete specificity (Howarth 2005: 332).

The problem-driven comparative approach based on the discourse analysis of particular case studies also makes a broader methodological contribution. Crucially, comparison enables explication of what, if anything, is context-specific in a given discursive context. This has particular significance for poststructuralist IR, which has tended to focus on the identity production of the United States. Comparison of the reproduction of state discourses on foreign and security policy and state identities thus facilitates spatial analysis of similarities and differences in the key components of the state. Comparison also gives alternative insights into the common-sense knowledge of identities, which is relevant in the face of criticism of discourse analysis for not taking us very far because the findings are often so obvious. The counter-argument is that we often do not have to look very far to find structures enabling and constraining the production of identities (Doty 1993: 308), and that discourse analysis allows (rather than forecloses) analysis of less transparent cases. Despite such obviousness, it facilitates explanation of how the commonsensical identities enabling and constraining action are arrived at. This study contributes to this debate in introducing a comparative element, suggesting that what was obvious in Britain was not necessarily obvious in

Finland, and vice versa. The obviousness of any particular finding or argument appears to be a relative phenomenon. In order to account for this relative character of social realities analysts should inquire more deeply into the common sense that shapes the identities and our reasoning.

In terms of its contribution to the literature on Europeanization, discourse analysis can enhance understanding of particular contexts (two EU member states in this study). It facilitates analysis and a deeper understanding of why variation occurs within seemingly similar contexts such as small member states and major member states. Specifically, the method applied in this book is valuable in terms of accounting for developments in domestic contexts over time. In analytical terms the research outcomes also support the attempt to move beyond dominant theoretical assumptions based on intergovernmental and supranational approaches. The findings suggest that Europeanization should be understood as a top-down and bottom-up process in which state identities are shaped by EU discourses that then feed back to the EU level (i.e. shape the EU discourse). As the methodological reflections suggest, the empirical starting point of the analysis – the discursive context of the member state – proved to be fruitful. However, in bringing the domestic arena back into the analysis of European integration, we should avoid thinking of the European and state-level of analysis as ontologically separate dimensions of our inquiries and rather see them as mutually constitutive. The stronger scholarly focus on local, regional and global processes that cut across conventional state boundaries gives this analytical proposition broader applicability.

Similarly, although the focus of this book is on conventional foreign and security policy and the state, the theory and methods blur the domestic/international distinction. In other words, the approach does not preclude the analysis of other kinds of political communities. Indeed, the value of analyses dealing with collective identities of various kinds of political communities such as the European Union is recognized. In terms of political analysis, the findings underline the need to account for increasingly overlapping local, regional and global identities. The poststructural reconceptualization of foreign policy embraced in this study and the recognition of Europeanization as a top-down and bottom-up process call for scholars to engage with diverse forms of political communities located on various levels of social and political interaction. The suggested added value of comparative discourse analysis deserves further research attention.

Notes

1 Introduction

1 The terminology used in the scholarly literature to refer to the institutional aspects and development of European integration varies. Terms such as the European Community (EC), European Communities (EC) and European Economic Communities (EEC) are often used to refer to the same political entity known as the European Union (EU) since the Treaty on the European Union (TEU) of 1992. Originally there were three Communities: the European Coal and Steel Community (ECSC), the European Atomic Energy Community (Euratom) and the European Economic Community (EEC). The three merged in 1967; since then it has become common to talk of the European Community. The term the European Union, and the abbreviated form the EU, are generally used in this book to mark this institutional development prior to 1992 as well, except when the reference is specifically to a certain treaty or institutional development, one of the three Communities, or where other writers or policy-makers are being quoted.

2 The CFSP was established by the TEU agreed in 1992. The Amsterdam Treaty clarified 'the possibility of a common defence policy' stated in conjunction with the CFSP in TEU, and established the European Security and Defence Policy (ESDP). This policy was renamed the Common Security and Defence Policy in 2010 in accordance with the Lisbon Treaty. The acronym CSDP is used to refer to the EU's defence policy since 1992 except when the reference is specifically to a particular Treaty or institutional development, or where other writers or policy-makers are being quoted.

2 The Europeanization of foreign policy

1 It is suggested that the debate between contemporary mainstream IR approaches, neo-realism and neo-liberalism, known as the neo-neo debate, is not between two world-views, and that they focus on similar questions and agree on a number of assumptions. As Lamy notes, it is assumed in both that states are value maximizers and that anarchy constrains their behaviour. However, a certain division of labour has been agreed between contemporary realists and liberals. Whereas neo-realists have tended to focus on security and military issues, neo-liberals concentrate on issues such as political economy, the environment and human rights (Lamy 2005: 215–218). Given the similarities and emergent consensus between these accounts some scholars have argued that we should talk not of a 'neo-neo debate' but of 'neo-neo synthesis' (Wæver 1996: 163–164).

2 This is not to suggest that realism was absent in the scholarly debates of the 1990s. Quite the reverse, it responded vigorously to criticism and significant theoretical development followed. In the early 2000s it has been regaining its position as the dominant approach to world politics, and it is difficult 'to avoid a sense that in the

twenty-first century realism is resurgent' (Williams 2005: 2). Nevertheless, as M.E. Smith (2004) suggests, realism's ontological assumptions resulting in a narrow conceptualization of integration as cooperation among states have made it an ill-suited approach to analysing recent developments in European foreign and security policy/ies. He argues, for instance, that increasing cooperation cannot be explained with reference to the three dominant EU member state(s) France, Germany and Britain. Although they are important, they have had distinctly different foreign and security policy aims in the post-Cold War world. Moreover, the role of the smaller member states in enhancing the cooperation has been greater than realists expected (M.E. Smith 2004: 20). Also Arter notes the contribution of the small states (Arter 2000), and Joenniemi suggests that small states are becoming more influential because they are less likely to have the 'hang ups' in relation to integration that the larger powers obsessed with questions of sovereignty may have (Joenniemi 1998).

3   For example, theories of interdependence suggest that as security concerns diminish among the set of states, and issues become increasingly entangled, the states are more likely to cooperate in managing the costs and benefits (Keohane and Nye 1977, M.E. Smith 2004: 21). As the following section suggests, this position resembles European-integration theories such as functionalism and Deutch's notion of security communities.

4   Deutsch identified two distinct kinds of security community. The first, the amalgamated security community, involved the formal merger of states in a larger community through institutional development, and was symptomatic of the neo-functionalist conceptualization of integration. The second, pluralistic community comprised entities in which the component states retained their separate identities. Integration, here, emerges without institutional fusion. (Rosamond 2000: 43)

5   Related to this, M. Smith describes the European order of the 1990s as complex, fluid and multilayered, thus raising important questions about sovereignty, autonomy and statehood (M. Smith 1994: 23, 42). Consequently, any analysis of the European order, including foreign policy, should (i) emphasize the strategies adopted by the state authorities in order to respond to the change; (ii) maintain a clear view of the ways in which the European order is changing because of the absence of consensus about the rules that clearly affect foreign policy action and strategies; and (iii) examine the crucial role played by the international institutions in setting limits on the legitimate behaviour of the states and other actors (M. Smith 1994: 43).

6   Knill also notes that the study of Europeanization has traditionally concerned developments on the supranational level (Knill 2001).

7   Börzel and Risse distinguish three major dimensions along which the domestic impact of Europeanization has been analysed, and processes of domestic change have been traced (Börzel and Risse 2000). First, there are more and more policy areas that are affected by policy-making in Brussels (Radaelli 2000, Caporaso and Jupille 2001, Knill 2001). Second, if policies are increasingly made at the European level there are likely to be consequences for domestic politics, defined as processes of societal interest formation, aggregation and representation. Studies have focused on how domestic actors strive to channel their interests into the European policy-making process (Greenwood and Aspinwall 1998, Raunio and Tiilikainen 2003), and how electoral and party politics are shaped in the face of integration (Aspinwall 2004). Finally, most works on the impact of Europeanization focus on domestic institutions, both formal and informal. Scholars have analysed whether and to what extent European processes, policies, and institutions affect domestic systems of interest intermediation (Jupille and Caporaso 1999, Knill 2001, M.E. Smith 2004).

8   White notes that the process began almost immediately after the Second World War when the fears of a resurgent Germany prompted the Dunkirk Treaty (1947) of mutual defence between Britain and France, followed by the Brussels Treaty (1948) extending the collective defence in Belgium, the Netherlands and Luxemburg. In the face of

increasing East–West tension manifested in the Berlin crisis in 1948 negotiations began to include the United States and Canada in collective European defence arrangements, which resulted in the North Atlantic Treaty (1949) establishing transatlantic defence arrangements (White 2001: 4).

9   'Civilian power Europe' is related to European diplomatic coordination carried out mainly on the economic level, and not in the traditional field of security and defence (M. Smith 2003: 559).

10 Keatinge's (1983) analysis focuses on Irish foreign policy, and Saeter (1984) applied a similar perspective to West Germany (both cited in Featherstone 2003: 10). The term Europeanization was also applied within the NATO context in the literature on European security, signifying the strengthening of the 'European pillar' , in other words the increasing influence and responsibilities of European states within the Alliance (Allen 1998).

11 Although the focus on the relationship between the EU and the domestic level of governance connects studies of Europeanization in different fields, scholars in the field of foreign policy are particularly keen to theorize this relationship. However, other fields have also moved in this direction. For instance, largely EU-centric and top-down-orientated comparative politics now also focus on institution building at the European level (Featherstone 2003: 13).

3   Foreign policy and state identity: towards comparative discourse analysis

1   Many social constructivists have attempted to solve the structure and agency problem by means of structuration theory, as articulated by Anthony Giddens. It is an ambitious theoretical attempt to transcend the dualism. Giddens prefers the word duality instead of dualism. Structure and agency are seen as two sides of the same coin, analytically separable but ontologically interwoven (Giddens 1976: 197, Hay 1995). This methodological claim has led to a well-established method of temporarily bracketing off agency – or structure-related factors. Basically this methodological choice involves isolating structural and agential factors for the practical purposes of the research. This allows analysis of the agential factors of national foreign policy-making, rather independently of the context (structural dimension), for instance. Alternatively, one could focus on the context (structural factors), such as the CFSP and the CSDP, and leave the agential factors aside. In the end these analytical engagements should be brought together.

2   More broadly this reflects the so-called 'levels of analysis problem' in IR, drawing on the separation of the domestic and international spheres of politics. Whereas in political science a state could be viewed as constituting some of the structures of a given society, in IR it is pre-dominantly an agent (reflecting different degrees of agency) operating in the anarchical system, often understood as the structure (Waltz 1979, Wendt 1992). It is therefore often considered a unitary actor, a 'pre-social' and 'exogenously given' political entity with a coherent identity. (S. Smith 2000: 160–162)

3   On methods see, Doty (1993), Campbell (1998), Milliken (1999), Laffey and Weldes (2004), for instance. On empirical contributions, see Doty on North-South Relations (1996), Campbell on US foreign policy (1993, 1998), Weldes on the Cuban missile crisis (1996), Muppidi on US-Indian Relations (1999).

4   Some of these authors might label themselves International Relations scholars. However, their research interests largely focus on European integration or the EU. On the other hand, some political scientists have explicitly problematized the international/domestic divide and have highlighted the interrelationship between the two.

5   Discourse analysis as an integration theory is anticipated by Ole Wæver (2004: 198). He notes that his categorization 'represents a picture that is much more logically structured than the experience "on the ground" where practitioners of discourse analysis will often feel that they simply analyse some European subject of interest'.

6 The works of Doty (1993, 1996), Campbell (1998), Weldes (1996) and Weldes *et al.*
   (1999) theorize US foreign policy.
7 According to Wæver (2004: 205) – the most prominent figure behind the approach –
   this frame of analysis is more traditional than many other discursive approaches in its
   focus on national spaces of political debate and in its explicit ambition to explain 'about
   which some poststructuralist discourse analysts remain sceptical'.

4 The Europeanization of Finnish foreign and security policy discourse: from neutrality to alignment identity

1 The arrangement was based on the 1948 Treaty for Friendship, Cooperation and
   Mutual Assistance (FCMA) with the Soviet Union, which specified that 'in the event
   of Finland, or the Soviet Union through Finland, becoming the object of an armed
   attack by Germany, or any other state allied with the latter, Finland will … fight to
   repel the attack independently or with assistance provided by the Soviet Union' (YYA-
   sopimus 1948, my translation).
2 This observation is based on a set of empirical material comprising the Parliamentary
   Defence Policy Council's estimate of developments in European Security
   (Parlamentaarinen puolustuspoliittinen neuvottelukunta 1990); the Report by the
   Council of State to Parliament on Foreign and Security Policy (Council of State 1995);
   two Reports by the Council of State to Parliament on Security and Defence Policy
   (Council of State 1997, Council of State 2001); and the Parliamentary debates on these
   documents (Eduskunta 1995a, 1995b, 1997a, 1997b, 2001a, 2001b).
3 Finland's international activity is often highlighted in foreign policy discourse.
   However, in the 1950s the policy leadership was indicating that Finland could not take
   part in Western European economic integration due to Soviet pressure. More recent
   and critical literature, however, suggests that the policy makers were highly self-
   conscious and self-restricting. On the other hand, Finland put forward two major
   international security initiatives during the Cold War. The first one was the Conference
   for Security and Cooperation in Europe (CSCE), which was further institutionalized
   as the Organization for Security and Cooperation in Europe (OSCE) in 1995, and the
   second one proposed a nuclear-weapons-free zone in Northern Europe. The OSCE has
   been widely viewed as the greatest achievement of post-war Finnish foreign policy,
   whereas the nuclear-free zone proved to be difficult for the Nordic countries that were
   NATO members.
4 After President Paasikivi's retirement Urho Kekkonen was elected as the president in
   1955. He stayed in office for twenty-six years. Whereas Paasikivi is often cited as the
   president who laid the foundations of the Finnish post-war foreign and security policy
   (Kekkonen 1957, Apunen 1977), neutrality is seen as Kekkonen's life-long vocation
   (Lipponen 2001). Paasikivi's policy, it is argued, was based on appeasement with the
   Soviet Union and the establishment of good-neighbour relations. Kekkonen, in turn,
   is predominantly viewed as the guardian of these good relations, and the president
   who promoted, consolidated and then institutionalized Finnish neutrality. Finnish post-
   war foreign and security policy is therefore labelled the 'Paasikivi-Kekkonen line'
   (Apunen 1977, my translation).
5 The terms 'particular kind of neutrality' and 'coloured neutrality' suggest that Finnish
   neutrality was spurious. In other words, the most important aim of Finnish foreign
   policy was to prevent Soviet military and political intervention rather than to acquire
   a neutral position in world politics.
6 The FCMA treaty constituted the basis of Finnish post-war foreign policy (Kekkonen
   1982, Väyrynen 1993). It included a security article and established a collective
   security guarantee between Finland and the Soviet Union. The treaty stated that if
   Finland was invaded and/or its territory was to be used to attack the Soviet Union,
   Finland would defend its territory with all means available, if needed, with Soviet
   assistance or together with the Soviet Union (YYA-sopimus 1948).

7 President Kekkonen was in office from 1956–1982, and has been regarded as the driver of the Finnish neutrality policy. He is also often seen as a president who used his constitutional powers extensively. The most important issue in terms of this study concerns Section 33 of the 1919 Constitution Act (overruled in 2000), with its general authorization for the direction of foreign policy: the relations of Finland with foreign powers shall be determined by the president.

8 The Soviet Union invaded Finland in November 1939. This led to the so-called Winter War, which ended in a truce after three-and-a-half months. As a result Finland had to cede 10 per cent of its territory, Finland, supported by Germany invaded the Soviet Union in 1941. This so-called Continuation War ended in June 1944, and as a result the 1940 borders were restored. Further, Finland lost its land link to the Barents Sea, and agreed to a Soviet military base next to Helsinki. It also agreed to force out the remaining German troops, which led to the third Finnish war, the so-called War of Lapland against Germany in 1944. (Brady n.d.)

9 When the Maastricht Treaty was agreed in 1992 the term European Union quickly replaced the term European Community in Finland. However, the latter term is still used in some specific legal and administrative discourses dealing with EU institutions and legislation of the first pillar, for instance. Because of the Lisbon treaty reforms (2009) the terms European Community is fading away in official documents and public discussion.

10 Constructing a square equal in area to a circle using only a straightedge and compass was one of the three geometric problems of antiquity. It was finally deemed impossible to solve in 1882 when pi was proven to be transcendental (see Weisstein, n.d.).

11 The 1948 Paris Peace Treaty included several military and weapons restrictions. Part III, Articles 13–22, limited the future troop strength to 34,400 soldiers, the navy to 4,500 individuals, and the air force to 3,000. There were also exclusions of equipment of an offensive nature, such as bombers, missiles, and submarines. Warships could not exceed a combined total of 10,000 tons. The air force could acquire up to sixty combat planes, but they were not to include bombers or fighter bombers. None of the services was allowed to construct, to procure, or to test nuclear weapons (Suomen rauhansopimus 1947)

12 During the EEA negotiations the foreign policy leadership had constantly argued that the EEA was sufficient for Finland and that there was no need to discuss EC/EU membership. Suddenly, when the EEA treaty was going through the ratification process in the Finnish Parliament the Government announced that it was not adequate to secure Finnish long-term trade interests given that Sweden (1990) and Austria (1989) had both applied for full EC membership (Rehn 1993: 205–207).

13 The terms deployed to capture the period of so-called 'rapid reorientation' (Joenniemi 2001) are illustrative. It was referred to as the 'Westernization' or 'Europeanization' of Finnish policy, and described as a move 'from Moscow to Brussels', 'from neutrality to alignment' (Forsberg and Vogt 2003, my translation). Notwithstanding the differences among these scholars, they broadly agreed on the diminishing importance of the East and of neutrality in the Finnish foreign policy. In contrast, the significance of the West increased, mainly through economic integration and the EU's foreign, security and defence policies, as well as NATO's Partnership for Peace programme (PfP).

14 In 1995 the foreign policy leadership indicated that it was privately pushed to clarify the Finnish position in several high-level meetings during the membership negotiations (Koivisto 1995: 548, 550).

15 The 1995 report is a 78-page document supplemented with maps and annexes. It was published in Finnish and translated into English. The analysis of the White Paper is based on the English version. The documentation of the related parliamentary hearings is in Finnish and the translations are mine. The Report has two main sections: (i) *The International Security Environment and Finland* (11–56); and (ii) *The Development of Finland's Security Policy* (63–69). The first section – some three quarters of the document – establishes what existed in terms of Finland's foreign and security policy

and clarifies its position and policies towards its external environment. The second part, a seven-page concluding section, outlines the development of Finnish security policy in the near future. (Council of State 1995).

Significantly, the 1995 white paper informed the subsequent security and defence policy reports in 1997 and 2001. Accordingly, it articulates a 'security environment' in which Finland found itself during the 1990s and beyond, and is the key document on Finland's foreign, security and defence policy of the 1990s. It addresses the changed external environment and clarifies Finland's changed position. As such it is an appropriate starting point for the analysis of the new Finnish security discourse.

16 By operational logic I mean a structure in which things are given meaning and simultaneously positioned vis-à-vis other subjects and objects (Doty 1993).

17 This polarized view of the East and the West in the debate on Finnish foreign policy and security is, of course, oversimplified. The representations are multifaceted and their meanings have never been fully established. For instance, several competing political opinions emerged during the time of autonomy (1809–1917) and the 'national awakening'. Whereas some of elite were favourable to Russia, others wanted to re-establish Finland's historical position as part of Sweden. The idea of national self-determination also ran high in both camps, and some prominent figures were openly hostile towards Russia (Harle and Moisio 2000: 72–82).

18 The research design is described in detail in Chapter 2.

19 The 1997 white paper, *The European Security Development and Finnish Defence*, and the 2001 paper, *The Finnish Security and Defence Policy*, are both 100 pages long, plus the annexes. The 1997 report is divided into two main sections: 'European Security Development and Finland', and the 'Development of Finland's Defence'. Whereas the first section (42 pages) articulates the environment within which Finland found itself in terms of security and defence, the second (45 pages) sets out the main guidelines for developing the Finnish defence policy. The 2001 paper comprises four main sections. Again the first section on 'the Security Environment and Finland's Policy' (43 pages) gives the context in which the Finnish policy is then outlined in subsequent sections on 'Developing Finland's Defence' (22 pages), 'International Crisis Management' (11 pages) and 'Precautionary Measures and Combating Threats to Society' (10 pages) (Council of State 1997, 2001).

20 The initiative was launched in 1997 by the Finnish prime minister, Paavo Lipponen, It did not cover traditional 'hard' security-policy issues, promoting 'soft' security issues instead and advocating strategies associated with economics, the environment and nuclear safety (Ojanen, Herolf, Lindahl 2000). The inclusion of non-EU member states in the initiative had implications for the EU's external relations, and has been linked to its emerging foreign and security policy.

5 The Europeanization of British foreign and security policy discourse: re-articulating the great-power identity

1 As George suggests, the hesitance to adopt the term EU after the Maastricht Treaty and usage of Communities and the EEC is an example of the British 'awkwardness' in relation to the rest of Europe (George 1998: 2). Moreover, the expression '(European) Common Market' used in Britain and the United States indicates a degree of exceptionality (George 1998: 2, Diez 2001).

2 As in the previous case here, too, I emphasize that my purpose is not to examine change and continuity in the British foreign and security *policy*, but to analyse the effect of the CFSP and the CSDP on the official discourse.

3 This material includes six Statements on Defence Estimates (SDEs) from 1990 to 1996 produced by the Ministry of Defence (Ministry of Defence 1990, 1991, 1992, 1993, 1994, 1995, 1996), the Strategic Defence Review (Ministry of Defence 1998); the 1999 Defence White Paper (Ministry of Defence 1999); the 2001 Ministry of Defence Policy

Paper on European Defence (Ministry of Defence 2001); a 1992 Conservative Party Election Manifesto (Conservative Party 1992), ten UK prime ministers' speeches addressing the British foreign and security policy and the developing CFSP and the CSDP (Thatcher 1990, Major 1994, Blair 1997a, 1997b, Blair 1998a, 1998b, 1998c, 1998d), the Joint British–French declaration on European Defence in St Malo (British–French Summit 1998); and parliamentary debates relating to SDR (House of Commons 1998), the 1999 Defence White Paper and the 2001 European Defence Paper in the House of Commons (House of Commons 2000a, 2000b and 2001).

4   The notion of decline underpins the seminal volume on British foreign policy edited by M. Smith, S. Smith and B. White (1988), for instance. As Allen (1988) notes, implicit in many of the chapters in this book is the argument that Britain has ceased to be a global power with global interests.

5   The failed Franco–British intervention in Suez in 1956 following Egypt's decision to nationalize the Anglo-French Suez Canal Company is often seen as a significant watershed in Britain's post-war history. Sanders, for instance, suggests that although Britain's power in the world was already in decline, the Suez Crisis heralded the large-scale withdrawal from the Empire and the shift towards Europe that occurred after the 1960s. (Sanders 1990: 88–89)

6   Neumann suggests that in contemporary discourses of European identity formation the East is used as a sign of otherness on the all-European, regional and national levels (Neumann 1998).

7   The East, characterized by political and economic instability that could lead to disputes and conflicts, was important, if not influential, in that it is constructed as a test of the EU's ability to establish stability. The developing South has a marginal role in the 1997 and 1998 foreign policy documents, in other words the discussions are Euro- and US-centric. Accordingly, the British subject position emerges in relation to the European Union and the United States in the 1998 data.

8   The analysis of the debates proceeded in two phases. First, I read the Official Reports of the UK Parliament, called Hansard, for the relevant time periods, with an eye on the debates concerning the SDR, the CFSP and the CSDP. Second, I chose seven debates for analysis: on the SDR, after its publication, on 8 July 1998 and 19 October 1998; on the European Union on 11 November 1998; on Foreign Affairs and Defence on 27 November 1998; and the post-St Malo debates on the European Council on 14 December 1998, on defence on 22 March 1999 and on Foreign and Commonwealth Affairs on 18 May 1999 (in the last two, European defence cooperation was addressed in distinct sections).

9   The acronym 'GPD 1' is used for the great-power discourse prior to the 1998 re-articulation and 'GPD 2' for the 1998 re-articulation.

10   The parliamentary debates in the House of Commons on foreign and security policy in 1999, 2000 and 2001 were examined. The analysis showed that EU foreign and security policy was one of the most hotly debated issues during this period. Two debates were chosen for closer analysis: (i) the debate on the 1999 white paper on 22 and 28 February 2000 and (ii) the debate on the European Security and Defence Policy on 19 March 2001, which explicitly addressed the issues clarified in the 2001 policy paper on European Defence.

6   Comparing the reproduction of state identities in Finland and Britain

1   President Koivisto's reasoning on the Baltic State question in 1991 is illustrative. He noted the British Prime Minister John Major's activism in finding a peaceful solution to the Baltic States' independence aspirations. His conclusion that after Major's talks with the Soviet Union there was no need for an active Finnish policy towards the Baltic States (Koivisto 1995) generated a representation of Finland as a passive and neutral state, and Britain as the major Western power in European security.

Bibliography

Adler, E. (1997) 'Seizing the middle ground: constructivism in world politics', *European Journal of International Relations* 3: 319–363.

Aggestam, L. (2004) 'Role identity and the Europeanisation of foreign policy' in Tonra, B. and Christiansen, T. (eds) *Rethinking European Union Foreign Policy*, Manchester: Manchester University Press.

Allen, D. (1988) 'Britain and Western Europe' in Smith, M., Smith, S. and White, B. (eds), *British Foreign Policy: tradition, transformation and change*, London: Unwin Hyman.

Allison, G.T. (1971) *Essence of Decision: explaining the Cuban missile crisis*, Boston, MA: Little, Brown and Company.

Andreatta, F. (1997) 'The Bosnian war and the new world order: failure and success of international intervention', *Occasional Papers*, no. 1, Paris: Institute for Security Studies for Western European Union.

Apunen, O. (1977) *Paasikiven-Kekkosen linja* (*Paasikivi-Kekkonen Policy*), Helsinki: Tammi.

Arter, D. (1995) 'The EU referendum in Finland on 16 October 1994: a vote for the west, not for the Maastricht', *Journal of European Public Policy* 33: 361–387.

Arter, D. (1996) 'Finland: from neutrality to NATO?', *European Security* 5: 614–632.

Arter, D. (2000) 'Small-state influence within the EU: the case of Finland's "northern dimension initiative"', *Journal of Common Market Studies* 38: 677–697.

Aspinwall, M. (2004) *Rethinking Britain and Europe: plurality elections, party management and British policy on European integration*, Manchester: Manchester University Press.

Avery, G. and Missiroli, A. (2007) 'Foreword', in Avery, G. *et al. The EU Foreign Service: how to build a more effective common policy*, EPC Working Paper, no. 28. Online. Available: www.epc.eu/TEWN/pdf/555858396_EPC%20Working%20Paper%2028%20 The%20EU%20Foreign%20Service.pdf (accessed 23 May 2008).

Bache, I. (2008) *Europeanization and Multi-Level Governance: cohesion policy in the European Union and Britain*, Lanham, MA: Rowman and Littlefield.

Berger, T.U. (1996) 'Norms, identity, and national security in Germany and Japan' in Katzenstein (ed.) *The Culture of National Security: norms and identity in world politics*, New York: Columbia University Press.

Biswas, S. (2002) 'W(h)ither the nation state? National and state identity in the face of fragmentation and globalization', *Global Society* 16: 175–198.

Blair, T. (1997a) 'Speech by the Prime Minister Tony Blair at the Lord Mayor's Banquet – Friday 10 November 1997'. Online. Available: www.number-10.gov.uk/output/Page 1070.asp (accessed 12 December 2002).

Blair, T. (1997b) 'Speech by the Prime Minister Tony Blair at the British/Indian Golden Jubilee Banquet – Thursday 13 November 1997'. Online. Available: www.number-10. gov.uk/output/Page1073.asp (accessed 12 December 2002).

Blair, T. (1998a) 'Prime Minister's speech to the French National Assembly – Tuesday 24 March 1998'. Online. Available: www.number-10.gov.uk/output/Page1160.asp (accessed 12 December 2002).

Blair, T. (1998b) 'Speech by the Prime Minister – change: a modern Britain in a modern Europe – Tuesday 20 January 1998'. Online. Available: www.number-10.gov.uk/ output/Page1150.asp (accessed 12 December 2002).

Blair, T. (1998c). 'Speech by the Prime Minister at the US State Department – Friday 6 February 1998'. Online. Available: www.number-10.gov.uk/output/Page1155.asp (accessed 12 December 2002).

Blair, T. (1998d) 'Speech by the Prime Minister on foreign affairs – Tuesday 15 December 1998'. Online. Available: www.number-10.gov.uk/output/Page1168.asp (accessed 12 December 2002).

Börzel, T.A. and Risse, T. (2000) 'When Europe hits home: Europeanization and domestic change', *European Integration Online Papers (EIoP)* 4(12). Online. Available: http:// eiop.or.at/eiop (accessed 12 July 2004).

Brady, J. (n. d.) 'Chronology of Finnish history', *Virtual Finland Portal*. Online. Available: http://virtual.finland.fi/netcomm/news/showarticle.asp?intNWSAID=25911 (accessed 12 January 2005).

Bretherton, C. and Vogler, J. (2006) *The European Union as a Global Actor*, 2nd edn, London: Routledge.

British–French Summit (1998) in Rutten, M. (compiled) (2001) *From St Malo to Nice: European defence: core documents*, Chaillot Paper, no. 47, Paris: The Institute for Security Studies for Western European Union.

Browning, C.S. (1999) 'Coming home or moving home?: "westernising" narratives in Finnish foreign policy and the reinterpretation of past identities', *FIIA Working Papers*, Helsinki: Finnish Institute of International Affairs.

Browning, C.S. (2003) 'Constructing Finnish national identity and foreign policy, 1809–2000' unpublished Ph. D. thesis, University of Wales at Aberystwyth.

Bulmer, S. (2007) 'Theorizing Europeanization', in Granziano, P. and Vink, M.P. (eds) *Europeanization: new research agendas*, Basingstoke: Palgrave.

Campbell, D. (1993) *Politics without Principle: sovereignty, ethics, and the narratives of the Gulf War*, Boulder, CO: Lynne Rienner Publishers.

Campbell, D. (1998) *Writing Security: United States foreign policy and the politics of identity*, Minneapolis, MN: University of Minnesota Press.

Caporaso, J.A. and Jupille, J. (2001) 'The Europeanization of social policy and domestic political change', in Green Gowles, M., Caporaso, J.A. and Risse, T. (eds), *Transforming Europe: Europeanization and domestic change*, Ithaca, NY: Cornell University Press.

Carlsnaes, W. (1993) 'Sweden facing the new Europe: whiter neutrality?' *European Security* 2: 71–89.

Carlsnaes, W. (2004) 'Introduction', in Carlsnaes, W., Sjursen, H. and White, B. (eds) *Contemporary European Foreign Policy*, London: Sage.

Carlsnaes, W., Sjursen, H. and White, B. (eds) (2004) *Contemporary European Foreign Policy*, London: Sage.

Christiansen, T., Jørgensen, K.E. and Wiener, A. (2001) 'Introduction', in Christiansen, T., Jørgensen, K.E. and Wiener, A. (eds) *The Social Construction of Europe*, London: Sage.

Clark, I. (1999) *Globalization and International Relations Theory*, New York and Oxford: Oxford University Press.

Conservative Party (1992) 'Conservative Party general election manifesto 1992', in Dale, I. (ed.) (1997) *Conservative Party General Election Manifestos 1900–1997*, London: Routledge.

Conservative Party (1997) 'Conservative Party general election manifesto 1997', in Dale, I. (ed.) *Conservative Party General Election Manifestos 1900–1997*, London: Routledge.

Council of the European Union (2000) *Military capabilities commitment declaration*, 1 December 2000, Brussels. Online. Available: http://register.consilium.europa.eu/pdf/en/00/st13/st13799.en00.pdf (accessed 26 May 2010).

Council of the European Union (2001) *Declaration by the Presidency on behalf of the European Union on the signing of the framework agreement in Skopje*, 13 August 2001, Brussels. Online. Available: www.consilium.europa.eu/ueDocs/cms_Data/docs/press Data/en/cfsp/11425.en1.doc.html (accessed 26 May 2010).

Council of the European Union (2003a) *Draft declaration on EU military capabilities*, 19 May 2003. Online. Available: http://register.consilium.europa.eu/pdf/en/03/st09/st09132-re02.en03.pdf (accessed 26 May 2010).

Council of the European Union (2003b) *Press release 11439/1/03 of 2522nd Council meeting*, 21 July 2003, Brussels. Online. Available: www.consilium.europa.eu/uedocs/cms_data/docs/pressdata/en/gena/76749.pdf (accessed 26 May 2010).

Council of the European Union (2003c) *A secure Europe in a better world: European security strategy*, 12 December 2003, Brussels. Online. Available: www.consilium.europa.eu/uedocs/cmsUpload/78367.pdf (accessed 26 May 2010).

Council of the European Union (2008) *Report on the implementation of the European security strategy – providing security in a changing world*, 11 December 2008, Brussels. Online. Available: www.consilium.europa.eu/ueDocs/cms_Data/docs/pressdata/EN/reports/104630.pdf (accessed 26 May 2010).

Council of State (1995) *Security in a Changing World: guidelines for Finland's security policy*, report by the Council of State to the Parliament 6 June 1995, Helsinki: Publications of the Foreign Ministry, J-paino ky.

Council of State (1997) *The Finnish Security and Defence Policy*, report by the Council of State to the Parliament on 17 March 1997, Helsinki: Oy Edita Ab.

Council of State (2001) *The Finnish Security and Defence Policy*, report by the Council of State to the Parliament 13 June 2001, Helsinki: Edita Plc.

Cramér, P. (1998) *Neutralitet och europeisk integration* (*Neutrality and European Integration*), Stockholm: Norstedts Juridik AB.

Delanty, G. and Rumford, C. (2005) *Rethinking Europe: social theory and the implications of Europeanization*, London: Routledge.

Deutsch, K.W. (1968) *The Analysis of International Relations*, Englewood Cliffs, NJ: Prentice Hall.

Diez, T. (1999) 'Riding the am-track through Europe; or, the pitfalls of a rationalist journey through European integration', *Millennium Journal of International Studies* 28: 355–369.

Diez, T. (2001) 'Speaking "Europe": the politics of integration discourse', in Christiansen, T. Jørgensen, K.E. and Wiener, A. (eds) *The Social Construction of Europe*, London: Sage.

Doty, R.L. (1993) 'Foreign policy as social construction: a post-positivist analysis of United States counterinsurgency policy in the Philippines', *International Studies Quarterly* 37: 297–320.

Doty, R.L. (1996) *Imperial Encounters: the politics of representation in north–south relations*, Minneapolis, MN: University of Minnesota Press.

Doty, R.L. (2000) 'Desire all the way down', *Review of International Studies* 26: 137–139.

Dover, R. (2007) *Europeanization of British defence policy*, Aldershot: Ashgate.

Driver, S. and L. Martell (1998) *New Labour: politics after Thatcherism*, Cambridge: Polity.

Duchêne, F. (1973) 'The European Community and the uncertainties of interdependence', in Kohnstamm, M. and Hager, W. (eds) *A Nation Writ Large?: foreign policy problems before the community*, London: Macmillan.

Eduskunta (Parliament of Finland) (1995a) 'Valtiopäiväasiakirjat lähetekeskustelu 6.6.1995: valtioneuvoston selonteko 1/1995' ('Parliamentary documents first hearing 6 June 1995: report by the Council of State to the Parliament 1/1995'), Helsinki: Eduskunta. Online. Available: www.eduskunta.fi (accessed 12 June 2002).

Eduskunta (Parliament of Finland) (1995b) 'Valtiopäiväasiakirjat palautekeskustelu 31.10., 1. ja 2.11. 1995: report by the Council of State to the Parliament 1/1995' ('Parliamentary documents second hearing 31 October, 1 and 2 November 1995: report by the Council of State 1/1995'), Helsinki: Eduskunta. Online. Available: www.eduskunta.fi (accessed 12 June 2002).

Eduskunta (Parliament of Finland) (1997a) 'Valtiopäiväasiakirjat lähetekeskustelu 17. ja 18.3.1997: valtioneuvoston selonteko 1/1997' ('Parliamentary documents first hearing 17 and 18 March 1997: report by the Council of State to the Parliament 1/1997'), Helsinki: Eduskunta. Online. Available: www.eduskunta.fi (accessed 12 June 2002).

Eduskunta (Parliament of Finland) (1997b) 'Valtiopäiväasiakirjat palautekeskustelu 27., 28. ja 30.5. 1997: valtioneuvoston selonteko 1/1997' ('Parliamentary documents second hearing 27, 28 and 30 May 1997: report by the Council of State to the Parliament 1/1997'), Helsinki: Eduskunta. Online. Available www.eduskunta.fi (accessed 12 June 2002).

Eduskunta (Parliament of Finland) (2001a) 'Valtiopäiväasiakirjat lähetekeskustelu 5., 6. ja 7.9.2001: valtioneuvoston selonteko 2/2001' ('Parliamentary documents first Hearing 5, 6 and 7 September 2001: report by the Council of State to the Parliament 2/2001'), Helsinki: Eduskunta. Online. Available: www.eduskunta.fi (accessed 12 June 2002).

Eduskunta (Parliament of Finland) (2001b) 'Valtiopäiväasiakirjat palautekeskustelu 19.12.2001: valtioneuvoston selonteko 2/2002' ('Parliamentary documents second hearing 19 December 2001; report by the Council of State to the Parliament 2/2002'), Helsinki: Eduskunta. Online. Available: www.eduskunta.fi (accessed 12 June 2002).

Fawcett, L.L.E. and Hurrell, A. (1997) *Regionalism in World Politics: regional organization and international order*, Oxford: Oxford University Press.

Featherstone, K. (2003) 'Introduction: in the name of "Europe"', in Featherstone, K. and Radaelli, C.M. (eds) *The Politics of Europeanization*, Oxford: Oxford University Press.

Fierke, K.M. and Wiener, A. (2001) 'Constructing institutional interests: EU and NATO enlargement', in Christiansen, T., Jørgensen, K.E. and Wiener, A. (eds) *The Social Construction of Europe*, London: Sage.

Forsberg, T. and Vogt, H. (2003) 'Suomen ulkopolitiikan eurooppalaistumien' ('The Europeanization of the Finnish foreign policy'), *Suomen poliittinen järjestelmä* (The Finnish Political System). Online. Available: www.valt.helsinki.fi/vol/spj/electures/forsberg-vogt.htm (accessed 23 February 2004).

Forster, A. (1998) 'Britain: still an awkward partner?', *Journal of European Studies* 6: 41–57.

Forster, A. (2000). 'Britain', in Manners, I. and Whitman, R. (eds) *The Foreign Policies of the European Union Member States*, Manchester: Manchester University Press.

Foucault, M. (1972) *The Archaeology of Knowledge*. London: Tavistock.

George, S. (1998) *An Awkward Partner: Britain in the European Community*, Oxford: Oxford University Press.

Giddens, A. (1976) *New Rules of Sociological Method: a positive critique of interpretative sociologies*, London: Hutchinson.

Gilpin, R. (1987) *The Political Economy of International Relations*, Princeton, NJ: Princeton University Press.

Gingsberg, R.H. (2003) *The European Union in International Politics: baptism by fire*. Lanham, MD: Rowman and Littlefield.

Giuliani, M. (2003) 'Europeanization in comparative perspective: institutional and national adaptation', in Featherstone, K. and Radaelli, C.M. (eds) *The Politics of Europeanization*, Oxford: Oxford University Press.

Glarbo, K. 'Reconstructing a common European foreign policy', in Christiansen, T., Jørgensen, K.E. and Wiener, A. (eds) *The Social Construction of Europe*, London: Sage.

Goetschel, L. (1999) 'Neutrality, a really dead concept?', *Cooperation and Conflict* 34: 115–139.

Græger, N., Larsen, H. and Ojanen, H. (2002) *The ESDP and the Nordic Countries: four variations on a theme*, Helsinki: The Finnish Institute of International Affairs.

Green Cowles, M., Caporaso, J.A. and Risse-Kappen, T. (eds) (2001) *Transforming Europe: Europeanization and domestic change*, Ithaca, NY: Cornell University Press.

Greenwood, J. and Aspinwall, M. (1998) *Collective Action in the European Union: interests and the new politics of associability*, London: Routlege.

Grevi, G. and Keohane, D. (2009) 'ESDP resources', in Grevi, G., Helly, D. and Keohane, D. (eds), *European Security and Defence Policy: the first 10 years (1999–2009)*, Paris: European Union Institute for Security Studies.

Haas, E.B. (1968) *The Uniting of Europe: political, social, and economic forces 1950–1957*, Stanford, CA: Stanford University Press.

Hansen, L. (2002) 'Introduction', in Hansen, L. and Wæver, O. (ed) *European Integration and National Identity: the challenge of the Nordic states*, London: Routledge.

Harle, V. and Moisio, S. (2000) *Missä on Suomi?: kansallisen identiteettipolitiikan historia ja geopolitiikka*, Tampere: Vastapaino.

Hay, C. (1995) 'Structure and agency', in Marsh, D. and Stoker, G. *Theory and Methods in Political Science*, London: Macmillan.

Hay, C. (2002) *Political Analysis: a critical introduction*, Basingstoke: Palgrave.

Hay, C. and Rosamond, B. (2002) 'Globalization, European integration and the discursive construction of economic imperatives', *Journal of European Public Policy* 9: 147–167.

Hay, C., Watson, M. and Wincott, D. (1999). *Globalisation, European Integration and the Persistence of European Social Models*, Brighton: Sussex European Institute.

Held, D. (1999) *Global Transformations: politics, economics and culture*, Stanford, CA: Stanford University Press.

Helsinki European Council (1999) *Presidency Conclusions*, 10 and 11 December 1999. Online. Available: www.consilium.europa.eu/ueDocs/cms_Data/docs/pressData/en/ec/ACFA4C.htm (accessed 26 May 2010).

Hey, J.A.K. (2003) 'Introducing small state foreign policy', Hey, J.A.K. (ed.), *Small States in World Politics: explaining foreign policy behaviour*, London: Lynne Rienner.

Hill, C. (1988) 'The historical background: past and present in British foreign policy', in Smith, M., Smith, S. and White, B. (eds), *British Foreign Policy: tradition, change and transformation*, London: Unwin Hyman.

Hill, C. (1993) 'The Capability-expectation gap, or conceptualizing Europe's international role', *Journal of Common Market Studies* 31: 305–328.

Hill, C. (1996a) 'United Kingdom: sharpening contradictions', in Hill, C. (ed.) *The Actors in Europe's Foreign Policy*, London: Routledge.

Hill, C. (ed.) (1996b) *The Actors in Europe's Foreign Policy*, London: Routledge.

Hix, S. (1994) 'The study of European Community: the challenge to comparative politics', *West European Politics* 17: 1–30.

Hix, S. (1999) *The Political System of the European Union*, London: Macmillan.

Hix, S. and Goetz, K.H. (2000) *Europeanised Politics?: European integration and national political systems*, Portland, OR: Frank Cass.

Hooghe, L. and Marks, G. (2001) *Multi-Level Governance and European Integration*, Oxford: Rowman & Littlefield.

Hopf, T. (1998) 'The promise of constructivism in international relations theory', *International Security* 23: 171–200.

House of Commons (1998) 'Commons Hansard debates text for Monday 19 October 1998', *Hansard – House of Commons Debates*. Online. Available: www.publications. parliament.uk/pa/cm199798/cmhansrd/vo981019/debindx/81019-x.htm (Accessed 12 October 2004).

House of Commons (2000a) 'Commons Hansard debates text for Monday 28 Feb 2000 – defence white paper', *Hansard – House of Commons Debates*. Online. Available: www.publications.parliament.uk/pa/cm199900/cmhansrd/vo000228/debindx/00228-x.htm (accessed 12 September 2004).

House of Commons (2000b) 'Commons Hansard debates text for Tuesday 22 Feb 2000 – defence white paper' (2000), *Hansard – House of Commons Debates*. Online. Available: www.publications.parliament.uk/pa/cm199900/cmhansrd/vo000222/debindx/00222-x.htm (accessed 12 September 2004).

House of Commons (2001) 'Commons Hansard debates text for Monday 19 Mar 2001 – European security and defence policy', *Hansard – House of Commons Debates*. Online. Available: www.publications.parliament.uk/pa/cm200001/cmhansrd/vo010319/debindx/10319-x.htm (accessed 12 September 2004).

Howarth, D.R. (2005) 'Applying discourse theory: the method of articulation', in Howarth, D.R. and Torfing, J. (eds) *Discourse Theory in European Politics: identity, policy and governance*, Basingstoke: Palgrave Macmillan.

Howarth, D.R. and Stavrakakis, Y. (2000) 'Introducing discourse theory and political analysis', in Howarth, D.R. Norval, A.J. and Stavrakakis, Y. (eds), *Discourse Theory and Political Analysis: identities, hegemonies and social change*, Manchester: Manchester University Press.

Howarth, D.R. and Torfing, J. (eds) (2005) *Discourse Theory in European Politics: identity, policy and governance*, Basingstoke: Palgrave Macmillan.

Howorth, J. (2001) 'European defence and the changing politics of the European Union: hanging together or hanging separately?', *Journal of Common Market Studies* 39: 765–789.

Howorth, J. (2004) 'Discourse, ideas and epistemic communities in the European security and defence policy', *West European Politics* 27: 211–234.

Hurd, D. (1994) 'Developing the common foreign and security policy', *International Affairs* 70: 383–393.

Hurrell, A. and Menon, A. (1996) 'Politics like any other?: comparative politics, international relations and the study of the EU', *West European Politics* 19: 386–402.

Hyde-Price, A. (2006) '"Normative" power Europe: a realist critique', *Journal of European Public Policy* 13: 217–234.

Hyde-Price, A. (2008) 'A "tragic actor"?: a realist perspective on "ethical" power Europe', *International Affairs* 84: 49–64.

Ingebritsen, C. (1998) *The Nordic States and European Unity*, Ithaca, NY: Cornell University Press.

Jachtenfuchs, M., Diez, T. and Jung, S. (1998) 'Which Europe?: conflicting models of a legitimate European political order', *European Journal of International Relations* 4: 409–446.

Jakobsen, P.V. (1997) 'The twelve and the crisis in the Gulf and northern Iraq 1990–1991', in Jørgensen, K.E. (eds), *European Approaches to Crisis Management*, Hague: Kluver Law International.

Jakobson, M. (1968) *Finnish Neutrality: a study of Finnish foreign policy since the second world war*, London: Evelyn.

Jakobson, M. (2004) 'Torjuntavoitto avasi tien rauhaan' ('Defence victory paved way to peace'), Helsingin Sanomat, 3 September 2004. Online. Available: www.hs.fi/artikkeli/ Torjuntavoitto+avasi+tien+rauhaan/1076153822466 (accessed 26 May 2010).

Joenniemi, P. (1998) 'From small to smart: reflections on the concept of small states', *Irish Studies in International Affairs* 9: 61–62.

Joenniemi, P. (2001) 'Finland in the New Europe: a herderian or hegelian project?', in Hansen, L. and Wæver, O. (ed) *European Integration and National Identity: the challenge of the Nordic states*, London: Routledge.

Johnston, A.I. (1996) 'Cultural realism and strategy in Maoist China', in Katzenstein, P. (ed) *The Culture of National Security: norms and identity in world politics*, New York: Columbia University Press.

Jupille, J. and Caporaso, J.A. (1999) 'Institutionalisation and the European Union: international relations and comparative politics', *Annual Review of Political Science* 2: 429–444.

Kagan, R. (2002) 'Power and weakness: why the United States and Europe see the world differently', *Policy Review Online*, no. 113. Online. Available: www.policyreview.org (accessed 13 March 2005).

Kalela, J. and Turtola, J. (1975) 'Suomen kansainvälisen aseman ja ulkopolitiikan kehitys toisen maailmansodan jälkeen' ('Development of Finland's international position and foreign policy after the Second World War'), in Väyrynen, R. and Hakovirta, H. (eds) *Suomen ulkopolitiikka (Finland's Foreign Policy)*, Tampere: Gaudeamus.

Kantola, A. (2002) *Markkinakuri ja Managerivalta: poliittinen hallinta Suomen 1990-luvun talouskriisissä (Market Discipline and Managerial Power: political governance in Finland's economic crisis in 1990s)*, Helsinki: Loki-kirjat.

Kantola, J. (2006) *Feminists Theorize the State*, Basingstoke: Palgrave.

Katzenstein, P. (1996) 'Introduction: alternative perspective on national security', in Katzenstein, P. (ed.) *The Culture of National Security: norms and identity in world politics*, New York: Columbia University Press.

Kekkonen, U. (1943) 'Good neighbourliness with the "hereditary enemy" – speech given at a meeting organized by the Swedish agrarian union in Stockholm, 7 December 1943', in Vilkuna, T. (ed.) *Neutrality: the Finnish position*, London: Heinemann.

Kekkonen, U. (1952) 'Losing the war, winning the peace – speech given at the unveiling of the war memorial in Lahti, Finland, 1 June 1952', in Vilkuna, T. (ed.) *Neutrality: the Finnish position*, London: Heinemann.

Kekkonen, U. (1957) 'Our policy of neutrality – speech given at a banquet in honour of N.A. Bulganin and N.S. Khrushchev in Helsinki, 7 June 1957', in Vilkuna, T. (ed.), *Neutrality: the Finnish position*, London: Heinemann.

Kekkonen, U. (1961) 'Finland's attitude to problems in world politics – speech given at the general assembly of the United Nations, 19 October 1961', in Vilkuna, T. (ed.), *Neutrality: the Finnish position*, London: Heinemann.

Kekkonen, U. (1961) 'Finland's position in international politics – speech given at the national press club, Washington, 17 October 1961', in Vilkuna, T. (ed.), *Neutrality: the Finnish position*, London: Heinemann.

Kekkonen, U. (1982) *A President's View*. London: Heinemann.

Kennan, G.F. (1974) 'Europe's problems, Europe's choices', a reprint from: *Foreign Policy* 14, Spring 1974.

Keohane, R.O. and Nye, J.S. (1971) *Transnational Relations and World Politics*, Cambridge, MA: Harvard University Press.

Keohane, R.O. and Nye, J.S. (1977) *Power and Interdependence: world politics in transition*. Boston, MA: Little, Brown.

Keränen, M. (2001) 'Vertaileva ja poikkikulttuurinen tutkimus: kaksi tapaa lähestyä muita maita' ('Comparative and cross-cultural research: two ways to approach other countries'), *Politiikka* (*Politics*) 43: 82–92.

King, G., Keohane, R.O. and Verba, S. (1994) *Designing Social Inquiry: scientific inference in qualitative research*, Princeton, NJ: Princeton University Press.

Knill, C. (2001) *The Europeanisation of National Administrations: patterns of institutional change and persistence*, Cambridge: Cambridge University Press.

Koivisto, M. (1995) *Historian tekijät: kaksi kautta II*, Helsinki: Kirjayhtymä Oy.

Krasner, S.D. (1983) *International Regimes*, Ithaca, NY: Cornell University Press.

Laclau, E. and Mouffe, C. (1985) *Hegemony and Socialist Strategy: towards a radical democratic politics*, London: Verso.

Laclau, E. and Mouffe, C. (1987) 'Post-Marxists without apologies', *New Left Review* 166: 79–106.

Laffey, M. and Weldes, J. (2004) 'Methodological reflections on discourse analysis', *Qualitative Methods* 2: 28–30.

Lamy, S.L. (2005) 'Contemporary mainstream approaches: neo-realism and neo-liberalism', in Smith, S. and Baylis, J. (eds) *The Globalization of World Politics: an introduction to international politics*, Oxford: Oxford University Press.

Landman, T. (2000) *Issues and Methods in Comparative Politics: an introduction*, London: Routledge.

Lankowski, C. (2001) 'Germany: a major player', in Zeff, E.E. and Pirro, E.B. (eds), *The European Union and the Member States: cooperation, coordination, and compromise*, London: Lynne Rienner.

Larsen, H. (1997) *Foreign Policy and Discourse Analysis: France, Britain and Europe*, London: Routledge.

Liebert, U. (2003) 'Between diversity and equality: analysing Europeanisation', in Liebert, U. *Gendering Europeanisation*, Brussels: P.I.E.-Peter Lang.

Lipponen, P. (2001) *Kohti Eurooppaa* (*Towards Europe*), Helsinki: Tammi.

Luif, P. (1995) *On the Road to Brussels: the political dimension of Austria's, Finland's and Sweden's accession to the European Union*, Laxenburg: Austrian Institute for International Affairs.

McCormick, J. (1996) *European Union: politics and policies*, Boulder, CO: Westview Press.

Macleod, A. (1997) 'Great Britain: still searching for status?', in Le Prestre, P.G. (ed.) *Role Quests in the Post-Cold War Era: foreign policies in transition*, Montreal and Kingston: McGill-Queen's University Press.

Major, J. (1994) 'Conservative Party conference speech 1994'. Online. Available: www.johnmajor.co.uk/1994.htm (accessed 23 July 2004).

Manners, I. (2006) 'Normative power Europe reconsidered: beyond the crossroads', *Journal of European Public Policy* 13: 182–199.

Manners, I. and Whitman, R. (2000) 'Introduction', in Manners, I. and Whitman, R. (eds), *Foreign Policies of the European Union Member States*, Manchester: Manchester University Press.

Marsh, D. and Hay, C. (eds) (1999) *Demystifying Globalization*, Basingstoke: Macmillan.

Milliken, J. (1999) 'The study of discourse in international relations: a critique of research and methods', *European Journal of International Relations* 5: 225–254.

Ministry of Defence (1990) *Statement on the Defence Estimates* (1990), London: UK Ministry of Defence.

Ministry of Defence (1991) *Statement on the Defence Estimates: Britain's defence for the 90s*, London: UK Ministry of Defence.

Ministry of Defence (1992) *Statement on the Defence Estimates*, London: UK Ministry of Defence

Ministry of Defence (1993) *Statement on the Defence Estimates: defending our future*, London: UK Ministry of Defence.

Ministry of Defence (1994) *Statement on the Defence Estimates*, London: UK Ministry of Defence.

Ministry of Defence (1995) *Statement on the Defence Estimates: stable forces on a strong Britain*, London: UK Ministry of Defence.

Ministry of Defence (1996) *Statement on the Defence Estimates*, London: UK Ministry of Defence.

Ministry of Defence (1998) *Strategic Defence Review: modern forces for the modern world*. Online. Available: www.mod.uk/issues/sdr/wp_contents.htm (accessed 24 April 2003).

Ministry of Defence (1999) 'Defence white paper'. Online. Available: www.mod.uk (accessed 12 March 2003).

Ministry of Defence (2001) 'European defence – Ministry of Defence policy paper'. Online. Available: www.mod.uk (accessed 12 March 2003).

Missiroli, A. (2007) 'Introduction: a tale of two pillars', in Avery, G. *et al. The EU Foreign Service: how to build a more effective common policy*, EPC Working Paper, no. 28. Online. Available: www.epc.eu/TEWN/pdf/555858396_EPC%20Working%20Paper%2028%20The%20EU%20Foreign%20Service.pdf (accessed 23 May 2008).

Mitzen, J. (2006) 'Ontological security in world politics: state identity and the security dilemma', *European Journal of International Relations* 12: 341–370.

Moisio, S. (2003) *Geopoliittinen kamppailu Suomen EU-jäsenyydestä* (*Geopolitical Struggle over Finland's EU Membership*), Turku: Turun yliopisto.

Moravcsik, A. (1991) 'Negotiating the single European act', in Keohane, R.O. and Hoffmann, S. (eds) *The New European Community: decision-making and institutional change*, Boulder, CO: Westview.

Moravcsik, A. (2001) 'Constructivism and European integration: a critique', in Christiansen, T., Jørgensen, K.E. and Wiener, A. (eds), *The Social Construction of Europe*, London: Sage.

Morgenthau, H.J. (1973) *Politics Among Nations: the struggle for power and peace*, New York: Knopf.

Möttölä, K. (1993) 'Puolueettomuudesta sitoutumiseen: turvallisuuspoliittisen perusratkaisun muutos kylmästä sodasta Euroopan murrokseen' ('From neutrality to alignment: security policy change from the Cold War to the European transformation'), in Forsberg, T. and Vaahtoranta, T. (eds) *Johdatus Suomen Ulkopolitiikkaan: kylmästä sodasta uuteen maailmanjärjestykseen* (*Introduction to Finnish Foreign Policy: from the Cold War to the new world order*), Tampere: Gaudeamus.

Muppidi, H. (1999) 'Postcoloniality and the production of international insecurity: the persistent puzzle of U.S.–Indian relations', in Weldes, J., Laffey, M. Gusterson, H. and Duvall, R. (eds) *Cultures of Insecurity: states, communities, and the production of danger*, Minneapolis, MN: University of Minnesota Press.

Neumann, I.B. (1998) *Uses of the Other: 'the east' in European identity formation*, Minneapolis, MN: University of Minnesota Press.

Nolan, C.J. (2001) 'The OSCE: nonmilitary dimensions of cooperative security in Europe', in Hidge, C.C (ed.) *Redefining European Security*, London: Garland Publishing.

Nuttall, S.J. (2000) *European Foreign Policy*, Oxford: Oxford University Press.

Official Journal (1992) *Treaty on the European Union*, C 191, 29 July 1992. Online. Available http://eur-lex.europa.eu/en/treaties/index.htm (accessed 26 May 2010).

Official Journal (1997) *Treaty of Amsterdam*, C 340, 10 November 1997. Online. Available: http://eur-lex.europa.eu/en/treaties/index.htm (accessed 26 May 2010).

Official Journal (2001) *Treaty of Nice*, C 80, 10 March 2001. Online. Available: http://eur-lex.europa.eu/en/treaties/index.htm (accessed 26 May 2010).

Ojanen, H. (2002) 'Theories at a loss? EU-NATO fusion and the "low-politicisation" of security and defence in European integration', *FIIA Working Papers* 35, Helsinki: The Finnish Institute of International Affairs.

Ojanen, H. (2006) *The EU and the UN: a shared future*, FIIA Report 13/2006, Helsinki: Finnish Institute of International Affairs.

Ojanen, H., Herolf, G. and Lindahl, R. (2000) *Non-Alignment and European Security Policy: ambiguity at work*, Helsinki and Bonn: The Finnish Institute of International Affairs and Institut für Europäische Politik.

Parlamentaarinen puolustuspoliittinen neuvottelukunta (Parliamentary defence policy council) (1990) *Arvio Euroopan turvallisuuspoliittisesta tilanteesta ja sen kehitysnäkemyksistä sekä niiden vaikutuksesta Suomen puolustuspolitiikkaan* (*Evaluation of European Security Policy Situation and Prospects of its Development and Their Impact on Finland's Defence Policy*), Helsinki: Parliament of Finland.

Pijpers, A. (1991) 'European political cooperation and the realist paradigm', in Holland, M. (ed.) *The Future of European Political Cooperation: essays on theory and practice*, London: Macmillan.

Puolustusministeriö (Ministry of Defence) (2001) 'Tiedotteita ja katsauksia 1/2001', 7 July 2001. Online. Available www.defmin.fi/index.phtml?463_m=592&463_o=10&s=263 (accessed 23 March 2010).

Puolustusministeriö (Ministry of Defence) (2004) 'Tiedotteita ja katsauksia 1/2004', 27 January 2004. Online. Available www.defmin.fi/files/254/1785_mts-tiedote1–2004_nettijulkaisu.pdf (accessed 23 March 2010).

Radaelli, C.M. (2000) 'Whither Europeanization?: concept stretching and substantive change', *European Integration Online Papers (EIoP)*, 4. Online. Available: http://eiop.or.at/eiop/ (accessed 12 March 2005).

Radaelli, C.M. (2004) 'Europeanisation: solution or problem?', in Cini, M. and Bourne, A. (eds) *The Palgrave Guide to European Studies*, Basingstoke: Palgrave Macmillan.

Raunio, T. and Tiilikainen, T. (2003) *Finland in the European Union*, London: Frank Cass.

Rainio-Niemi, J. (2008) *Small State Cultures of Consensus: state traditions and consensus-seeking in the neo-corporatist and neutrality policies in post-1945 Austria and Finland*, Helsinki: University of Helsinki.

Redmond, J. (1997) *The 1995 Enlargement of the European Union*, Aldershot: Ashgate 1997.

Regelsberger, E., Schoutheete, P.D. and Wessels, W. (1997) *Foreign Policy of the European Union: from EPC to CFSP and beyond*, London: Lynne Rienner.

Rehn, O. (1993) 'Odottavasta ennakoivaan integraatiopolitiikaan?: Suomen integraatio-politiikka kylmän sodan aikana ja sen päätösvaiheessa 1989–92', in Forsberg, T. and Vaahtoranta, T. (eds) *Johdatus Suomen Ulkopolitiikkaan: kylmästä sodasta uuteen maailmanjärjestykseen* (*Introduction to Finnish Foreign Policy: from the Cold War to the new world order*), Tampere: Gaudeamus.

Rieker, P. (2005) 'Europeanization of Nordic security: the European Union and the changing security identities of the Nordic states', *Cooperation and Conflict* 39: 369–392.

Rosamond, B. (2000) *Theories of European Integration*, Basingstoke: Macmillan.

Ruggie, J. (1993) 'Territoriality and beyond: problematising modernity in international relations', *International Organization* 47: 139–174.

Rutten, M. (2001) 'British–French Summit, St Malo, 3–4 December 1998', in Rutten, M. (compiled), *From St Malo to Nice: European defence: core documents*, Chaillot Paper, no. 47, Paris: The Institute for Security Studies for Western European Union.

Salminen, E. (2000) *Suomi-kuva Venäjän ja EU:n lehdistössä 1990–2000*, Helsinki: Suomalaisen kirjallisuuden seura.

Sanders, D. (1990) *Losing an Empire, Finding a Role: an introduction to British foreign policy since 1945*, New York: St Martin's Press.

Sandholtz, W. and Zysman, J. (1989) '1992: recasting the European bargain', *World Politics* 42: 95–128

Sauder, A. (1999) 'France's security policy since the end of the Cold War', in Hodge, C. C. (ed.) *Redefining European Security*, London: Garland Publishing.

Sjursen, H. (2001) 'The Common Foreign and Security Policy', in Andersen, S. and Elianssen, K. (eds) *Making Policy in Europe*, London: Sage.

Sjursen, H. (2003) 'Understanding the common foreign and security policy: analytical building blocs', *ARENA Working Paper Series*, no. 9 . Online. Available: www.arena.uio.no/publications/working-papers2003/papers/03_09.xml (accessed 26 May 2010).

Sjursen, H. and Smith, K.E. (2004) 'Justifying EU foreign policy: the logics underpinning EU enlargement', in Tonra, B. and Christiansen, T. (eds) *Rethinking European Union Foreign Policy*, Manchester: Manchester University Press.

Smith, H. (2002) *European Union Foreign Policy: what it is and what it does*, London: Pluto Press.

Smith, K.E. (2003) *European Union Foreign Policy in a Changing World*, Cambridge: Polity.

Smith, M. (1994) 'Beyond the stable state?: foreign policy challenges and opportunities in the new Europe', in Carlsnaes, W. and Smith, S. (eds), *European Foreign Policy: the EC and changing perspectives in Europe*, London: Sage.

Smith, M. (2003) 'The Framing of European foreign and security policy: towards a post-modern policy framework?' *Journal of European Public Policy* 10: 556–575.

Smith, M., Smith, S. and White, B. (1988) 'Introduction' in Smith, M., Smith, S. and White, B. (eds) *British Foreign Policy: tradition, change and transformation*, London: Unwin Hyman.

Smith, M.E. (2000) 'Conforming to Europe: the domestic impact of EU foreign policy co-operation', *Journal of European Public Policy* 7: 613–631.

Smith, M.E. (2004) *Europe's Foreign and Security Policy: the institutionalization of cooperation*, Cambridge: Cambridge University Press.

Smith, S. (1994) 'Introduction: foreign policy theory and the new Europe', in Carlsnaes, W. and Smith, S. (eds) *European Foreign Policy: the EC and changing perspectives in Europe*, London: Sage

Smith, S. (2000) 'Wendt's world', *Review of International Studies* 26: 151–164.

Squires, J. (1999) *Gender in Political Theory*, Cambridge: Polity Press.

Suomen rauhansopimus (1947) (The peace treaty of Finland) (1947), *Finlex.* Online. Available: www.finlex.fi/fi/sopimukset/sopsteksti/1947/19470020 (accessed 12 March 2005).

Tank, P.G. (1998) 'The CFSP and the nation-state', in Eliassen, K.A. (ed.) *Foreign and Security Policy of the European Union*, London: Sage

Taylor, P. (1994) 'Functionalism: the approach of David Mitrany', in Groom A.J.R. and Taylor, P. (eds) *Frameworks for International Co-operation*, London: Pinter.

Thatcher, M. (1990) 'Speech at lord mayor's banquet', Online. Available: www.margaret thatcher.org/Speeches/displaydocument.asp?docid=108241&doctype=1 (accessed 23 April 2004).

Thatcher, M. (2002) *Statecraft: strategies for a changing world*, New York: Harper Collins.

Tiilikainen, T. (1998) *Europe and Finland: defining the political identity of Finland in Western Europe.* Aldershot: Ashgate.

Tiilikainen, T. (2001) 'Finland in the EU', in Huldt, B., Tiilikainen, T., Vaahtoranta, T. and Helkama-Rågård, A. (eds) *Finnish and Swedish Security: comparing national policies*, Stockholm, Helsinki and Berlin: Swedish National Defence, Finnish Institute of International Affairs and Institut für Europäische Politik (Berlin).

Titscher, S. (2000) *Methods of Text and Discourse Analysis.* London: Sage.

Tonra, B. (2000) 'Denmark and Ireland', in Manners, I. and Whitman, R. (eds) *The Foreign and Security Policies of European Member States*, Manchester: Manchester University Press.

Tonra, B. (2001) *The Europeanisation of National Foreign Policy: Dutch, Danish and Irish foreign policy in the European Union*, Aldershot: Ashgate.

Tonra, B. (2003) 'Constructing the Common Foreign and Security Policy: the utility of a cognitive approach', *Journal of Common Market Studies* 41: 731–756.

Tonra, B. and Christiansen, T. (eds) (2004) *Rethinking European Union Foreign Policy*, Manchester: Manchester University Press.

Torfing, J. (1999) *New Theories of Discourse: Laclau, Mouffe and Zizek*, Oxford: Blackwell.

Torfing, J. (2005) 'Discourse theory: achievements, arguments, and challenges', in Howarth, D.R. and Torfing, J. (eds) *Discourse Theory in European Politics: identity, policy and governance*, Basingstoke: Palvgrave Macmillan.

Tugendhat, C. and Wallace, W. (1988) *Options for British Foreign Policy in the 1990s*, London: Routledge.

Van Evera, S. (1997) *Guide to Methods for Students of Political Science*, Ithaca, NY: Cornell University Press.

Väyrynen, R. (1990) 'Puolueettomuuden uudet poliittiset ulottuvuudet' ('New political dimensions of neutrality'), in Väyrynen, R. (ed.) *Suomen Puolueettomuuden Tulevaisuus* (*The Future of Finland's Neutrality*), Helsinki: WSOY.

Väyrynen, R. (1993) 'Kylmästä sodasta uuteen maailman järjestykseen: Suomen ulkopolitiikan kansainvälinen ympäristö' ('From Cold War to new world order: the international environment of Finland's foreign policy'), in Forsberg, T. and Vaahtoranta, T. (eds) *Johdatus Suomen Ulkopolitiikkaan: kylmästä sodasta uuteen maailman-järjestykseen* (*Introduction to Finnish foreign policy: from the Cold War to the new world order*) (eds), Tampere: Gaudeamus.

Vihavainen, T. (1991) *Kansakunta Rähmällään: suomettumisen lyhyt historia*, Helsinki: Otava.

Vihavainen, T. (2001) 'Finland, Stalin and Germany in the 1930s', *Virtual Finland – your window to Finland.* Online. Available: http://virtual.finland.fi/netcomm/news/show article.asp?intNWSAID=25928 (accessed 2 April 2002).

Vilkuna, T. (ed.) (1970) *Neutrality: the Finnish position by Urho Kekkonen*, London: Heinemann.

Vink, M.P. and Graziano, P. (2007) 'Challenges of a new research agenda', in Granziano, P. and Vink, M.P. (eds) *Europeanization: new research agendas*, Basingstoke: Palgrave.

Wæver, O. (1996) 'Rise and fall of the inter-paradigm debate', in Smith, S. Booth, K. and Zalewski, M. (eds) *International Theory: positivism and beyond*, Cambridge: Cambridge University Press.

Wæver, O. (1998) 'The sociology of a not so international discipline: American and European developments in international relations', *International Organization* 52: 687–727.

Wæver, O. (2002) 'Identity, communities and foreign policy: discourse analysis as foreign policy theory', in Hansen, L. and Wæver, O. (ed.) *European Integration and National Identity: the challenge of the Nordic states*, London: Routledge.

Wæver, O. (2004) 'Discursive approaches', in Wiener, A. and Diez, T. (eds) *European Integration Theory*, Oxford: Oxford University Press.

Wallace, H. (2000) 'Policy-making in the European Union', in Wallace, H. and Wallace, W. (eds) *The New European Union Series*, Oxford: Oxford University Press.

Wallace, W. (1991) 'Foreign policy and national identity in the United Kingdom', *International Affairs* 67: 65–80.

Wallace, W. (1992) 'British foreign policy after the Cold War', *International Affairs* 68: 423–442.

Walt, S. (1987) *The Origins of Alliances*, Ithaca, NY: Cornell University Press.

Waltz, K.N. (1979) *Theory of International Politics.* New York: Random House.

Weber, C. (1998) 'Preformative states', *Millennium* 27: 77–95.

Weisstein, E.W. 'Circle squaring', *MathWorld.* Online. Available: http://mathworld. wolfram.com/CircleSquaring.html (accessed 12 December 2004).

Weldes, J. (1996) 'Constructing national interests', *European Journal of International Relations* 2: 275–318.

Weldes, J. (1999) 'The cultural production of crises: U.S. identity and missiles in Cuba', in Weldes, J., Laffey, M., Gusterson, H. and Duvall, R. (eds) *Cultures of Insecurity: states, communities, and the production of danger*, Minneapolis, MN: University of Minnesota Press.

Weldes, J., Laffey, M. Gusterson, H. and Duvall, R. (1999). 'Introduction: constructing insecurity', in Weldes, J., Laffey, M., Gusterson, H. and Duvall, R. (eds) *Cultures of Insecurity: states, communities, and the production of danger*, Minneapolis, MN: University of Minnesota Press.

Wendt, A. (1992) 'Anarchy is what states make of it: social construction of power politics', *International Organization* 46: 391–425.

Wendt, A. (1999) *Social Theory of International Politics*, Cambridge: Cambridge University Press.

White, B. (2001) *Understanding European Foreign Policy*, Basingstoke: Palgrave.

White, B. (2004). 'Foreign policy analysis and the new Europe', in Carlsnaes, W., Sjursen, H. and White, B. (eds) *Contemporary European Foreign Policy*, London: Sage.

Williams, M.C. (2005) *The Realist Tradition and the Limits of International Relations*, Cambridge: Cambridge University Press.

Wodak, R. (1999) *The Discursive Construction of National Identity*, Edinburgh: Edinburgh University Press.

Wong, R. (2005) 'The Europeanization of foreign policy', in Hill, C. and Smith, M. *International Relations and the European Union*, Oxford: Oxford Univeristy Press.

YYA-sopimus (1948) 'Sopimus ystävyydestä, yhteistoiminnasta ja keskinäisestä avunannosta Suomen tasavallan ja Sosialististen Neuvostotasavaltain Liiton välillä' ('Treaty of friendship, cooperation and mutual assistance between the Republic of Finland and the Union of Socialist Soviet Republics'), *Finlex*. Online. Available: www.finlex. fi/fi/sopimukset/sopsteksti/1948/19480017 (accessed 12 June 2004).

Zielonka, J. (2002) 'Understanding European foreign policy', *Political Science Quarterly* 117: 152–153.

Index

For Product Safety Concerns and Information please contact our EU
representative GPSR@taylorandfrancis.com
Taylor & Francis Verlag GmbH, Kaufingerstraße 24, 80331 München, Germany